A

ABDUL QA   N

20

SHOPPING FOR BOMBS

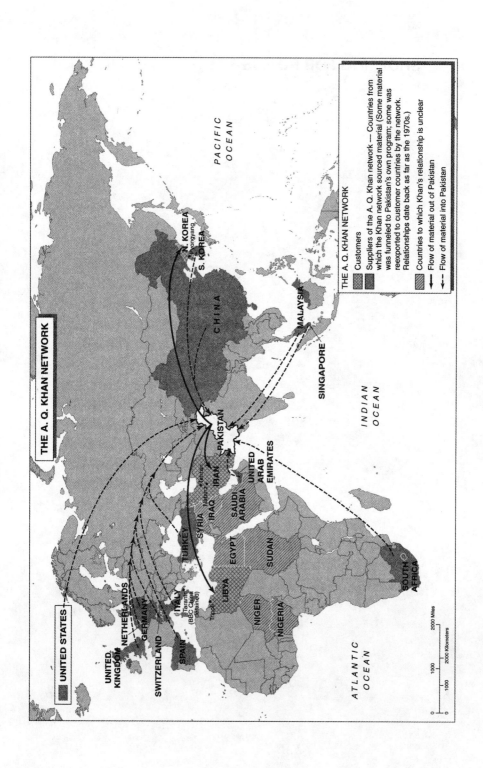

THE A. Q. KHAN NETWORK

THE A. Q. KHAN NETWORK

- Customers
- Suppliers of the A. Q. Khan network — Countries from which the Khan network sourced material (Some material was funneled to Pakistan's own program; some was reexported to customer countries by the network. Relationships date back as far as the 1970s.)
- Countries to which Khan's relationship is unclear
- Flow of material out of Pakistan
- Flow of material into Pakistan

UNITED STATES

UNITED KINGDOM
NETHERLANDS
GERMANY
SWITZERLAND
SPAIN
ITALY
Taranto (BBC Client detained)

TURKEY
SYRIA
Natanz
IRAQ
IRAN
Tehran
PAKISTAN
UNITED ARAB EMIRATES
SAUDI ARABIA
EGYPT
LIBYA
Tripoli
SUDAN
NIGER
NIGERIA
SOUTH AFRICA

CHINA
N. KOREA
Pyongyang
S. KOREA
MALAYSIA
SINGAPORE

PACIFIC OCEAN
INDIAN OCEAN
ATLANTIC OCEAN

0   1000   2000 Miles
0   1000   2000 Kilometers

SHOPPING FOR BOMBS

Nuclear Proliferation, Global Insecurity, and the Rise and Fall of the A. Q. Khan Network

GORDON CORERA

OXFORD
UNIVERSITY PRESS
2006

OXFORD

UNIVERSITY PRESS

Oxford University Press, Inc., publishes works that
further Oxford University's objective of excellence
in research, scholarship, and education.

Oxford   New York
Auckland   Cape Town   Dar es Salaam   Hong Kong   Karachi
Kuala Lumpur   Madrid   Melbourne   Mexico City   Nairobi
New Delhi   Shanghai   Taipei   Toronto

With offices in
Argentina   Austria   Brazil   Chile   Czech Republic   France   Greece
Guatemala   Hungary   Italy   Japan   Poland   Portugal   Singapore
South Korea   Switzerland   Thailand   Turkey   Ukraine   Vietnam

Published by Oxford University Press, Inc.
198 Madison Avenue, New York, NY 10016
www.oup.com

Oxford is a registered trademark of Oxford University Press

Library of Congress Cataloging-in-Publication Data
Corera, Gordon.
Shopping for bombs : nuclear proliferation, global insecurity, and
the rise and fall of the A. Q. Khan network / Gordon Corera.
p. cm.
ISBN-13: 978-0-19-530495-4 (cloth)
ISBN-10: 0-19-530495-0 (cloth)
1. Nuclear nonproliferation.
2. Security, International.
3. Khan, A. Q. (Abdul Qadeer), 1936–
I. Title.
JZ5675.C67 2006
623.4'5119092—dc22
2006012510

1 3 5 7 9 8 6 4 2
Printed in the United States of America
on acid-free paper

In memory of Bernard Corera

Contents

TARANTO, ITALY

October 4, 2003

IT WAS JUST AFTER MIDNIGHT when the *BBC China* made its unscheduled stop. It would be gone again in two hours. The German Secret Service had contacted the ship's owners in Hamburg, Germany, asking for help. The owners radioed the vessel as it passed through the Suez Canal instructing it to change course. "Don't ask any questions," the captain was told. Waiting in the cold night air, the team at the dock in Taranto knew they would have to work fast to identify five forty-foot cargo containers by serial number and then remove them from amongst the more than two hundred on board. The *BBC China* had to resume its voyage without anyone knowing what had happened. Its ultimate destination was the Libyan capital Tripoli.

The containers' journey had begun in August in a factory in Malaysia. A close-knit team working between America's CIA and Britain's Intelligence Service received a tip-off in mid-September that a consignment of important goods had arrived at the bustling hub of Dubai's free-trade zone where they would be loaded onto a tramp steamer.

By the time the team had identified the boat as the *BBC China*, it had already left port. After a frantic search, it was found slowly snaking its way through the Suez Canal. From then on, the ship was closely watched. But until the containers were finally prised open at the port in Italy, the tension was palpable amongst those involved in the operation. What if they were filled with soft toys?

The interception of the *BBC China* had come after a difficult, even depressing summer for the small team working jointly between America's Central Intelligence Agency and Britain's Secret Intelligence Service (formally known as SIS although often known as MI6). Over the previous years, they had pieced together a picture of an unprecedented global black market, supplying the most deadly nuclear technology to some of the world's most dangerous states. They had watched and waited for an opportunity to break the network but it had proved frustratingly difficult and slow. Meanwhile, the network was still churning out more sensitive material and looking for more customers. Then in the spring of 2003, a golden opportunity seemed to have arisen when MI6 was contacted by one of the network's customers who wanted to talk. But by the summer, negotiations with Libya had stalled. Thanks to the intelligence penetration of the network, the United States and UK knew that the Libyans were being far from honest about what they were up to. Was this going to be another lost opportunity? Something had to be done to force the issue.

The opening of the containers led to a wave of relief from the team. Inside were thousands of aluminium components—positioners, casings, pumps, and flangers. There were all packed in wooden boxes bearing the logo SCOPE. No one but a trained expert would have known that these were for a centrifuge, the device that enriches uranium, the heart of a clandestine nuclear program.

The United States and UK kept the interception of the *BBC China* secret from the wider world for many months, but within hours they set in motion a chain of events to exploit its fleeting diversion. A senior MI6 officer would call his Libyan opposite number and demand an explanation. Within weeks, a team of CIA and MI6 officers would finally be taken into the heart of Colonel Gadaffi's nuclear project. Soon after, the Libyan leader would shock the world by announcing he was giving up something that few realized he had—an active nuclear weapons program.

And for the man who had provided almost that entire capability, including the cargo of the *BBC China,* this was also the beginning of the end. The curtain was slowly coming down on the decades-long career of Pakistani scientist, spy, and national hero, A. Q. Khan, who had been peddling his wares as a salesman of the darkest most closely held nuclear secrets. As with the Libyans, the endgame would not be without its bumps along the road. A week before the *BBC China*'s interception, the CIA director had begun the process of putting Khan out of business in a meeting with Pakistan's leader in the unusual confines of a suite in a New York hotel. In a detailed briefing that stunned President Musharraf of Pakistan, George Tenet had explained just how much the U.S. government knew regarding Khan's activities. And within hours of the *BBC China*'s interception, a senior U.S. diplomat would arrive in Islamabad to drive home the message that the time for action had come. The end was at hand for Khan and his network. But those few individuals had already managed to do untold damage by spreading the most secret, dangerous nuclear technology across the world.

Introduction

ALTHOUGH IT HAD BEEN MONTHS IN PREPARATION, President Eisenhower was still rewriting his speech on the morning of December 8, 1953. His plane circled for half an hour before landing at LaGuardia airfield in New York. From there, he traveled to the United Nations where an audience of three and a half thousand was waiting for an address that would come to define the world's approach to nuclear technology for the coming decades.

In the few, but eventful, years since Hiroshima and Nagasaki, the United States was already losing its monopoly on nuclear weapons. More and more states were seeking the bomb as part of the relentless quest for security, power, and prestige in the international arena. Intense scientific research, atomic espionage, and an occasional helping hand from others were in turn delivering this deadly capability to the doorsteps of more and more states. The arms race between the United States and the USSR and the spread of nuclear weapons would be the defining national security challenge of the coming years. Eisenhower's speech was designed to inaugurate a public debate on how this proliferation challenge should be met. In his diary, he wrote of his "clear conviction that the world was racing toward catastrophe."[1]

The president began his UN address with the stark message that the U.S. stockpile already exceeded by many times the explosive power of all the bombs, munitions, and shells dropped in every theatre of World War II. "But the dread secret, and the fearful engines of atomic might, are not ours alone," he continued. "So my country's purpose is to help us move out of the dark chamber of horrors into the light. . . . It is not enough to take this weapon out of the hands of the soldiers. It must be put into the hands of those who will know how to strip its military casing and adapt it to the arts of peace. The United States knows that if the fearful trend of atomic military build-up can be reversed, this greatest of destructive forces can be developed into a great boon, for the benefit of all mankind." He proposed that those countries with the bomb should begin to disarm and contribute nuclear material from their stockpiles to a bank that would be controlled by an international atomic energy agency. In turn, other countries around the world would reap the enormous positive benefits of the peaceful atom. After a few seconds, those in the hall began to applaud thunderously. Eisenhower's speech became known as "Atoms for Peace" and its impact was to be far more controversial than its idealistic tone suggested.

The International Atomic Energy Agency (IAEA) came into being in 1957 but it never became the steward for a stockpile of surrendered nuclear material in the way that Eisenhower had envisaged. The notion of adapting the new technology to "peaceful arts" had more success. Under Atoms for Peace, countries around the world were encouraged to develop their own civilian nuclear energy programs. Reams of U.S. documents were declassified, scientists came to be trained in the United States, and both nuclear material and research reactors were supplied to dozens of nations. This unprecedented dispersal of nuclear technology was driven by a combination of genuine idealism, Cold War superpower rivalry, and stark commercial interests emanating from the nuclear industry.

As the spread of technology galloped ahead, the great disarmament Eisenhower envisioned never gathered steam. In 1968 the Non-Proliferation Treaty would codify a bargain in which the existing five nuclear weapons states (the United States, USSR, China, France, and Great Britain) were to negotiate in "good faith" to disarm. Meanwhile the non-nuclear states would be guaranteed assistance in developing civilian nuclear programs in return for agreeing not to pursue their own weapons.

In the mid-1970s, the optimistic vision of Atoms for Peace began to crumble. In those years of accelerating proliferation, there was a palpable sense of a rolling tide that threatened to break. Old certainties were shattered by India's 1974 nuclear test. Clearly, developing countries were capable of mastering the dark technology of weapons after all. Adding insult to injury, India had used expertise and even material supplied by the United States under Atoms for Peace. How much longer would it be before others followed suit? It was now abundantly clear that the notion that the peaceful atom and the destructive atom could be kept separate was false. The two were inextricably linked and the spreading of nuclear knowledge and technology for ostensibly peaceful purposes was also spreading the bomb.

It was at this point that Abdul Qadeer Khan stepped onto the stage. In the story of the spread of nuclear technology over the last thirty years, this elusive figure casts a blurred but unmistakable shadow over proceedings. From Pakistan's own clandestine program, born in an era of shifting nuclear sands and driven by fear of India, to today's equally unstable international security environment, Khan is the sometimes visible but often unseen thread drawing together what might appear an otherwise disparate array of events in the story of the spread of nuclear weapons. It was he more than any other individual who undermined the idealistic structure fashioned by Eisenhower.

The former CIA Director George Tenet has reportedly described Khan as "at least as dangerous as Osama bin Laden," a label richly deserved given that Khan has wreaked havoc on attempts to restrain one of the greatest threats facing the world today, the spread of nuclear technology.[2] Khan was responsible not only for developing the nuclear capability in his native Pakistan but also for building an unrivalled, clandestine procurement network that spanned the globe. Many states have longed for the power that nuclear weapons are perceived to provide, but the technical challenges had appeared insurmountable to all but a few. And so they might have remained, until Khan began looking for customers and shifting his exceptional business model from import to export. This book attempts to do some justice to this complex tale, even as the true scale of the damage Khan wrought remains unclear to this day.

This is also a story that cannot be understood, however, without recognizing that for many people, and not just in his native Pakistan, Khan was—and remains—a hero. Many developing countries perceive a profound duplicity in a handful of states denying to others the technology that they refuse to relinquish. Critics argue that the United States particularly has sought to maintain a restrictive cartel on nuclear weapons. For the West, the spread of the bomb may be a nightmare, heightening global insecurity and making it more likely the weapon will be used. But for any individual nation facing its own particular challenges the bomb may represent the notion, real or imagined, of security. For Pakistanis, Khan delivered the security and prestige that his country so desperately desired, and he was feted for it accordingly.

Understanding the sharp dichotomy of perception over Khan also helps unlock some of the reasons why the existing architecture to control the spread of nuclear weapons is in such profound trouble. Khan's defiance of the West was not just an individual act but one that exemplified a deeper divergence of values that has yet to be bridged, a questioning of the attitudes that underpin the non-proliferation system. Khan himself always hated his caricature in the West as a "madman," arguing that his demonization was born out of frustration at how he undermined Western plans to project its power across the world. Like many others, he despised the non-proliferation system, but uniquely, Khan managed to bring it to its knees.

Most countries with nuclear weapons have engaged in atomic espionage. Most have also proliferated nuclear technology based on perceived strategic priorities—the United States to the UK, France to Israel, the Soviet Union to China, China to Pakistan. Khan was different. Here was an individual willing to proliferate to any country that was ready to pay—including Iran, North Korea, and Libya. And for the first time a dangerous array of products was available entirely in the private sector, outside of state control, creating what Mohammed El-Baradei, the head of the nuclear watchdog the IAEA, calls a "Wal-Mart of private-sector proliferation."[3] In short order, thanks to Khan's network with its "one-stop shopping," a country—any country—could take huge steps towards becoming a nuclear power.

While it may be tempting to over-individualize the story, to present A. Q. Khan as the lone villain, a comic book or spy film caricature, the "A. Q. Khan network" was very much a network. Khan was a middleman: a broker for businesses willing to supply and for states wanting to buy, he fused the commercial greed of the former with the strategic interests of the latter. His activities provide a unique window into a shadowy world in which a small group of nations worked collaboratively to develop advanced missile and nuclear technology out of sight of the rest of the world, technology that then became the foundation for a global trade that will far outlast its most famous contributor.

Why did Khan do it? Khan is often portrayed as either an agent of the Pakistani state or an entirely rogue actor. But each of the deals Khan cut was different—they differed in timescale, in scope, and in terms of what motivation lay behind them. Understanding this is vital in unlocking one of the frequently asked questions about Khan's activities—just how much did the Pakistani government know? The evidence is murky, fragmentary, and often circumstantial, but for Pakistan, almost any answer is an uncomfortable unhappy one. Either they knew nothing and their most sensitive national security programs were essentially out of their control or they knew of Khan's actions and failed to stop them. Either answer has profound consequences for understanding how easily the bomb can spread to more and more countries.

Given the damage he inflicted, why wasn't he stopped? Calling the emergence and resilience of the A. Q. Khan network a failure of intelligence is too simplistic. Khan's activities and the existence of a network around him were known about in Western intelligence for decades. But intelligence itself is not enough. The question is how it is used. There were periods when the trail went cold and warnings signs were missed but the intelligence was often hazy, right to the end, partly because programs developing weapons of mass destruction are the most closely held and closely guarded secrets of the most secretive regimes. Furthermore, knowing something is not the same as being able to do something about it. The problem all along was not so much uncovering Khan's activities as finding a way of acting against him. If there was a long-term failure, it was as much a failure of policy and political will, one revolving around America's strange, convulsive relationship with Pakistan, as it was of intelligence. For too long, the West was distracted.

As the second half of the book reveals, Khan's network was eventually broken through an effective harnessing of the different tools of intelligence and diplomacy. Khan did immeasurable damage but he could have done much more if he had not been stopped when he was. Despite this victory, the entire nuclear non-proliferation system is creaking at the seams. Today, like the mid-1970s, the world again faces the fear that, beginning with customers of Khan like Iran and North Korea, we may be at the cusp of a new era of accelerated proliferation. In a post-9/11 era with its pervasive sense of insecurity, a sense in part heightened by Western policy, more states seem to be keeping their options open and watching and waiting to see which way the tide breaks. Iran's ambitions may well signal the death knell of the current non-proliferation system because of the fear—so far not backed by definitive proof—that it is manipulating the system's weaknesses by exploiting its legal right to civilian power to garner technology that can also be used for a weapons program.

But whatever happens in the case of Iran, the broader problems revealed by A. Q. Khan's story remain with us. Right from the start in Eisenhower's day, a fundamental problem has been that the same core technologies can easily be diverted from producing power to weapons. In a world of transnational networks, international terrorists, and rapidly developing technology, preventing the spread of nuclear weapons is becoming more important but ever harder. Thanks to the Khan network, much of the equipment and knowledge for developing nuclear technology is no longer controlled by states—it is in the marketplace. Putting this genie back in the bottle may be impossible.

This book is not a biography of Khan, nor is it a detailed history of the technical characteristics of his network. It is rather an attempt to explain the questions of wider relevance. Why did Khan do what he did? Why wasn't he stopped? What are the complexities involved in halting the proliferation of nuclear weapons? The story of A. Q. Khan cannot be understood in isolation, in isolation from his status in Pakistan and its nuclear program, in isolation from his broader business network, or in isolation from the broader strategic context of interaction between rogue states trading technology. Much still remains unknown. The final answers lie with a man under house arrest in Islamabad, out of touch with the outside world, and out of reach of those who want to talk to him.

Part 1

RISE

CHAPTER 1

Roots

DUSK WAS JUST BEGINNING TO FALL as jubilant Indian paratroopers flooded onto the Ramna Green racecourse in Dhaka, East Pakistan. Celebratory gunfire echoed around the city. It was December 16, 1971, and in just thirteen days, India had crushed Pakistan's proud army. The leader of the Pakistani forces in the East, Lieutenant General "Tiger" Niazi, normally a bombastic, self-assured figure who had promised to fight to the last man, looked shell-shocked as he waited on the grass to sign the formal instrument of surrender. Wearing his trademark beret, Niazi was close to tears as he sat, surrounded by smiling Indian officers, at the wooden desk. After signing the type-written sheets, he stood, shook hands, stripped off his epaulettes, and then handed over his revolver to his Indian opposite number, the turban-clad Lieutenant General Aurora. Niazi was driven away in a jeep as Aurora was lifted on the arms of the crowds. With defeat, Dhaka was set to become the capital of the newly independent Bangladesh, its people having risen up, with Indian support, against unequal rule by the rest of Pakistan to the West. The nation of Pakistan had been dismembered and its very survival seemed to be at question. Despite rumors of the imminent appearance of the U.S. Seventh Fleet, none of Pakistan's supposed allies had come to its aid.

The TV pictures of the scene at Ramna and of the Pakistani Army's humiliation at the hands of its mortal enemy, India, were shown only once in West Pakistan. As soon as they appeared, a torrent of complaints flooded the country's sole TV channel and the army questioned whether the broadcast was a deliberate attempt to undermine its position.

But thirty-five hundred miles away in Europe, there were no such controls. In Belgium, a Pakistani student about to finish his doctorate watched the images of his nation's humiliation with a sense of horror and disbelief. He was plunged into depression. His misery prevented him from working for days. And out of his anger rose a deep resolve and determination that such a catastrophe should never be allowed to occur again and that he would play his part in preventing it.[1]

Abdul Qadeer Khan had not come to Europe as a spy. The young scientist arrived as a student in the early 1960s at a time of heady optimism. The belief that the marvels of nuclear technology were to be spread around the world amidst a culture of open scientific exchange still held sway and Khan would benefit greatly from this openness. As he began first his academic and then his professional career, colleagues and friends saw an amiable, lanky Pakistani who was comfortable living in the West and seemed to embody the cooperative, internationalist ethos of the times. But what few recognized was that beneath the calm, quiet facade ran a deep seam of nationalism and purpose.

Khan had been born in the town of Bhopal in British India in 1936, just over a decade before India and Pakistan were violently wrenched apart. In the bloody partition of 1947, millions were killed as Muslims fled from India to Pakistan and Hindus from Pakistan to India. As a witness to the chaos, events left deep scars on the boy. "The situation was relatively calm compared to what was happening in the rest of India and Pakistan," Khan would later recall of his hometown, "but still I can remember trains coming into the station full of dead Muslims." A fiery picture of the last train out of India still hangs in Khan's study in his home in Islamabad. In 1952 Khan decided he had no future in India and left to join his brothers in Pakistan. He made the journey over the border alone. The train ride, filled with harassment, intimidation, and violence, would remain etched in his memory. "At one train station the soldiers pulled gold jewelry off of Muslim women and pulled the earrings out of their ears," he remembered decades later. "Every valuable possession was taken from the passengers, and ticket checkers refused to return your ticket unless they were illegally gratified. I had been traveling with a pen that my brother gave me when I passed my exams, and just as I was crossing out of India, a border guard reached towards me and snatched it from my pocket. The pen had almost no monetary value, but the guard's behavior hurt me, and it was something I'll never forget."[2]

In Pakistan, Khan attended school and then university in the teeming city of Karachi. He proved to be a hard worker. His father was a headmaster at a school in the city and Khan planned to be educated in Europe, then return home to teach at a university. And so Khan set off for Europe in his mid-twenties. At first, he was overwhelmed by homesickness but would stay for more than a decade. He studied first in West Berlin, then in the Netherlands, and finally in Belgium where he completed his Ph.D. In doing so he built up not only scientific expertise but also a wide support network of academic sponsors and friends who were all too happy to help a pleasant, young Pakistani student along his way. Some would continue to help him later when his ambitions became darker. Those who knew Khan in this period remember an affable young man who had an uncanny knack of easily getting to know people from all over the world. While studying in Delft, in the Netherlands, he bumped into a young Dutch student named Henk Slebos in a coffee room in the university who was also studying metallurgy. Since they lived in rented rooms near each other, they decided to begin traveling to college together. "He was a serious student," Slebos recalled of his friend. "He was not what one would call a 'bon vivant.'" Slebos himself was a playful character and something of a practical joker, in contrast to the more earnest Pakistani. The two remained close friends over the years and eventually Slebos became an important associate of Khan.[3]

A. Q. Khan has had a greater impact on nuclear proliferation than any other individual in the last three decades, yet his story begins with simply a case of the right man at the right time in the right place. As he finished his Ph.D. in 1971, an opening came up for which his particular skills were ideally suited. Khan was trained as a metallurgist, not a nuclear scientist as is often assumed. Professor M. J. Brabers who supervised his thesis heard about a job at FDO (Physical Dynamics Research Laboratory) in the Netherlands and put in a good word. Without this job offer, Khan would most likely have ended up an unknown academic or engineer. On the strength of his professor's recommendation, Khan sailed through the interview and began work in May 1972, the moment when FDO was introducing the latest, most advanced nuclear technology. FDO was a subcontractor to Ultra Centrifuge Nederland (UCN). In turn, UCN was the Dutch wing of URENCO—an international consortium founded in 1971 that consisted of the UK, Germany, and the Netherlands which was at the forefront of Europe's attempts to develop the latest, most advanced centrifuge technology for nuclear fuel. Nuclear power was seen to represent a future of cheap, plentiful energy and Europe wanted its own supply of enriched uranium fuel that was independent of the United States. URENCO was their answer.

URENCO's cutting-edge operations were incongruously located in the sleepy town of Almelo set in rolling green countryside. Housed within a vast hall in the company's plant stood a regimented field of thousands of tall, slender cylinders connected together by a maze of metal piping. These were "cascades" of centrifuges, the machines that produced the nuclear fuel. Fissile material is the essential ingredient in nuclear programs because it can be split apart to release energy (in a controlled way for power, uncontrolled for weapons). But developing fissile material is far from easy. Natural uranium can be mined from the ground but only about 0.7 percent of it consists of the more fissile U235 isotope, the rest being U238. So the concentration of U235 has to be increased by a process known as enrichment. Uranium enriched to 5 percent U235 can be used as fuel for a nuclear power reactor, but if it continues to be enriched by the same process to around 90 percent, it can be used for a weapon. There are different enrichment methods based around separating U235 by exploiting its minutely lighter weight. One of these is using centrifuges. A rotor within the centrifuge cylinder casing spins uranium gas at incredibly high speeds, separating out the lighter U235 isotope so it can be gradually siphoned off. Each machine only enriches the gas a tiny amount and so the slightly more concentrated output of one machine is fed into the next centrifuge in a larger configuration of connected machines called a cascade. The technical challenges in building a single working centrifuge are considerable—each consists of a hundred parts and many of these have to be engineered to within a thousandth of a millimeter and able to withstand incredibly high speeds. One tiny mistake and the centrifuge will spin out of control, often crashing into other machines and destroying the entire cascade.

URENCO hired Khan because it was shifting to a new German-designed centrifuge model that required the translation of reams of documents. Khan's new job was to serve as part translator-part scientist. From his years as a student, Khan was fluent in English, Dutch, and German, and his metallurgical expertise was useful in analyzing what types of metal could stand up to the stress of spinning at high speeds and coping with corrosive gas. To begin his job, Khan had to obtain security clearance from the Dutch Security Service, which supervised URENCO. That procedure did not prove to be an obstacle. The process was sloppy: no one saw any great danger from a young scientist from a poor, undeveloped country like Pakistan who had been settled in Europe for more than a decade. It was the first of many examples of a lax attitude to security that ultimately proved embarrassing for URENCO and the Netherlands.

As he began work, Khan found it remarkably easy to come across sensitive information, often taking papers home over the weekend to work on. He had been given clearance to see material marked "restricted" but not the next levels of classification, "confidential" and "top secret," yet that didn't stop him from getting access to information at these higher levels. Khan was supposed to work in one of a number of small offices beyond a perimeter fence from the main building at Almelo and he was supposed to only enter the main plant with an escort. However, according to staff who worked there at the time, almost immediately after starting work he began making trips inside the secret centrifuge plant by himself, acquiring an inside understanding of the secret technology. Staff at URENCO drove over from Germany with classified designs, drawings, and specifications for the new centrifuge carried in a diplomatic pouch. Khan would then translate the documents and draft engineering requirements.[4] No one asked any questions as Khan wandered round with his notebook. At one point a colleague saw Khan taking notes in Urdu, his native tongue, but he claimed he was just writing a personal letter—a claim that was readily accepted. A Dutch government report later noted that there had been an "open atmosphere." Even though his specialty was in the field of metallurgy, his gaze merrily wandered across a much broader variety of information. Crucially, he was not just learning how the centrifuge worked but how it was put together and who supplied the parts that made the whole.

Meanwhile, Khan lived what appeared to be an ordinary, family life at his home in the quiet suburb of Zwanenburg. In a post office in 1963 he had met Hendrina, a quiet, friendly Dutch–South African woman. They married in the Pakistani Embassy in The Hague, and the two showed all the signs of being a young couple in love, constantly holding hands. Frits Veerman started work at FDO in the 1960s and was later introduced to his new colleague, Khan, with whom he would eventually share an office. "He was a friendly man and he took a lot of interest in his fellow workers," recalls Veerman. Despite a somewhat stern face, Khan was an easy-going young man and would often bring in sweets for his colleagues. The two men soon became friends and Veerman frequently ate dinner (usually Pakistani food rather than European) at Khan's home on evenings or weekends, getting to know Khan's wife as well as his daughters Dina and Ayesha. It was Veerman who would eventually be one of the first to realize that Khan was leading a double life.

Khan embarked on his life as a spy in the autumn of 1974. There is no evidence that he was recruited. Rather, a sense of wounded national pride seems to have grown in the wake of the 1971 defeat. This led Khan to volunteer himself: he wrote a letter on September 17 through Pakistan's embassy in Belgium to the country's Prime Minister Zulfikar Ali Bhutto and offered his services to his nation. He told Bhutto that he should consider the enrichment route to developing fissile nuclear material for a bomb, that he had the know-how to accomplish it, and that he wanted to return to help. His motivation appears primarily patriotic—a chance to put his contacts and access at his country's service.

Khan's timing was exquisite. His offer had come at a critical juncture, just as Pakistan's nuclear program was shifting gears. There had been a low-level civilian program since 1954, when an American "Atoms for Peace" exhibition toured the country, touting the wonders of nuclear power. This led to the establishment of the Pakistan Atomic Energy Commission (PAEC) and eventually the purchase of a small nuclear reactor supplying energy. But the humiliating capitulation at Ramna shook Pakistan's political, military, and strategic foundations to the core and set Pakistan on a new path.

Although it was the Indian test of a nuclear explosive in 1974 that finally drove Pakistan towards the bomb, the initial impetus came earlier, born out of the catastrophic defeat of 1971. In 1970 Pakistan's first national elections had exposed a country that was deeply divided politically as well as geographically. Pakistan had been formed less than a quarter of a century before as two entirely separate territories, East and West Pakistan, with no common border and India in between them. The residents of East Pakistan were resentful because they were treated as second-class citizens and locked out of the best jobs in the army and civil service by West Pakistanis—and so, out of the elections came polarization and then unrest. In March 1971 West Pakistan had ordered a crackdown in the East that descended into brutality, eventually triggering the intervention of India and a catastrophic defeat.

The lessons of that defeat would define Pakistan military and strategic thinking for decades to come. These were, firstly, that India could not be trusted and was bent on Pakistan's destruction; secondly, that when it came to the crunch, despite whatever "security guarantees" they may offer, the United States (and other allies) could not be relied upon to provide meaningful military support to protect the nation; and finally, as a result of these other two lessons and since it was now painfully evident that Pakistan could not match India with conventional military force, nuclear weapons were the only way of levelling the playing field and ensuring the survival of the nation.

Four days after the surrender at the Ramna racecourse, President Yahya Khan resigned and Zulfikar Ali Bhutto assumed power. The charismatic, flamboyant Bhutto had a near messianic sense of destiny and of his own role in restoring the country's shattered pride. "I was born to make a nation, to serve a people, to overcome an impending doom," he wrote at the end of his life.[5] He had also long been an advocate of a nuclear weapons program. During the 1960s when concern was growing over India's activities, Bhutto, then a cabinet minister, had begun to develop a keen interest in the subject. In 1965 he'd uttered his famous promise: "If India builds the bomb, we will eat grass or leaves, even go hungry, but we will get one of our own. We have no other choice."

On taking office Bhutto wasted little time in making his dramatic move. On January 20, 1972, he summoned together the country's top scientific and military minds for a secret meeting. Some scientists came from as far as the United States hoping to help their homeland. The meeting was planned for the previous week in the town of Quetta, but winter storms coming in from Afghanistan forced Bhutto to move it to the lawn of a colonial mansion in Multan. At the meeting Bhutto started slowly and worked himself up into a fury. In one of the eloquent rhetorical outbursts for which he became well known, Bhutto made clear to the assembled group that he intended to restore their country's honor. Would they join him in this great patriotic task? "The meeting was pure showmanship and vintage Bhutto. It was rather like a jamboree . . . There was a great deal of enthusiasm and joy," recounted Bhutto's press secretary Khalid Hasan who attended the meeting and provided the first account of it a few years later to the BBC. "He said 'We're going to have a bomb' like 'We're going to have a party.' And he said 'Can you give it to me?' So they started shouting like schoolchildren. They said 'Oh yes, yes, you can have it, you can have it.' And Bhutto was very amused and he said "Much as I appreciate your enthusiasm these are serious matters but in any case this is a very serious political decision which Pakistan must make and perhaps all third would countries must make one day because the time is coming. So can you do it?' They said 'we can do it given the resources and the facilities.' So Bhutto said 'I can find you the resources and I can find you the facilities.'"[6] Bhutto asked how long it would take to build a bomb. The scientists said five years. He replied that he wanted it in three and promised to spare nothing to support the scientists in their quest. Pakistan would stand tall again.

At the meeting, younger scientists like the British-educated Sultan Bashiruddin Mahmood voiced their support for the bomb.[7] A few of the older generation expressed their concerns about whether it really was possible or desirable to move towards nuclear weapons. Bhutto tolerated no dissent and a scientist named Munir Khan replaced one of the doubters, the chair of Pakistan's Atomic Energy Commission (PAEC), during the actual meeting. An elegant well-spoken man, Munir Khan came from an established family and had been educated in the United States on a Fulbright scholarship before working for the International Atomic Energy Agency (IAEA) in Vienna. But while he supported the building of the bomb, his time in the West made him the target for critics and rivals who questioned his loyalties.[8] A. Q. Khan was not involved at this stage. No one outside this small coterie knew it, but Pakistan had embarked on its long journey to becoming a nuclear power.

Much has been made of the notion of an "Islamic Bomb" and the idea that Bhutto was seeking to create something for the entire Muslim world. In practice, Bhutto was driven by the more prosaic reality of dealing with India's conventional military advantage and emerging nuclear program, as well as by a nationalistic desire to show that Pakistan really was capable of building its own bomb. Bhutto's motivation was not primarily religious —rather he was a developing-world nationalist who asked why only the Western world should be allowed nuclear weapons. This too, would be A. Q. Khan's creed—the notion that the bomb should not be the sole preserve of Western powers. However, the rhetoric of the "Islamic Bomb" did prove particularly useful when it came to finding the money for a program. Pakistan was a poor country and a nuclear weapons program would cost billions of dollars in clandestine funding. From where was it to come?

In the weeks after the Multan meeting, Bhutto went on a world tour of twenty countries, focusing particularly on the Middle East. During this trip, Bhutto planted the international roots of Pakistan's program that would nurture it in the long term. Amongst the stops was Libya. There, Bhutto met with Libya's young, new leader, Colonel Gadaffi. "The atmosphere was beautiful," later recounted Khalid Hasan, Bhutto's press secretary, who had accompanied him on the trip. Thousands of expatriate Pakistanis living in Libya turned out to greet Bhutto. "It was evening when we landed in Tripoli and we could see nothing but people . . . Gadaffi was there, and he come onto the tarmac and embraced Bhutto, and I think kissed him on both cheeks."[9] The visit was short, a night and a day, but of enduring importance. Gadaffi took Bhutto to his house where his wife had put on traditional Pakistani dress in a tribute to their guest. The two men hit it off and found much in common with their revolutionary nationalist rhetoric. Pakistan was also grateful that Libya had provided military assistance in 1971 and now there was the chance to work together.

Gadaffi had taken power in 1969 at the youthful age of twenty-seven. He had been born in the desert to a simple, nomadic Bedouin family before joining the military (where he trained briefly in Britain) before returning home to become the leader of a small group of revolutionary officers. Overthrowing the king of Libya in a coup, the young leader's ambitions were expansive: he immediately set the country on an anti-colonialist and anti-western course. Gadaffi was charismatic and supremely self-confident and wasted no time in making clear he wanted a nuclear weapon—"the sword of Islam" as he described it.[10] At this time, his desire for the bomb was driven by status and self-image—it would give the Libyan leader the place on the world stage that he coveted so much.

Whilst he had the wealth from oil, Gadaffi had none of the technology or scientific base for his own program. In 1970, within months of taking power, he sent an emissary to make rather naïve approaches to try and buy a bomb from China. The emissary was quickly rebuffed. Now Bhutto had arrived in Libya looking for money. Why not strike a deal with the Pakistanis? Libya would provide the funds and the Pakistanis would develop the weapon. Secret meetings took place in Paris in 1973. An Organisation of the Islamic Conference (OIC) meeting in February 1974 in Lahore saw Bhutto cement his position with the Islamic world and particularly with the Libyan leader, naming the city's cricket stadium after him. Munir Khan, the new chief of Pakistan's nuclear program, also provided a tour of Pakistan's nuclear reactor in Karachi to Gadaffi. An iconic photograph shows Bhutto and Gadaffi with their fists clenched during the summit. Addressing a mammoth crowd at the newly christened Gaddafi Stadium, the Libyan leader declared that his country was ready to sacrifice its blood if Pakistan were ever threatened: "Our resources are your resources," he promised.[11] Cash began to be flown from Tripoli outside of normal accounts. By 1976 declassified files revealed that the United States had received intelligence indicating that a financing deal did exist—although it saw it as being for "some unspecific future nuclear co-operation."[12]

Libya had expected full access to the technology but it did not take long before Gadaffi began to feel shortchanged.[13] Pakistanis meanwhile were wary of the insistence that joint projects had to be located in Libya even though the manpower and expertise was coming from Pakistan.[14] The relationship faded. Bhutto may have played up the notion of an "Islamic bomb" amongst fellow Muslim states to garner support but privately he realized there were limits to the benefits of such a notion to Pakistan and its acceptability to the West, warning his daughter that the world would accept a Pakistani bomb but not an Islamic one.

In his travels, Bhutto also courted financing from the Gulf States, including Saudi Arabia. These countries were flush with cash from revenues following the 1973 oil crisis and wanted to counter a possible Israeli bomb. Defeat at the hands of Israel in 1973 had shattered Arab and Muslim pride and led to a new impetus to try and use technology to level the playing field. Many Arab countries worried, however, that if one of them were to move too fast down the nuclear path, they would risk being attacked by Israel (as happened to Iraq in 1981). A Pakistan program—seen by the world as a counter to that of India—was less likely to be stopped. Lacking the technological base to develop its own program, Saudi Arabia was highly supportive of Pakistan's program, secretly offering financing, it is believed, in return for security guarantees or access to the technology.[15] When it came to Pakistan's nuclear capacity, "the Saudis regard Pakistan as a trustworthy friend who will come to Saudi Arabia's assistance whenever the occasion arises," argued former Pakistani Ambassador to Saudi Arabia Shahid Amin.[16] Payments from the Gulf States to Pakistan are suspected to have passed through the Bank of Credit and Commerce International (BCCI), a shadowy institution founded in Pakistan that funded Pakistan's nuclear quest amongst an array of other shady dealings.[17]

Bhutto brought on board his most crucial ally when he paid a number of visits to Beijing, the first in January 1972, again in May 1974, and then a critical visit in the summer of 1976.[18] Bhutto had pioneered closer relations with the Chinese from the 1960s when he was foreign minister. Bhutto recognized that China was keen to help Pakistan in order to counter India with whom it had fought a brief war in 1962. From the early 1970s Chinese tanks and aircraft were increasingly visible at Pakistan's national military parades as it replenished stocks used up in the 1971 war. Economic and technical support also began heading to Islamabad. Bhutto described gaining China's support as "my greatest achievement and contribution to the survival of our people and our nation" and the culmination of eleven years of work. Beijing's aid was also to prove of enduring significance for Khan. Secretly, Bhutto had also gained China's agreement to help build a nuclear bomb.[19] China was to be the silent partner in Pakistan's program, providing it with crucial technical help in its early years.

At just after eight o'clock in the morning on May 18, 1974, in the desert village Pokhran in Rajasthan, India tested what it called a "peaceful nuclear explosive." The strange designation came about because India still wanted to retain something of the moral high ground it had always tried to occupy. But it had increasingly come to see the non-proliferation regime as a means by which the West was preventing India from developing its own technology and achieving its own security.[20] India's decision was driven as much by domestic considerations as broader international strategy, a desire to show that it could transcend its colonial past and master the science that had previously been the preserve of the West. That was coupled with a desire to be seen as a global player and send a message to its neighbors, China more so than Pakistan.

But it was in Islamabad that India's test had the greatest impact. Suddenly, the program Bhutto had begun with such a flourish in 1972 acquired a real sense of urgency. It was no longer a mere option to be pursued, it was now an imperative. The test also had its impact on Abdul Qadeer Khan watching events from the Netherlands. It seems to have been the tipping point that led Khan to turn to atomic espionage and to make his skillful pitch in the letter to Bhutto a few months later. It was India's test that made Khan's offer so tempting to Pakistan's leader. Khan's entreaty caught the attention first of Bhutto's military secretary who then handed it to the prime minister himself. "He seemed to be talking sense," Bhutto wrote in the margin of the letter and passed it on to Munir Khan telling him to arrange a meeting.[21] So Khan traveled to Pakistan at the end of 1974 for a series of secret meetings with officials, using the code-name "Karim" and staying at the house of a relative in Karachi.[22] Khan later claimed he met with the prime minister himself, although that may not have been the case.[23] He was told that his services would be required but that he should stay a little longer in the Netherlands to garner as much expertise as he could.

Back in the Netherlands, by the end of 1974, Khan's work as a stealer of secrets became increasingly bold. Cars with diplomatic plates from Pakistan's Embassies in France and Belgium would be parked at his house until the early hours of the morning. In October 1974 he was allowed to spend sixteen invaluable days in the so-called "brainbox" of Almelo where the most sensitive work was undertaken.[24] He was supposed to be escorted but frequently went in alone—the door was left wide open for Khan to undertake his most important piece of espionage, gaining access to the very latest plans for the G-2 centrifuge. By 1975 Khan had access to the information that would become the basis of his career as Pakistan's hero and an international proliferator. He stole the designs for almost every centrifuge on the drawing board, URENCO officials would later admit.[25] The parts found on the *BBC China* nearly thirty years later as well as the discoveries found on the ground in Iran and Libya (and which are hidden somewhere in North Korea) would all be derivatives of those centrifuges being developed in the mid-1970s in the Netherlands. The designs were invaluable. Knowledge, not physical material, was the essence of Khan's work and the secret to his success.

During 1975, Sultan Bashiruddin Mahmood, one of the younger scientists who had voiced his support for the bomb at Bhutto's meeting in Multan and had subsequently been appointed as a key figure, came to Europe to begin the search for the technology that could support a nuclear program. Khan came over from Holland to see him and both men stayed in the attic of a Pakistani diplomat's house. Soon after, vital drawings and blueprints began to flow from Khan through an intermediary, including the names of suppliers. This allowed purchasers to start knocking on the doors of various businesses.[26] During 1975, as he became more brazen, Khan also became more careless. His friend, Frits Veerman's suspicions began to be aroused, not least by Khan's rather haphazard security, hardly the actions of a trained spy. At the Khan household, Veerman spotted centrifuge drawings and in their shared office space, he began to overhear phone conversations with people in Pakistan and individuals from Pakistani embassies in Europe relating to centrifuge technology. Khan would talk about sensitive details quite openly in front of Veerman. Veerman told his managers at FDO three times. "I said he was spying but they didn't believe me at first." Their reaction was to deny it was possible and to do nothing. The lax security at FDO even allowed groups to come over from Pakistan on a handful of occasions to visit the facility and for Khan to send discarded centrifuge parts to Pakistan.[27]

Finally, by late 1975, the managers at FDO were beginning to wake up to the fact that they might have a problem. A French company was asked by the Pakistani Embassy in Belgium to find a special foil, knowledge of which was highly restricted and could only have come from someone with inside knowledge of the URENCO program. By October FDO had contacted Dutch authorities to express their concerns. It has only recently become clear that from this point, Khan was coming under official scrutiny. Just how closely he was watched and by whom is a matter of debate. Ruud Lubbers, who was minister for Economic Affairs in 1975, has claimed that the Dutch authorities considered arresting Khan but were stopped by the CIA. "The Americans wished to follow and watch Khan to get more information," Lubbers told Dutch radio three decades later. However, U.S. officials involved at the time deny this was the case and say that it was the Dutch who had Khan under surveillance, who failed to pick him up, and who never realized that he might flee. Khan's friend, Henk Slebos, has also claimed that Khan was in regular contact with the Dutch Security Service during the time he worked at URENCO. "He met them on a regular basis," claims Slebos, although the purpose of the meetings is unclear.[28]

So why was he not picked up? Security officers at the plant also said they noticed Khan behaving suspiciously and asking questions outside his area but when this was reported to superiors they said not to do anything. The most likely explanation for this inactivity is that the security services thought it would be more valuable to watch Khan and try and work out what he was up to. If so, it was the first of a number of costly mistakes, many of them stemming from an underestimation of Khan's ability and the danger he posed. Instead of being arrested, Khan was simply promoted away from involvement in the centrifuge program but left a free man. With the shuffling of his job, Khan realized the game was up. But he already had stolen the information he needed. Within two months, on December 15, 1975, he left, telling everyone he was going on a brief holiday to Pakistan. His wife later wrote to friends that a bout of yellow fever would keep him away for another two months. During his return to Pakistan, Khan decided the time had come for him to return and take control of the enrichment program. He soon submitted his resignation letter to his old employers.

Khan had left suddenly but his contact with his old firm did not stop. Orders came into FDO from Pakistan for equipment (some of which was still supplied). Khan also wrote a number of letters to Veerman. In January 1976, almost immediately after returning to Pakistan, Khan wrote saying he was sick and had to remain in bed but was missing the chicken and other food in Holland. He then asked for help with information on components and designs.[29] In another letter he asked Veerman to come to Pakistan on holiday, but Veerman became suspicious when Khan insisted that the Pakistani government pay for all the expenses and he declined. By the summer of 1976, Khan's letters to Veerman (often passed on by hand via a visiting Pakistani scientist or someone from the embassy) began to ask for classified, highly specific technical information. "Very confidentially, I request you to help us. I urgently need the following for our research programme," Khan wrote asking for information on the etches of pivots used in the bottom of centrifuges. "I shall be very grateful if you could send a few negatives for the pattern . . . I hope you will not disappoint me."[30] This time when Veerman showed his letters to FDO directors, the reaction was anger rather than disbelief. These letters were eventually used against Khan when was he was put on trial in absentia in Holland in 1983.[31] Dutch Security Service officers also came to see Veerman with photos of Pakistanis who had served abroad under diplomatic cover to see if he could identify any of them.[32] They had realized the danger of the spy in their midst too late.

Khan did not suffer fools gladly and could be prickly and brusque, not least with those who worked for him. And on his return to Pakistan at the end of 1975, Khan's fierce ambition was soon all too evident as he begun to elbow others aside. Sultan Bashiruddin Mahmood ran an early pilot enrichment program at Sihala in Northern Pakistan and A. Q. Khan initially worked under Mahmood as his director of research and development. On April 19, 1976, he wrote a letter to Munir Khan, the head of the entire nuclear program, expressing frustration, "I am not at all satisfied with it and could have contributed at least ten times of what I have been able to do."[33] Friction soon emerged between A. Q. Khan and the more staid, less flamboyant and aggressive Munir Khan, the start of a rivalry that would last for decades with profound consequences. Khan seemed to resent Munir's status and began to question whether he really was committed to delivering the bomb.

A. Q. Khan had a useful ability to get close and to remain close to whoever was in power in Pakistan at the time. He soon persuaded Bhutto that everything was going far too slow on enrichment and that he needed his own organization to get the process moving. Khan had the great advantage of being the only person in the entire Pakistan program who had ever actually seen a working centrifuge. By July 1976 Engineering Research Laboratories (ERL) was established as an independent organization under Khan's control, reporting directly to the prime minister, not to the Pakistan Atomic Energy Commission (PAEC) or the rest of the nuclear establishment under Munir Khan. This provided A. Q. Khan with the power base and with the autonomy and secrecy that allowed him to do so much. A three-member board would eventually be established to oversee the organization consisting of A.G.N. Kazi (to provide funding), Ghulam Ishaq Khan (to liaise with the military), and Agha Shahi (to deal with foreign relations and protect Khan and his work against foreign pressure).

Finding a home for Khan's secret plant was the next task. Khan himself took charge of this process, scouting out a number of sites. His feet became bloody from thorns as he trod miles round the hills searching for the perfect hideaway. By September 1976 he had settled on the locality of Kahuta. Even though it was in an earthquake zone, Khan said he didn't want his scientists to be out in the wilderness but near the capital, Islamabad. The terrain also offered the possibility of building underground, which would secure the most sensitive work against attack. The compensation for the parcels of land needed to make up the one-hundred-acre site was so generous that locals queued up to offer their property.

Kahuta's secretive work was known as Project 706. At the start, it consisted of a leaky, broken down building, full of bats. "It was literally a shed," said one person involved from the very beginning who remembers the sense of excitement and purpose that surrounded the task. "We understood at that time, this project was make or break for the country. It was the most important mission for the government." From the start, security was exceptionally tight. "It was more secure than the prime minister's house," said one senior military official associated with Kahuta. "We were very vigilant. We were very aware of the U.S. trying to put in spies."[34] Staff and their families were told to socialize with each other and not talk to strangers. Local shepherds and residents were told to keep watch for any suspicious activities around the plant. Kahuta would not remain secret for long though.

Once again, broader events were conspiring to make Khan the right man at the right time in the right place. Ironically, it was a piece of successful U.S. counter-proliferation action that would give Khan his next break. 1977 saw the arrival in Washington of the Carter administration, which had campaigned on placing a higher priority on nuclear non-proliferation. For the first time since the peaceful and military aspects of nuclear technology had been decoupled under Atoms for Peace, the spread of nuclear power was linked directly with that of the spread of nuclear weapons. The Indian explosion of 1974 had shaken the complacent non-proliferation system to the core. That India had used a civilian nuclear power infrastructure to develop the bomb shattered preconceived notions of what was possible. It led to a new sense that the problem of nuclear proliferation was suddenly accelerating beyond traditional powers and into new aspiring nations. Suddenly, Atoms for Peace seemed like a much more dangerous slogan than it had in previous, more optimistic times.

At the same time, more countries were seeking nuclear technology for a mix of commercial and strategic motives. Nuclear power looked more attractive partly as a result of the oil crisis of 1973, which had created concerns over energy dependency, and partly because it provided the potential for weapons. A domino effect meant that as more countries were seen as possibly going down that path, others felt they needed to follow. In the mid-1970s, there was a palpable sense of proliferation accelerating. By 1975 the Shah of Iran was talking about starting a massive nuclear power program. Iraq responded by signing a deal with the French for a reactor. Brazil, Argentina, South Korea, and Taiwan were also believed to be pursuing programs—all of which could lead to the nuclear bomb.

As well as mounting demand, there were also a growing number of countries willing to supply nuclear equipment. Because of the rich spoils, there was intense competition to become a purveyor of nuclear technology. Germany was negotiating a deal with Brazil, France with Pakistan. The situation risked spiraling out of control. In the immediate wake of the Indian test, the United States had halted new contracts to supply nuclear fuel. Previously, by supplying discount fuel it had dissuaded others from entering the market. But now the Europeans sensed a business opportunity and the riches on offer were vast and tempting—the CIA estimated that international nuclear exports could gross forty to fifty billion dollars over the following five years.[35] Business interests were a powerful lobby everywhere including in the United States. President Carter appointed Joseph Nye, a cerebral academic who also enjoyed the cut and thrust of diplomacy, to be the lead diplomat on the subject. Nye soon found that in addition to battling Europeans who disliked the administration's moralistic tone, his new post also engaged him in vicious internal politics with those keen to secure contracts for nuclear energy. Over the previous decades, an influential network had built up of scientists, engineers, bureaucrats, and businessmen engaged in nuclear power, a network that often crossed national boundaries and that formed a powerful lobby on behalf of nuclear energy. "I can remember one official from one of the companies telling me he would try and get me fired because he disagreed with my policy. It didn't work," recalls Nye.[36]

The United States was determined to stem the tide. By the late 1970s, the CIA was beginning to learn of Pakistan's interest in nuclear weapons. But it was convinced that any Pakistani nuclear weapons program would draw on plutonium not enriched uranium. There are two paths to developing nuclear weapons. One is developing fissile material for a bomb through uranium enrichment. The other involves reprocessing spent fuel from a nuclear power reactor to make a plutonium bomb. For this route, alongside a civilian nuclear reactor, all that's needed is a specialist reprocessing plant to separate out the plutonium from the highly radioactive spent fuel rods—the plutonium can then either be used for a weapon or as further fuel for a reactor. Few in the West thought that any non-Western country could develop the technological know-how to develop its own enrichment process, and so up to the late 1970s plutonium was seen as the primary problem to watch out for. Stopping countries from buying reactors and reprocessing plants was the task at hand, or so it appeared.

Plutonium was indeed Pakistan's initial preferred option for the bomb. It had obtained a reactor, which began operating in Karachi in 1972. With a reprocessing plant, Pakistan could have the material to make up to fifteen or twenty bombs a year. A contract was signed in March 1973 with a French company to provide just that capability. But India's May 1974 tests caused major complications. Suddenly, the world woke up to the possibility that so called "less-advanced" nations might actually be able to arrive at nuclear weapons technology using the nuclear power technology supplied by the developed world.

But how could countries be stopped? In the following months, a nascent non-proliferation regime emerged to try and control technology exports. Rather than try to provide security guarantees to countries like India and Pakistan to reduce their desire for nuclear weapons, the existing weapons states decided to try to deal with supply rather than demand by restricting the export of equipment. The London Club (later to become the Nuclear Suppliers Group) was designed to stop the kind of competitive spiral in which one country would sell sensitive items for fear that if they didn't someone else would—and take the profit. For Joe Nye, stopping Pakistan from getting a reprocessing plant was a top priority. He first traveled out to Islamabad to meet Pakistani officials but met with a dead end. There was no chance of them cancelling a legitimate contract, they informed him curtly.

The next stop was France to see if they could be convinced. France believed that nuclear energy was the future and that it could capture more of the market, especially because the United States was coming to be seen as a less reliable exporter after threatening to curtail supplies based on foreign policy considerations. Nye's job was to convince the French that the Pakistanis would misuse their technology. The CIA had already managed to recruit spies in Pakistan's nuclear program. And by January 1976 this human intelligence, as well as highly classified satellite imagery, had shown that Pakistan wanted the capability provided by the French for much more than an energy program. "We discovered some pretty good evidence that they were doing experiments that were related to making a weapon," recalls Nye. He flew to Paris to confront the French with the evidence. "I talked to Foreign Ministry people and they had a hard time taking it on board." The person who made the difference was André Giraud, the head of the French Atomic Energy Commission. "I remember him saying to me 'If this is true—and we will have to make sure of that for our ourselves—it may require us to change our policy—which is a very straightforward type of response.'"[37] The French did their checking and the deal was off.

One avenue had been successfully closed but it had merely diverted Pakistan down another where Khan was busy at work. The blocking of the French deal in 1978 was on the surface a major blow to Pakistan's nuclear ambitions. But while it may have pushed forward the time scale for Pakistan to obtain nuclear material, it was also a moment when Khan and his work could move center stage. With his knowledge of enrichment technology, his expertise suddenly became not just a backup option to the preferred plutonium route but the only realistic way for Pakistan to get its hands on weapons-grade material. The enrichment route was also much easier to keep clandestine since it did not require a large, purchased facility such as a reprocessing plant but could be put together piecemeal and hidden. Many were sceptical about whether a country like Pakistan could manage to develop its own technically advanced enrichment program. These sceptics were not only in the West, but also on the three-man board that managed Khan's activities and amongst the businessmen who supplied Khan with technology. But Khan would prove them all wrong.

Khan quickly found a way of subverting the new non-proliferation system, developing methods he would apply throughout his career. He understood that trying to buy entire enrichment plants was not realistic—it was too obvious and would be blocked in no time. However, thanks to his time studying URENCO he knew exactly who supplied every part to make the latest centrifuge. Buying these parts direct from suppliers or through middlemen would be harder for Western intelligence agencies to detect. It would also play to the greed of European suppliers happy to make a sale without asking questions about where their specialized equipment might eventually end up. Khan was learning that commercial greed could be his greatest ally. Almost all of the equipment in Kahuta—the equipment that would be used to make the weapons material for Pakistan's bombs—came from Europe. And this procurement network, which Khan began in the mid to late 1970s, in turn became the basis for Khan's proliferation network of the following decades. "A country which could not make sewing needles, good and durable bicycles or even ordinary durable metal rods was embarking on one of the latest and most difficult technologies," Khan later said of this period. "We devised a strategy by which we could go all out to buy everything that we needed in the open market to lay the foundation of a good infrastructure and would then switch over to indigenous production as and when we had to. My long stay in Europe and intimate knowledge of various countries and their manufacturing firms was an asset."[38]

Teams spanned out across the world usually working out of Pakistan's embassies. Diplomatic pouches which could not be searched or Pakistan's official airline were sometimes used for shipping sensitive items. Front companies were set up but Pakistan often found that using existing businesses and asking them to help in their patriotic duty was often the most effective route. There was often little disguising what the purchasers were after or from where the information came . In some cases, businesses were shown the actual copies of blueprints from URENCO and asked how much it would cost for a particular product. When they were quoted a price, the Pakistani buyers would tell the surprised businessmen to raise it by another 50 percent. It was no wonder that so many suppliers knew they were on to a good thing with Khan and would stay with him for so many years and keep quiet about his activities.

In 1976, Pakistani teams—including Khan himself and his number two, a scientist called G. D. Alam—made the pilgrimage to Switzerland's "Vacuum Valley," a series of small industrial villages along the Rhine that had become a hub for specialized centrifuge equipment. On their shopping trip, they found a business named CORA Engineering, which would provide a custom-made uranium conversion facility. The facility converts uranium into gas to be fed into the centrifuge and turns it back into a solid after being enriched. CORA saw no problem in the deal. "What can lead to a nuclear weapon that is the question of course," responded an executive when reporters challenged him later. "Nuts and bolts can lead to a nuclear weapon. Where do you draw the line?"[39] The unit was so large it had to be flown on three specially chartered C-130 planes to Pakistan along with other material from Switzerland.

The purchasing team also paid a visit to Vakkuum Apparate Technik (VAT), which was willing to provide the vacuum tube and valve equipment required for an enrichment plant. VAT queried the Swiss government as to whether this broke export controls but since only complete centrifuges were on the restricted list the government saw no reason to object even though the final purpose was obvious. Switzerland's support for free trade and neutrality in international affairs made it a willing exporter, not least because it may have seen some advantage in having indigenous technology should the country ever need its own nuclear program. However, no government was keen to lose out in the growing lucrative export market for nuclear technology by being tougher on their companies than other governments. Friedrich Tinner was the export manager for VAT and met Khan when he came to Switzerland. The two men forged an enduring relationship, still meeting nearly a quarter of a century later, long after Tinner had left VAT and founded his own firm.[40]

In some cases, suppliers must have known what the purpose was, in other cases they may have been deceived, or the lure of large amounts of cash may have persuaded them to deceive themselves. Germany was another major purchasing hub for nuclear equipment, with the company Leybold Heraeus helping with a uranium hexafluoride handling plant as well as other items. An employee of Leybold, Gotthard Lerch, traveled over to Pakistan and would, like Friedrich Tinner, remain in touch with Khan long after the initial deal had run its course, setting up his own company in Switzerland after he left Leybold in 1985.

Though perfectly willing to sell equipment, Germany blocked the sale of the raw material—uranium yellowcake—that Pakistan had looked to buy through a middleman. Pakistan found another route. The African state of Niger boasts few natural resources. But the one thing it does have, buried deep in the Sahara desert, hundreds of miles from anywhere, is raw uranium. Huge craters lie in the desert where it is mined in searing temperatures, creating what looks from afar like an inverted pyramid with layered walls. After being mined, the ore is milled, crushed, and purified before being dried into uranium oxide—commonly known as yellowcake. The yellowcake is later turned into gas—uranium hexafluoride (UF6 or "Hex") at a conversion plant—which is then pumped into centrifuges to be enriched.

The key figure in Niger in the mid-1970s was again the Libyan leader, Colonel Gadaffi. Libya and Niger had enjoyed a prickly relationship over the years but Gadaffi had supported a coup that brought Colonel Seyni Kountche to power in 1974. Gadaffi saw the selling of uranium to Pakistan as a means of reinforcing Libya's role (and protecting his investment) in Pakistan's nuclear program. Convoys would travel 150 miles from the mines to an airstrip at Agadez and then fly across the Sahara to Tripoli. Some of the material would then be flown on to Karachi in Pakistan. Kountche was quite open about the sales, "We are selling to Pakistan and if the IAEA doesn't carry out proper supervision that's a matter for its own conscience." But since Niger sold its uranium to Libya, which then shipped some of it on to Pakistan, there was no way for the nuclear material watchdog, the IAEA, to know what Pakistan had.[41] The CIA was aware by January 1977 of Pakistan's approach to Niger but thought it was for energy needs rather than the bomb and wasn't aware of an actual transfer (nearly thirty years later, it would be able to confirm the transfer when it finally got access into Libya).[42] Eventually, Pakistan, like most other aspirant nuclear countries, would work to develop its own indigenous uranium mining capacity but Niger, like many of the locations and characters from Khan's earliest days, would play a part later in his story.

Khan had an uncanny ability to maintain contacts with individuals who were useful and draw them into his network. Many of the scientists from Europe who had taught him visited Pakistan soon after Khan returned—although they deny helping build a bomb. Often the professors would get their air tickets free or half price courtesy of the Pakistan government. Khan's college friend from their time studying metallurgy at Delft, Henk Slebos, was one such visitor. After a brief spell in the navy, he went to work for another URENCO subcontractor before starting his own company whose website would later boast that it specialized in "technical purchasing": "we find hard-to-get objects for customers all over the world." In 1976 Slebos went to Pakistan for the first time. He was said to have code-named his work supplying Khan "Operation Butter Factory." The following year a business partner reported his suspicions to the Dutch Security Service and Slebos was investigated but not stopped. He would be a key supplier for Khan and Pakistan to the very end, despite the odd run-in with the authorities. He was unlucky in October 1983 when unions at a Dutch airport were checking every package as a result of a labor dispute. In Slebos's luggage they found a U.S.-made oscilloscope heading for Pakistan via the United Arab Emirates (UAE). He spent no time in jail.[43] "Business was never interrupted," he later said of the aftermath of the arrest.[44]

Even when Khan and his network caught the attention of Europe's authorities, they were underestimated. A key moment came in Britain in 1978 when the sale of specialist high-frequency inverters from Swindon-based Emerson Electric became public. The inverters were the same type used by British Nuclear Fuels in their uranium enrichment and ensured a precise and constant power supply to centrifuges—vital when they are spinning extremely fast. After the sale of an initial first batch, a scientist who worked at the company said in a BBC documentary that anybody who was anybody in the company had a pretty shrewd idea what the inverters were intended for but everyone thought that the Pakistanis would not know what to do with them.[45] There was a company joke that the inverters would rust away in cases. That mix of willful naïveté and arrogance about Pakistan's capability would prove a recurring theme. A few weeks after the first order the firm's management was shocked to receive a telex asking for more than a million pounds worth of inverters with a list of sophisticated modifications that showed the recipients knew exactly what they were doing. This sale did not go ahead but Pakistan already had enough inverters to run several thousand centrifuges and the knowledge to make more themselves.

Another of Khan's suppliers also appears for the first time in the context of the Emerson deal. Peter Griffin first met Khan through a bizarre coincidence. One of Khan's suppliers in London called up Griffin thinking he was involved with a company of a similar name but Griffin managed to cut a deal for some parts anyway. Khan was a frequent visitor to London until the early 1980s, staying at the home of an old college friend. So one evening, Griffin found himself having dinner with Khan and a number of other men in a Pakistani restaurant not far from Westminster and the Houses of Parliament. Over a dinner of rice and curry, Khan was quiet, amusing, and charming. He was so quiet that it wasn't clear how important he was and that he was actually in charge of the team. But at one point a question was directed at a senior Pakistani military officer, who pointed at Khan and said "he is the boss." Griffin placed an order with Emerson for more inverters at a point when it was legal but when they were added to the British government's list of controlled items the deal was stopped and he never shipped any inverters to Khan. Griffin went on to become a regular supplier of a variety of equipment for Khan, everything from hospital lifts to lighting, all entirely legal he maintains.[46] He was careful to ensure that shipments conformed to the then current export controls. Griffin was never prosecuted and only had goods detained three times in twenty-five years. Each time the goods were returned to Griffin and subsequently exported to Pakistan.

When a British member of Parliament, Frank Allaun, brought up the fact that some inverters had been sold to Pakistan from the UK, the government launched a full-scale investigation. An inquiry by Minister of Energy Tony Benn found the sale was technically completely legal although the inverters were quickly added to the export control list. The London Club was already starting to struggle to outpace the proliferators. After being denied more inverters, Pakistani purchasers simply started buying the parts with which to assemble the inverters themselves, forcing Britain to twice expand the control list in 1979. As Britain imposed more stringent controls in the late 1970s, Khan complained in a letter, "the Britishers are stalling it more than before. They are even stopping nails and screws." In another letter he added, "All our material has been stopped, everywhere they are delaying it. Now we will have to do some work ourselves."[47]

The growing publicity did not stop Khan, quite the opposite. Khan was becoming famous in Pakistan and around the world as the mysterious figure building the Pakistani bomb. He seemed to relish it. There was no shortage of people queuing up to make money. Khan said that after the initial burst of publicity "we received several letters and telexes. Many suppliers approached us with the details of machinery and with figures and numbers of instruments they had sold to Almelo. In the true sense of the word they begged us to purchase their goods. And for the first time the truth of the saying 'they would sell their mother for money' dawned on me. We purchased whatever we required."[48]

In CIA headquarters in Langley, Virginia, experts were beginning to put together the pieces of what was happening in Pakistan. By 1979 they realized that Khan had brought together pretty much everything needed to make his own centrifuge plant. This led to some desperate last-minute attempts to stop sales. In February, U.S. embassies in the Netherlands, France, Switzerland, and West Germany sent out urgent warnings to European governments that Pakistan's efforts should be taken seriously.[49] State Department officials traveled over for briefings. President Carter wrote to the German chancellor warning that two German firms were doing business with Pakistan's program. But the companies reported that they had already carried out deals supplying inverters and valves, vacuum pumps, brazing furnaces, and measuring equipment over the preceding three years.[50] By now much of the damage had already been done and many of the key parts were in place.

In Pakistan Bhutto was the initial driver of the nuclear weapons program, but the desire for the bomb proved to be a constant through Pakistan's subsequent violent political convulsions. Bhutto had fallen out with Pakistan's all-powerful army and elections in 1977 led to accusations of vote rigging. This was followed by domestic unrest, martial law, and finally a coup. Bhutto himself (and some of his friends to this day) argued that the United States and the CIA had been behind the coup as punishment for his pursuit of nuclear weapons and willingness to stand up to American pressure. Bhutto claimed that during a tense August 1976 visit, Henry Kissinger threatened "to make a horrible example" of him for his pursuit of the bomb. Whether those words were actually used or not, Pakistan's new leader, the smooth, ambitious General Zia ul-Haq, showed no sign of wavering in his support for the program or altering the policy—the national consensus was too strong that the bomb was the route to security. Bhutto had kept the program under his own wing with scientists reporting to him partly to increase his power base against the military, but now the army took control of the program, a hold that they have never relinquished even when civilian government was later restored. Khan himself was sorry to lose his initial sponsor and even requested mercy for Bhutto but Bhutto would be hung in 1979. Khan himself was too valuable for Pakistan to lose and his unique role continued.

In the late 1970s the United States struggled to find a coherent and settled policy to deal with Pakistan's nuclear ambitions, vacillating between censure and cooperation with little balance between sticks and carrots. The U.S.-Pakistan relationship has never been easy, a story marked by periods of intense cooperation followed by fallings out and mistrust with no even keel or constancy. From the mid-1970s, concerns over the nuclear program meant the aid tap was switched on and off repeatedly as sanctions were imposed but never for long enough or severely enough to have any chance of deterring Pakistan. Military aid was used at other times to boost Pakistan's sense of security and thereby, it was hoped, reduce its perceived need for weapons but this was never enough to convince Pakistan that it could overcome India's conventional advantage and counter the idea that getting the bomb was a matter of national survival. The strange rhythm of close cooperation, interspersed with periods of sanctions and neglect proved largely ineffective and created mistrust.

The United States considered more drastic options to deal with A. Q. Khan and the Pakistan program, including covert activity or air strikes against Kahuta, once presented in a paper by Ambassador Gerrard Smith (hastily denied when reported by the American media), another time by Joseph Nye. Secretary of State Cyrus Vance asked Nye to outline the pros and cons of covert action or air strikes in a private memo rather than an official government paper to avoid potential diplomatic embarrassment if it leaked. "What I wrote at the time was that it would be very difficult to pull off successfully," recalls Nye. "There were too many unknowns and too many moving parts." As would be judged the case when debating whether to strike other countries' nuclear programs in the future, the high costs coupled with the limited prospects of success meant the idea was shelved.

Washington may have considered air strikes too risky, but Pakistan took every precaution. French anti-aircraft missiles were installed around Kahuta to protect against air strikes whether from the Americans, Indians, or Israelis. Security was tight. Kahuta was becoming a place of legend and curiosity for many in and out of Pakistan. Signs on the road for miles leading up to Kahuta warn that no foreigners are allowed near and any who tried risked trouble. Pakistan initially denied Kahuta even existed.

U.S. diplomat Robert Galluci flew to Pakistan in 1979 for the first of many visits to confront General Zia over the nuclear program. Having seen satellite photography of this mysterious location he was determined to try and see it for real. There was no intelligence value in going, just curiosity. Gallucci convinced a reluctant U.S. ambassador to provide a young political officer, Marc Grossman, to take him and an intelligence analyst on the outing. Grossman was due to leave Islamabad in a week so if he got expelled as a result it would not be much of a problem. The small party picked up a jeep from the embassy motor pool and headed out. As they approached the barbed-wire fences that surrounded Kahuta, Grossman talked his way past a guard by saying that they were going for a picnic, and glimpsed Kahuta's sprawling workshops from a hillside. "Zia actually said to me when I showed him overhead photography that this could be a cowshed—well it would have been the largest cowshed in the universe," recalls Gallucci.[51] Gallucci got away with the visit—and the intelligence analyst managed to take some useful photographs. Unfortunately, the next week the French ambassador tried to replicate the feat and he and his driver were badly beaten (as was a British journalist who tried to interview Khan at his house). When told of the incident with the French ambassador, Zia reportedly said, "I wish it had been the American bastard."[52]

India's nuclear test had also led to alarm in the U.S. Congress. A new tide of congressional activism over proliferation began to emerge with profound consequences for U.S. foreign policy. For decades, there has been a perpetual tussle between Congress and the administration over whether the executive was doing enough on proliferation and whether it was too soft on Pakistan. In 1976 Congress passed the Symington Amendment barring U.S. military and economic aid to any country that imported nuclear technology not under IAEA safeguards. It was enforced in April 1979 when

CIA analysts announced they were convinced of the existence of Pakistan's clandestine enrichment program and of the role of A. Q. Khan. This was almost certainly the result of recruiting a spy within the facility or program. Aid was cut off and U.S.-Pakistan relations began to decline precipitously with rows over human rights as well as the nuclear issue.

On November 21, 1979, a mob of fifteen thousand Pakistanis stormed the U.S. embassy in Islamabad and set fire to it after rumors swept the city of U.S. involvement in the seizing of the Grand Mosque in Mecca, Saudi Arabia. A young CIA officer, Gary Schroen, who was trapped inside for six hours, remembers that there was little help from the Pakistani government. "When we got out on the roof there were Pakistani Army people just standing around. No one was doing anything to stop the rioting."[53] The U.S.-Pakistan relationship looked strained to the point of snapping. The pressure was growing on Pakistan's nuclear program and Khan's work.

But the pressure from Washington didn't last. Stopping proliferation was about to play second fiddle to other concerns. Just as the details of Pakistan—and Khan's—procurement activities were becoming public, the drive to stop Pakistan ran out of steam. This happened at a crucial point as Pakistan was moving past the point of no return at which it had enough technology to go it alone.

In December 1979 the whole strategic calculus over U.S.-Pakistan relations was transformed. U.S. spy satellites showed a major Soviet military force had been placed on the Afghan border and CIA Director Stansfied Turner told President Carter that the Soviets were "in the starting blocks." Once the Soviets went in, it was decided to expand an existing limited CIA covert-action program by using stolen stockpiles of Soviet small arms, mortars, and rockets to arm Afghan freedom fighters or mujahideen. This would allow Washington and Islamabad to fight the Soviets but with a level of deniability. It was to be a critical moment in U.S. policy towards Pakistan. For a crucial decade, just as the nuclear program was gathering pace, proliferation was to be subordinated to broader priorities. Prioritizing the Afghan issue over proliferation was a rational policy choice, especially in the context of the Cold War. But it was one that would have consequences. These were to prove critical years for Pakistani procurement from the West and for the first international deals selling the technology on to other states. "It changed our whole relationship with the Pakistani government," remembers CIA officer Schroen. "We went from anger and almost a break in relations to almost best of friends again." The Symington Amendment was lifted and aid resumed. Initially, Carter offered four hundred million dollars in economic and military aid but Zia described this as "peanuts" (perhaps a deliberate provocation to the Georgian peanut farmer) and, sensing the shifting political winds in the United States, held out for more. Within a few months Jimmy Carter was out of office and under President Reagan, Zia got much more. In 1981, the United States agreed to a five-year $3.2-billion aid package as well as increased support for the covert program of arming the mujahideen. Alexander Haig explicitly told Pakistani Foreign Minister Agha Shahi, "we will not make your nuclear program the centrepiece of our relations," making clear that nuclear development could go on as long as it didn't result in a test or anything that would draw congressional ire.[54] The Reagan administration believed that Carter had been too restrictive on nuclear exports, damaging the U.S. nuclear industry. Rather than operate a universal policy, the new administration decided that it would make decisions over exports based on a country's relationship with the United States and broader foreign policy priorities.[55]

For Pakistan, the Afghan conflict provided an excellent opportunity to restore ties with the United States, turn the aid tap back on, and ensure that the United States would—if not turn a blind eye—then at least take a less severe view of the nuclear program as well as other developments. Beneath the smooth exterior that Zia presented to Western negotiators, he was personally very religious and began to Islamize the military and the state.[56] The Afghan campaign created a culture of jihad in the country and began to alter the nature of Pakistan's state and society. The inflow of vast sums of money from the United States and Saudi Arabia helped build up the Inter-Services Intelligence Agency (ISI) into a powerful behemoth, cementing a growing alliance between Islamists and the military and a close defence relationship with Saudi Arabia and Prince Turki al-Faisal, the head of Saudi Arabia's intelligence agency, who visited Pakistan sometimes as much as five times a month.[57]

The U.S. administration worried little about these developments and instead was focused on one goal: making the Soviets bleed. How explicit was the deal of the United States turning a blind eye to Pakistan's nuclear development (short of testing a bomb) in return for help in Afghanistan? Robert Gallucci, who negotiated with Zia for over a decade, believes it was clearly understood. "There was an assurance given by Zia to Alexander Haig when he was secretary of state, which had three parts. One: we will not build nuclear weapons. Second: we will not embarrass you. Thirdly: we will not transfer the technology. And he broke all three."[58]

CHAPTER 2

The Bomb

IT WAS A WINTER MORNING and Richard Barlow was sitting in his office on the third floor of CIA Headquarters in Langley, Virginia, anticipating a quiet day. But when he answered his phone, he immediately snapped to attention. It was a colleague from the Department of Energy who had an intriguing tip off. In October 1986 the Toronto sales office of a Pennsylvania steel company had been contacted with an unusual request. A Pakistani-born Canadian businessman, Arshad Pervez (known as "Archie") had enquired about buying highly specialized maraging steel made by only seven companies in the United States. The marketing manager of the company knew the steel was on a controlled list of exports and he reported his suspicions to customs officials. Eventually, the information had found its way to Barlow. At that moment, Barlow couldn't have foreseen how the case would plunge him into the vicious internal politics surrounding proliferation and Pakistan. In the end the treacherous divide between the interests of intelligence in dealing with proliferation and the interests of diplomacy in prizing certain relationships over the naked truth would engulf him. Barlow would find that his opponent, Khan, was far better protected by the U.S. government than he was.

Barlow was a sandy haired, enthusiastic young analyst at the CIA. He had written his undergraduate thesis in the late 1970s on Pakistan's nuclear program, concluding that the problem was a lack of will on the part of the United States to apply policies that might stop Islamabad from developing the bomb. A high flyer, he had become the only person assigned at the CIA to work full time on Khan's network and was closely following his procurement activities—including a number of suspected purchases within the United States. "I became concerned about an enormous level of activity by the Pakistanis we were tracking in various ways," recalls Barlow, "and no one was doing anything about it."[1] Barlow was zealous in his pursuit. "He was something of a tiger," former colleague Robert Gallucci remembers. By the mid to late 1980s, U.S. intelligence had a good understanding of Khan's far-reaching procurement network. Sensitive items were being transhipped through Dubai, Europe, and sometimes Singapore or Hong Kong using false end-user certificates promising that items would end up at institutions like universities rather than their real destination—Kahuta, the site of Khan's secret activity. Major banks were involved in providing the finance for the shipments. The Bank of Credit and Commerce International (BCCI) was providing about three hundred thousand dollars for the Pervez deal. At the CIA, there was no shortage of detailed intelligence outlining the global scope and ambition of Khan's procurement networks but deciding what to do with this information and when and how to act against the network was a different matter.

The significance of the Pervez tip off was all too clear to Barlow. The specialized steel was for centrifuge rotors, the part of the machine that spins round at high speed within a casing. The P-1 design at Kahuta used aluminum rotors that were prone to shattering and Khan was busy upgrading to the more efficient P-2 design that used maraging steel. The size of the order made clear that Pakistan was intending a massive expansion of their enrichment program, while simultaneously promising the U.S. government that it would restrain its activity.

As they began to watch Pervez, Barlow and his colleagues made a conscious decision not to tell the State Department's Bureau of Near East and South Asia Affairs, which ran Pakistan policy, about their suspicions. They feared their colleagues would tip off the Pakistanis by issuing a diplomatic protest—known as a demarche—over Pervez's activities, as they had done with others in the past. If a protest were issued, it would alert the Pakistanis that the United States knew of the deal. There was disquiet in parts of the CIA and U.S. law enforcement agencies over the way in which the detail provided in demarches revealed the nature and extent of the U.S.

intelligence penetration of Pakistani procurement and nuclear activities. The United States had penetrated deep into the heart of Pakistan's nuclear program. There was little it didn't know. But was it more important to protect those sources and learn more or to risk revealing them by confronting Pakistan?

Determining exactly how much of one's hand to reveal is just one of the many strategic dilemmas that efforts to stop nuclear proliferation encounter. When it comes to proliferation, it isn't just a matter of collecting enough intelligence. Much more difficult may be working out what to do with the knowledge one has collected. Early on snippets of information may point to suspicious activity but are rarely sufficient to justify decisive action of a diplomatic, let alone military, nature. Whether in the case of Pakistan in the 1980s or Iran two decades later, confronting governments suspected of proliferation or suspected of harboring businesses involved in proliferation is not straightforward. Too little evidence and the country will simply deny its veracity or ask for more proof. But if too much evidence is shared then the source of the intelligence—usually either a human spy or electronic surveillance—will be all too obvious and open to elimination. Wait too long in watching a program and gathering intelligence, however, and it can be too late—a country can reach the point of no return with its nuclear program. Once a country has the indigenous capability to drive on towards the nuclear threshold, further attempts to restrict imports or procurement will be irrelevant. As nuclear capabilities progress, the problem may become clearer to the outside world, but stopping it becomes that much harder. Working out where on the continuum to intervene is a major problem and has always been the source of tension between those who collect intelligence and those who have to decide if and how to act on it.

In the early 1980s U.S. demarches were having little effect, including on European allies. The United States would often serve one demarche after another to countries whose businesses were selling to Pakistan but they were ignored, partly because Europeans accused the United States of failing to keep its own house in order. The U.S. government issued about one hundred communiqués to the West German government alone over exports to Pakistan during the 1980s.[2] Around seventy German firms are thought to have supplied Pakistan but most U.S. complaints were simply ignored. In one 1986 West German Economic Ministry internal memo, an official casually stated that U.S. intelligence warnings of planned nuclear exports to South Asia "usually land in my wastepaper basket."[3] During the 1980s only two officials were assigned to review twelve thousand application for licenses to export nuclear related technology. West Germany was an export-driven economy and commercial instincts prevailed.

Rather than go through diplomatic channels and risk losing Pervez, Barlow and his team decided to take a new approach. They began to formulate a plan to arrest their target. Catching proliferators red-handed can be tricky, especially with regards to the amount of evidence needed to prove that they knew they were helping a weapons program. By June of 1987, the trap was carefully set—an undercover agent posed as a steel salesman and met Pervez at the bar of Toronto's Hilton Harbour Castle Hotel. From there, they went up to a hotel room. Another officer was next door videoing the encounter through a camera concealed in a TV set. Pervez checked on his forty-five thousand-dollar kickback and then commented that the order might only be the start—also on the shopping list was beryllium, which can be used in nuclear weapons to form a shell around the fissile material. Then Pervez told the undercover agent, "the Kahuta client is ready . . . It's going to the Kahuta plant."[4] There was now no doubt about the destination. "He was either very, very bright or very, very dumb," said one investigator at the time. "In the end, I think he was dumb."[5] After the meeting at the hotel room, a container was sent to Pennsylvania to ship the steel and when Pervez turned up to inspect the shipment and finish the deal in July 1987 he was arrested.

Pervez was only the middleman. The investigation revealed that the real buyer was far more interesting—a retired brigadier from the Pakistani Army called Inam ul-Haq who ran a front company for purchasing components for the nuclear program, whose role was well understood in the CIA. In turn, he was the link in the chain connecting the sale to both A. Q. Khan and the Pakistani government. Barlow believes that senior figures at the State Department deliberately prevented the arrest of ul-Haq, who was supposed to have arrived with Pervez in Pennsylvania in July, but who never showed. "He was tipped off by people in our government. Very high-level people—indirectly to his government."[6] Eventually, ul-Haq would be arrested in Germany and extradited to the United States. However, in 1987 the Pervez case, because of the clear trail back to Khan and Pakistan, was igniting a political firestorm in Washington.

In 1984 a group of Pakistanis had been stopped in Houston trying to export fifty krytons—electronic triggering switches for nuclear weapons. Two members of the group were released after spilling the beans and revealing that the Pakistan Atomic Energy Commission had ordered the parts.[7] When questioned, General Zia claimed that the krytons were for revolving lights, like the type put on top of ambulances. Congress was not happy. In 1985, in the wake of the kryton affair, Congress passed the Solarz Amendment—named after New York Congressman Stephen J. Solarz. The amendment required that aid should be cut off to any country found to be trying to export sensitive items from the United States for a nuclear weapons program. The aim was to convince Pakistan that it would not be in its interests to keep trying to procure within the United States. The Pervez case seemed to leave no room for doubt that this was exactly what Pakistan had continued to do. "My first reaction was that this was outrageous," remembers Solarz.[8] It looked like a deliberate slap in the face by Pakistan in the wake of the new law. The problem was that news about Pervez broke just as a massive new military and economic aid package to Pakistan was coming before Congress. The aid was intended, in part, as a reward for Pakistan's support for the mujahideen in the indirect war against the Soviets in Afghanistan. Now it was under threat.

Alarm bells went off all over the CIA's Directorate of Operations, the State Department, and the White House as it became clear to supporters of the Afghan operation that the Pervez case might mean the rupturing of the relationship that supplied the Afghan rebels. The stance of prioritizing anti-communism over counter-proliferation was logical in the 1980s, although it was not universally shared across the government. Much of the tension then (as always) lay between those whose job it was to deal with proliferation and those who dealt with regional issues such as South Asia or the Middle East. One group prioritized dealing with proliferation wherever it was found even if this damaged relations with a particular country, the other group believed that maintaining close relations with a country (in this case Pakistan) served broader diplomatic priorities (such as winning the war in Afghanistan). This friction existed within the State Department and CIA. There were clashes between the CIA's Directorate of Operations who would ally with the State Department regional teams against officers in the CIA analytical Directorate of Intelligence who sided with State Department proliferation officials.

There were also occasional problems with allies, who often had different priorities. Throughout the 1980s, the UK was also tracking Khan very closely—even closer than the United States by some accounts. They were "at least as interested as we were" remembers Barlow who would travel over to London for meetings with his opposite numbers from MI6. "In general cooperation was productive, but there was tension as the UK government did not share fully our policy goals. They didn't completely buy into the Afghan thing. There was quite a bit of tension over it. They felt that proliferation was more important than we did and they felt we were not doing enough."[9]

But the Afghan operation was a priority for the White House and the top of the CIA. The relationship between the top officials at the CIA and Pakistan was intense—CIA Director Bill Casey flew secretly to Pakistan a number of times to check on the Afghan operation and dined with Zia at his residence, Army House, in Rawalpindi. Many viewed avoiding destabilizing the Pakistani government and ensuring its cooperation in helping America fight its wars as the top priorities, well above dealing with proliferation.

For Barlow, the stark choice offered between fighting the Cold War and dealing with proliferation was a false one. "You could have done both," he believes. "It was basically a question of more effectively using our leverage of economic and military aid. We drew lines in the nuclear sand and when Zia crossed them, we just drew another line. The 'powers that be' felt that if we pushed it and cut off aid or even part of it, that Zia wouldn't help us and wouldn't funnel aid to the Afghans. I didn't agree with that. The Pakistanis didn't want the Russians on their border any more than we did. They weren't doing it for us. They had their own reasons. People were not willing to call his bluff. He had us wrapped around his finger and Zia played us brilliantly."

Inside Congress, the threat that the Pervez case posed to the Afghan aid package caused a major stir among the supporters of the anti-Soviet crusade. A huge lobbying campaign was launched led by the flamboyant Texan Congressman Charlie Wilson who had driven forward covert aid to Afghanistan with a near-messianic anti-communist zeal.[10] Others joined in—

at a dinner at Pakistan's embassy, former National Security Adviser Zbigniew Brzezinski told Solarz that cutting off aid would lead to a Soviet triumph in Afghanistan and an anti-American government in Islamabad. In response, Solarz summoned the CIA to explain and Richard Barlow came over from Langley to give a highly classified briefing to Congress about Pakistan's activities. Previously, other individuals had briefed Congress on the Pakistan issue but had painted a very different, and less complete, picture. Barlow was asked whether those involved in the Pervez case were agents for the Pakistani state and whether there had been any other activity since the kryton affair. Although a colleague tried to cut him off, Barlow proceeded to explain the clear and close links to the Pakistan government in both the Pervez case and also a number of other cases he'd been watching. Many of the congressmen seemed surprised at the strength of the conclusions and the scale of the activity. Clearly, they'd not been aware just how much evidence existed—had the administration been hiding this from them? "My very strong impression is they didn't completely level with us," recalls Solarz of the other officials who had briefed Congress prior to Barlow. "They knew a lot more than they were willing to say."[11]

Charlie Wilson fought back—organizing a delegation of seven congressmen to go to Pakistan and meet Afghan mujahideen, even encouraging the delegation to give blood for medical use by the fighters. They were also introduced to President Zia who promised at an official state dinner that the Pakistani nuclear program was peaceful. Earlier in 1987, Zia told an interviewer that he thought the "United States of America—the senators and congressmen—will look to the higher national interest rather than this tiddly-widdly nuclear program."[12]

In the end, Wilson's arm-twisting worked—the day after Archie Pervez was convicted in December for his role in the attempted sale, a congressional conference committee promised another $480 million to Pakistan. In January, the White House invoked the Solarz Amendment as it was obliged to but then immediately issued a waiver (as it had been given the ability to do under the legislation) meaning the aid would continue. Charlie Wilson would later recall his efforts as "my greatest achievement in Congress."[13]

For Barlow, the whole affair was taking a nasty turn. As soon as he stepped back into his office after briefing Congress, his phone began to ring off the hook. High-level people were not happy. His briefing had deeply upset a number of colleagues at the CIA Directorate of Operations and the State Department because it made clear that those who had been briefing Congress before had not been providing a full picture. They began to exert pressure to sideline Barlow. Not long after, managers removed his responsibility for tracking Khan and Pakistan. Barlow decided to quit. The first hints had just appeared of Pakistan and Khan negotiating to pass on some kind of technology, possibly to Iraq. But after his departure, cases investigating Khan were shut down and the treatment of Barlow sent out a strong message across the intelligence and non-proliferation community. Strategic interests had won out over intelligence, fighting in Afghanistan over proliferation, A. Q. Khan over Barlow. "It was observed by all my colleagues that a message was coming from the highest level—don't screw with this stuff. Don't embarrass our friends." The prioritization of the diplomatic relationship would render the intelligence findings moot, and the lack of resources applied to Khan at this critical point would prove to have a lasting legacy.

The impact of U.S. policy protecting Khan may also have extended overseas. Despite the growing interest in his activities, Khan continued to visit Europe in the 1980s. Ruud Lubbers claims that in 1986 the United States again pressured Dutch authorities not to re-open the case against Khan so that the CIA could continue following him, "I was told that the secret services could handle it more effectively," recalled Lubbers who was then prime minister. The details are murky although it is possible that at this point the United States was trying to avoid causing trouble with Pakistan and saw watching Khan as more useful in order to collect intelligence. Barlow believes that an opportunity was missed during these years to stop Khan early. "We knew who the people were. It's not that hard to shut down these networks," argues Barlow. "We might not have stopped the Pakistani bomb by that point but we certainly could have shut down their buying networks and in doing so—even if we weren't aware of it—we would have shut down what became their selling networks." The wealth of intelligence over this period might have presented the best opportunity to stop Khan early, but the chance was lost.

By the 1980s Khan was safely embedded within the Pakistan program and was protected by his indispensable function for his government in building the bomb and by his government's indispensable function for the United States in pursuing the Afghan campaign. Deep inside Kahuta, Khan spent the decade perfecting his centrifuges, emerging occasionally to issue provocative statements about his progress. Khan later claimed that the first enrichment began at Kahuta on April 4, 1978, and that he was "producing substantial quantities of uranium by 1981."[14] This is likely to be an exaggeration of the ease with which Khan mastered enrichment. In fact, many of his early designs didn't work properly and there were immense technical problems. When Khan's deputy at Kahuta, G. D. Alam, was observing the first test of a centrifuge from an adjoining room, the glass case containing the machine exploded so violently that pieces were embedded in the ceiling and left there as a memento. The next test device exploded as soon as the uranium hexafluoride gas (or UF6) was introduced. On June 4, 1978, the first prototype finally succeeded in a tiny amount of enrichment. Khan wrote a letter to his board on June 10 boasting, "We are now probably the 5th country in the world which has succeeded in enriching uranium."[15]

Enough progress had been made for President Zia to rename Engineering Research Laboratories as Khan Research Laboratories (KRL) on May 1, 1981. Thanks to his own salesmanship and bureaucratic skill, Khan's star was on the rise. As his prestige grew so did his autonomy. Thanks to Khan's propaganda and also that of the government, Pakistan's nuclear program was becoming an important symbol of the nation's independence, pride, and sovereignty, in part in direct opposition to the United States and its pressure to halt or even "roll-back" the program. "Kahuta is an all-Pakistani effort and is a symbol of a poor and developing country's determination and defiance to submitting to blackmail and bullying," said Khan.[16]

Western intelligence agencies confidently believed there was a pile of junk growing outside the plant as rotors broke when spun at high speed. Initially, the United States overestimated the difficulties Khan faced. "We believe that the Pakistanis have experienced difficulty in making their centrifuge machines work and that the Pakistanis have not yet produced any significant quantities of enriched uranium," read a 1983 State Department memo.[17] In the same year a classified CIA report estimated that Kahuta wasn't yet working and that once it was, it would still take two to three years to produce material for a bomb. There was no doubt in Washington though that the facility had one goal—nuclear weapons. New intelligence proved beyond any doubt that Khan was moving beyond simply enrichment to building a bomb. The same CIA document reported that in 1982 procurement agents long associated with KRL had ordered specialized metal components for a nuclear explosive device from European companies. The CIA said that in response to these developments, the United States approached the Pakistan government at the highest levels to express concern. The response was typical—"after initial discussion, we noted a shift in emphasis from procurement of weapons components themselves to procurement of machinery necessary for their manufacture." In other words, the same lesson from enrichment had been applied to nuclear weapon components—when discovered, simply shift from buying parts to manufacturing your own. Diplomatic demarches and warnings were only serving to alert procurers that they were being watched and had to shift their approach.

Khan's power and influence were growing. The importance of the pursuit of nuclear weapons meant success was prioritized above worrying over corruption or effective oversight, allowing Khan to run rampant. Kahuta was becoming a state within a state with Khan its undisputed leader. KRL was also a closed world unto itself. It would eventually include its own housing for workers, school for their children, and even a small hospital.[18] KRL itself had fifteen technical divisions as well as security, medical, and,— curiously, two finance divisions. Workers received 80 percent more pay than other government employees of the same rank and a 15 percent bonus as well as better conditions than those of the Pakistan Atomic Energy Commission (PAEC). The autonomy extended to finances. "No one looked. No one asked," conceded one former Pakistani diplomat with regards the KRL budget, "[Khan] was very generous for everyone who worked for him and knew him."

With his primary task of enriching uranium well underway, Khan began to diversify KRL's activities into the sale of conventional weapons to both the Pakistani military and other countries. As with his nuclear work, Khan's work was derivative rather than original. He often bought equipment from China and then reverse engineered it so that he could build his own version. KRL might have been autonomous from political control but it was tightly integrated into Pakistan's military-industrial complex with its intensely close connections between the military, government engineers and scientists, and private contractors. The military in Pakistan had become a major player in the economy as well as government, running large business conglomerates and providing additional income. KRL was part of this wider world. Khan himself boasted in 1991 that he had six thousand engineers and scientists working at Kahuta and had manufactured $350 million of missiles and mines.[19] KRL also sold surface-to-air missiles, anti-tank systems, mine exploders, laser targeters, and rocket launchers. There was much money to be made from this line of work with kickbacks to line the pockets of generals along the way and make them amenable to Khan. It would also serve as useful for cover for his other, less public activities.

When it came to the business of nuclear weapons and the capability to deliver them to targets in India, the culture was "you get it, I don't care how and I don't care about consequences. This was the national policy," says one Pakistani military officer.

Running a clandestine nuclear procurement, enrichment, and weapons program inevitably creates a hidden world within a state, a place that prying eyes are not allowed to peer into. In Pakistan there was the additional complexity of a deep and bitter rivalry between the two major wings of the nuclear program. On the one hand was the PAEC—the established senior partner and the more overt side of Pakistan's nuclear activities. On the other was Khan Research Laboratories—the more secretive newcomer. Each wanted to be the lead organization when it came to building the bomb and claim the glory. The program was highly compartmentalized and different parts often had no conception of what others were working on. The rivalry was intense.

The task of Khan's labs was originally confined to enrichment, but Khan would become known as the father of the Pakistani bomb. How much truth is there to the title or was it simply a brilliant piece of myth building? Those opposed to Khan claim that his contribution to the bomb was "no more than 5 percent" of the entire effort, yet he managed to "hijack" what was actually performed by hundreds of scientists and engineers.[20] The dispute over who did what in building the bomb is bitter and persists to the present day and provides some clues to Khan's later activities.

The rivalry was most rancorous when it came to building the actual bomb. At its most basic, turning fissile material into a bomb is relatively straightforward. With a gun-type device, one chunk of highly enriched uranium is fired into another, creating a chain reaction. As was the case with the bomb used in Hiroshima, the design is so simple it can be made without any testing. However, it does require a large amount of fissile material.

More advanced is the implosion device in which a precisely shaped charge of high explosives is detonated to compress a sphere of fissile material (either plutonium or uranium) so that it creates a super-critical mass and a nuclear explosion. The better the designs, the less fissile material is required. Maximizing the power for the minimum amount of material gives you more bombs. Ensuring the precision of the device and its timings and triggers requires extensive design and testing work.

Khan claims he wrote to Zia in 1982 saying he had enriched uranium and now wanted to build a warhead. After receiving the go-ahead (and the instruction to not tell anyone), two years later, he claims, the task was complete as KRL conducted a cold test (a cold test involves triggering the implosion device to check if it works but without using fissile material). Khan maintains that Zia's deputy stole the papers and handed them over to PAEC who then claimed they had done the work. Therefore Khan claims the 1998 tests were based on his design.[21] Meanwhile, PAEC officials claim that as far back as 1974 they'd been given the task of warhead design and were the first to do cold tests in 1983. The likelihood is that Zia became impatient by 1981 at the pace of PAEC's work (nearly sacking Munir Khan) and so took the expensive decision of creating two parallel weaponization programs to introduce an element of competition. PAEC probably did get there first but Zia ensured material flowed back and forth between the teams without them knowing it, leading to accusations of copying, which inflamed tensions.[22] In a desire to stoke patriotic pride and boost his own reputation, Khan's own account of his work on the weapons design neglects to mention a key fact: he did not do all the work itself.

Khan had a strange habit of carrying around documents relating to a weapons design in his briefcase, a habit that persisted until intelligence officers reported it to Zia who told him to keep them in a safe. But, according to one account, before this happened, U.S. intelligence officers managed to get access to A. Q. Khan's luggage in a hotel room during one of his trips abroad in the early 1980s.[23] Rifling through his papers they reportedly found a document proving Pakistan was in receipt of outside help: a drawing of a simple but effective nuclear bomb and the steps needed to make it. It was clear that the design had come from China. Beijing had handed over a full, proven weapons design, thought to be based on a Chinese test in 1966. Previously, countries had helped allies with the design

of weapons (the United States with the UK for instance) but never before
had one simply handed over an entire design. It was the same Chinese
design that would be found in another bag in Libya two decades later—
and the question of where else it might have gone is one of the great mysteries, and worries, surrounding Khan's activities.

After its 1976 deal with Bhutto, China proved to be a crucial partner in
Pakistan's nuclear program. "If you subtract Chinese help, there wouldn't
be a Pakistani program," argues nuclear proliferation analyst, Gary
Milhollin.[24] The relationship continued under Zia with the Chinese President paying a visit to Pakistan in April 1984. In the 1970s and 1980s,
there was no doubt that this was a state-to-state deal and that Khan was a
key intermediary. "It was a China-Pakistan relationship but Khan was the
guy with the contacts," says Richard Barlow. "He opened the door . . .
China was absolutely instrumental in assisting Pakistan's nuclear program
through Khan."[25] Khan made many visits to China during the 1980s, including one for weapons design training in the early 1980s and again in
November 1988.[26]

In some ways, China is the first example of Khan trading nuclear secrets, long before his other deals. From the 1970s to the early 1980s, China
was keen to get its hands on Western nuclear technology, even asking the
Iranians to pass on copies of contracts with the West. Khan knew that in
the URENCO designs he had something valuable that could be offered to
other countries and that he had a global niche in the market that he could
exploit. China, meanwhile, had a relatively weak centrifuge enrichment
program and was keen for Khan's assistance. It was also keen to see more
nuclear powers in the world and particularly to see its rival India kept at
bay. Pakistan arguably received more than they gave in the deal. As well as
help with reactors and the weapons design, Pakistan also received nuclear
material—either weapons-grade uranium or uranium hexafluoride according to differing accounts, which allowed Khan to test his centrifuges at the
early stages.[27] Chinese scientists were also present at Kahuta, possibly helping out or possibly observing. Khan continued traveling to China until the
end of his career, although because he was dealing with state corporations
it was hard to know whether the Chinese government was involved in his
activities. Chinese officials often stayed at Khan's guesthouse next door to
the residence. Pakistan's Foreign Minister Yakub Khan was also reported

to be present at the Chinese Lop Nor test site to witness a test in May 1983, and there has been speculation that the Chinese actually tested a Pakistani weapon. Khan however denied that he ever received designs or any other help from China: "If we produce a hamburger, the West will say that it has been copied by McDonald's."[28]

The design was invaluable to Khan and to Pakistan. It short cut a huge amount of difficult work in developing a weapon and even more importantly working out how to reduce its size so that it could be carried on a missile. Having a tested design allows a country to develop warheads with a level of confidence and secrecy and without having to take the diplomatically dangerous step of carrying out its own nuclear test. By 1983 the CIA was warning that China had provided assistance to the Pakistan program. Initially, this had been seen as largely centered on supporting the Karachi power reactor. But a secret briefing memo from the State Department added, "We now believe cooperation has taken place in the areas of fissile material production and possibly also nuclear device design."[29] This would help stymie a China-U.S. nuclear cooperation deal. Khan's agents had used the Chinese weapons design to tour round Europe procuring elements to put it together giving U.S. intelligence a good sense of what Pakistan had. Having the design would also help Khan keep up the pace in his battle with PAEC, which was trying to develop its own version. It would keep him in the game and solidify his status and reputation.

By 1987 the United States had gained more intelligence on the China-Pakistan relationship and wanted to confront Pakistan so Lawrence Livermore National Laboratory was asked to mock up a small model of the weapon based on the Chinese design using the intelligence picked up from procurement patterns. When Pakistan's Foreign Minister came to the State Department, he was taken to a room. A sheet was removed to reveal a football size mockup of the bomb along with a model of the entire Kahuta plant. But the minister still denied any relationship between Islamabad and Beijing or work on the bomb. The United States told the Pakistanis that a Chinese source had provided the information "at great personal risk." However, Pakistani officials were convinced that the Chinese spy story was cover for the fact that the CIA had a highly placed agent within their program whom the United States was trying to protect.[30] Extensive investigations were conducted into the subject and senior Pakistani intelligence officials believe that the CIA cultivated and recruited a scientist in the early 1980s who had access to all key locations including Kahuta and may even have planned a technical sabotage with the CIA that was foiled.[31] Whether the U.S. acquired the specific intelligence from China, Kahuta, or from A. Q. Kahn's luggage, the reality was that the U.S. had multiple sources of intelligence—derived from human spies and technical devices—which gave it an incredibly detailed picture.

The level of knowledge within the CIA about Pakistan's nuclear progress would cause increasing discomfort to both politicians and the intelligence community. It would repeatedly reveal that America's close ally was lying to it again and again and breaking one agreement after another. In 1982, during a visit to Washington, President Zia had assured President Reagan that Pakistan would not develop nuclear weapons. Zia, like Iranian leaders decades later, protested that there was no intention of developing a bomb and that Pakistan was simply exercising its legitimate right to develop peaceful nuclear technology. "I have said it on top of my voice. . . . we are not making a bomb . . . we are sold to the idea of stopping nuclear proliferation in the world. But where the difference has arisen is that I say it is the right of any developing country to acquire the modern technology and amongst the modern technology is the nuclear technology, nuclear technology for peaceful purposes." However, it did not take long for U.S. intelligence assessments to question whether Pakistan was being true to its word.[32]

In 1984 Khan publicly announced in one of many boastful newspaper interviews that Kahuta was enriching uranium and while it was not enriching to the concentration needed for weapons, it could do so in a short time if ordered.[33] The White House was also receiving intelligence that year pointing to enrichment taking place. In September President Reagan wrote a letter to General Zia warning him not to enrich above 5 percent or there would be consequences (restricting the Pakistani program rather than stopping it entirely was now the limit of U.S. ambitions). But simultaneously, forty thousand more Soviet troops went into Afghanistan and the conflict there began escalating. In November Zia gave written assurances that he would abide by the limit (which was fairly meaningless since enriching to 5 percent is the hardest part of the process, enriching further to weapons grade takes only a matter of days once cascades are reconfigured). But within a year, the CIA gained fresh intelligence that Pakistan had violated the deal. Again, the United States drew lines in the sand. And again, Zia crossed them. In 1984 the U.S. ambassador in Islamabad said of his CIA's station chief's work, "Collection efforts on the Pakistani effort to develop nuclear weapons is amazingly resourceful and disturbing. I would sleep better if he (CIA Station Chief Howard Hart) and his people did not find out so much about what is really going on in secret and contrary to President Zia's assurances to us."[34] The statement was a tribute to the extent to which intelligence was making life difficult for policymakers to retain their charade about Pakistan's intentions.

The twists and turns the administration took to preserve its alliance with Pakistan and turn a blind eye to the nuclear program became increasingly tortuous. So much so that Senator John Glenn reckoned that successive administrations "practiced a nuclear non-proliferation policy bordering on lawlessness."[35] In 1985 the U.S. Congress passed the Pressler Amendment, which required that the administration certify at the start of each fiscal year that Pakistan did not possess a nuclear device. A 1986 National Intelligence Estimate concluded that Kahuta had enriched sufficient weapons-grade uranium and had all the parts for a device. It judged Pakistan could have a bomb within two weeks of making a decision and was only "two screwdriver turns" from assembling a weapon.[36]

Yet the administration continued to certify to Congress that Pakistan did not have a nuclear weapon through the late 1980s, despite this evidence to the contrary. The administration got around this by saying Pakistan hadn't stockpiled or put together every single element for a bomb but the justifications bordered on the absurd. "In my view it was irrefutable evidence," remembers Richard J. Kerr who was then deputy director of intelligence at the CIA, "the argument always came down to a political judgment and that judgment was made on the basis not whether or not there was a weapon but whether that was a convenient time to declare that they had a weapon." Pakistan was simply too important an ally to lose. The intelligence was fixed to fit the policy.

Meanwhile, Pakistan edged closer and closer to the nuclear threshold. From 1987 Pakistan stepped up its efforts on the nuclear front—partly in response to a massive Indian military exercise called Brass Tacks. Hundreds of thousands of Indian troops gathered not far from the border. Pakistan interpreted the exercise as a threatening move and possible precursor to war. Khan himself made one of his occasional public interventions in the form of an interview, which caused huge shockwaves. "What the C.I.A.

has been saying about our possessing the bomb is correct," he said, hoping to send out a signal to the Indians of Pakistani intent and capability. "They told us Pakistan could never produce the bomb and they doubted my capabilities, but they now know we have it."[37] Khan's boast caused huge embarrassment, not least for the U.S. administration, which was telling Congress that there was no sign yet of a Pakistani bomb. Khan was soon forced to withdraw his remarks but Pakistani officials would later admit that they possessed the bomb from this year.[38] By the end of the 1980s, Pakistan had the bomb but chose not to make a formal entry into the nuclear club. The public display of a test would lead to India following with a test, and then Pakistan taking the blame for going first. U.S. aid was also too valuable to waste.

But then in 1988, the settled pattern began to change. Firstly, the Soviet Union, suffering enormously in Afghanistan partly thanks to the introduction of U.S.-supplied Stinger missiles, announced it would withdraw. It was on the surface an extraordinary triumph—although one whose legacy would be increasingly debated after September 11, 2001. And then in August 1988, Pakistan's politics were again thrown into turmoil after General Zia died under still unexplained circumstances. His C-130 aircraft crashed into the ground on its way to Islamabad, killing both the president and the U.S. Ambassador to Pakistan, but there were no signs of mechanical failure. The sudden departure of Zia left Pakistan's politics, and its nuclear program, at a crossroad.

In November 1988, Pakistan went to the polls. Despite attempts by parts of the army and intelligence services to stop her, Benazir Bhutto, the daughter of Zulfikar, emerged triumphant. For Washington, the new charismatic, Western-educated, and democratically elected prime minister seemed to present an excellent new partner with whom to work. With the Afghan campaign winding down, there was no doubt that it was going be harder for the United States to certify Pakistan did not have the bomb, but that problem had to be balanced against supporting Benazir Bhutto. Her June 1989 visit to Washington was going to be critical in cementing the new relationship.

However, the appearance of power was an illusion. Even though elections had taken place, Benazir was shut out of the nuclear program and had little influence over its course. Khan himself has claimed that no Pakistani government had ever interfered with his production. "It is a national project and no government ever caused any obstacle." [39] Over time his autonomy had increased. Under Zulfikar Bhutto, Khan had reported to the Prime Minister alone. That same system persisted under Zia with Khan having direct access to the president and no other chain of command or system of control around him. Only one or two other officials were appraised of Khan's activities and they had little influence over nuclear policy. These included the Foreign Minister Yakub Khan and the Finance Minister Ghulam Ishaq Khan. On Zia's death, a new power structure arose. Technically a troika of three would oversee the entire nuclear program—the president, prime minister, and army chief. Initially, this was comprised of Ghulam Ishaq Khan who had become president, General Mirza Aslam Beg who was army chief, and Benazir Bhutto. In practice, the relationships were intensely personal. President G.I. Khan was particularly close to A. Q. Khan because he had been involved with the program as far back as the 1970s. Khan once said that Ghulam Ishaq Khan guarded the nuclear program like a rock, as civilian governments came and went, and that he visited Kahuta every month to see progress.[40] He would be Khan's defender but it would be the army who would have most direct control over running the nuclear program. The prime minister would be left in the dark.

In practice the lack of formalized command channels meant it was not clear who had final oversight or authority over the nuclear program, providing Khan much freedom. One section of Pakistan's leadership could promise other countries, such as the United States, one thing whilst another section like the military took a different, even contradictory path. If any contradictory policies were then discovered, the blame could always be shifted to another power center within the state, allowing leaders a level of deniability over whatever was happening. Khan also learned to effectively work the system by playing off different leaders to get approval for whatever he wanted.[41] Later, the different parts of the political troika fought each other for supremacy. And because the nuclear program was the touchstone of the nation's security, if one power center tried to gain control over the nuclear program, then the others would see it as a threat to their authority and resist. This gave Khan free reign so long as he delivered the goods.

But as Bhutto was heading to Washington in 1989, there was little doubt amongst the intelligence experts that she had no real influence over the program. In a secret paper written just before the visit, CIA analysts ac-

knowledged that Bhutto was "unlikely to gain control over nuclear decision making anytime soon."[42] Before the election Bhutto had indicated
that she might slow down the nuclear buildup in order to secure continued U.S. support as the Afghan cooperation began to subside. This may
well have aggravated suspicions with the military that she might be willing
to sell out the prized nuclear option. At a meeting just before her departure
for Washington attended by the president, General Beg, and A. Q. Khan
she suggested capping production of fissile material so she had something
to offer (even though Pakistan was technically still supposed to be abiding
by the 1984 cap).[43] Disquiet grew amongst the supporters of the program.
Some CIA analysts believed that her position was "not clear and possibly
not relevant at this stage." A paper warned that while she might give private assurances during her visit over enrichment "whether she could deliver on these commitments is another matter" and also noted that fellow
Pakistanis would closely watch her on the visit. Some officials wanted to
pretend that Benazir was the right person to deal with and she could deliver but the intelligence analysts were right. Before being "allowed" to
take power, Bhutto had to give assurances that she would not interfere
with nuclear policy, Afghan policy, or the internal policies of armed forces.[44]
Benazir Bhutto never even visited KRL—she wasn't formally banned, but
knew better than to ask, according to friends.

Determined to show the new Pakistani leader how much was known
about the program, CIA Director William H. Webster organized a briefing
for Bhutto soon after she arrived in Washington, D.C. She was taken to
Blair House, a guesthouse for visiting dignitaries just across the road from
the White House. Inside there was a highly unusual presentation from the
head of the CIA to a foreign leader about their own nuclear program.[45] The
show included a mockup of the Pakistani bomb. What was truly shocking
to Benazir Bhutto was that U.S. intelligence knew more about the nuclear
program than she did. She had not even seen the bomb herself and she was
being shown a model by the CIA.

The next day she met President George H. W. Bush who told her that
Pakistan would be certified as not having a nuclear weapon in 1989. However, he made clear it would not be possible to do so the following year
unless she guaranteed Pakistan would not assemble the weapons and would
continue to halt enrichment above 5 percent. To help shore up her position

back home and prevent the military from criticizing her too much in achieving this, she was offered the sale of a number of much-desired F-16 aircraft for $1.6 billion.[46] This seemed to serve everyone's interests. Bhutto appeared at a joint session of Congress and said, "we do not possess nor do we intend to make a nuclear device. That is our policy." On the surface, it all looked like a success. No one mentioned to Congress or the American public that the CIA actually believed that the prime minister's confident statement was irrelevant and that Pakistan already had the bomb.

Remarkably, Richard Barlow found himself once again caught up in the internal Washington politics surrounding Pakistan. After leaving the CIA, Barlow ended up at the Pentagon working on proliferation issues in the office of the Secretary of Defence Dick Cheney. His first taste of trouble came in February 1989 in London when he was meeting with counterparts from British intelligence. The question came up over how much control Bhutto really had over the nuclear program. The MI6 officials made it clear they thought she had none and that her assurances were effectively meaningless. Barlow agreed, but other American officials resisted accepting that notion. It risked undermining the strategy of building her up as a viable partner and the great hope for a democratic Pakistan. Even during Bhutto's visit in June, fresh intelligence flowed into Washington suggesting that her guarantees did not count for much. After the visit, a contentious debate emerged over whether Pakistan could adapt the F-16 aircraft the United States was selling to carry nuclear weapons.

In August of 1989 Barlow learned that defense officials were appearing before Congress (who had to sign off on the deal) testifying that the F-16s were not capable of delivering nuclear weapons without extensive modifications beyond the capacity of Pakistan, such as replacing the entire wiring harness and changing computer systems. Barlow believed he was witnessing another attempt to mislead Congress as only simple, tiny changes would be needed to the fighters since the Pakistanis did not have complex U.S. nuclear weapons, arming, firing, or fusing systems and did not need pinpoint accuracy in their delivery systems. He had expressed this view in an intelligence assessment designed to go up to Defence Secretary Cheney. But as soon as Barlow protested to his bosses that Congress was being misled, the knives again came out from those whose interests and policies he was challenging. Barlow's views on the F-16 risked preventing a massive sale that would bring in money as well as serve the diplomatic priority of supporting Benazir Bhutto. Eventually, behind Barlow's back, the paper was rewritten so that it supported the sale. Barlow was fired, a victim of strategic priorities triumphing over intelligence.

Pakistan and Khan pressed on. Once again, it did not take long for Pakistan to take another critical step forward on the nuclear road. In the spring of 1990, another crisis flared with India, this time over Kashmir. Troops and tanks massed on each side of the border. General Beg had been emboldened by Iranian support, as well as a desire to distance his country from the United States, and decided to move forward both on Kashmir and the nuclear program. Enrichment and production resumed after having been halted before the 1989 Bhutto visit to Washington.[47] At the peak of the crisis, according to one report, intelligence came in that General Beg had authorized the assembly of at least one nuclear weapon.[48] Satellite imagery suggested Pakistan might be preparing to use it against India. Senior U.S. officials scurried to defuse the crisis, warning Pakistan's President G. I. Khan that he risked defeat and isolation if he listened only to his hawks like General Beg.[49]

With that crisis, the program had been pushed on towards its final step—the assembly of weapons—not least in the knowledge that because of the end of the Afghan war, certification by the United States was probably imminent and so there was little to loose. Bhutto was trapped. She lacked the leverage with the Pakistani military to deliver a halt to the nuclear program and gain support from the United States. And for the Pakistani Army and the Inter-Services Intelligence Agency (ISI) she lacked the leverage to deliver U.S. support (or at least an absence of sanctions) as they pushed forward. By August 1990 she was out of power. She sometimes claimed this was the result of a "nuclear coup" in which she'd been removed for interfering too much with the program, although the reality was that the nuclear issue was only part of a broader conflict with the military.

There had been a vicious battle with the ISI, and especially its chief Hamid Gul, who did everything to stop her from coming to power and then to drive her out, even after he had been removed from post. According to former Pakistani official Husain Haqqani, Hamid Gul and his deputy put out word to Islamists that "the ISI had intelligence that Benazir Bhutto has promised the Americans a rollback of our nuclear program. She will prevent a mujahideen victory in Afghanistan and stop plans for jihad in Kashmir in its tracks."[50] These three causes became the touchstone of Pakistani strategic thinking but also of political discourse through the 1990s with powerful support behind each of them. Ensuring an Islamist client state in Afghanistan to give Pakistan "strategic depth" against India was a major priority. The skills developed by the ISI in training the mujahideen in Afghanistan were also now being transferred to the arena of Kashmir to support a new insurgency against India. This was led by militant groups who were technically independent but in reality under the tutelage of the ISI. Finally, the bomb was a symbol of Islamic achievement in the teeth of foreign opposition and the Islamists came to see themselves as the program's guardian, with Khan its larger-than-life, quasi-mystical symbol. Khan himself cleverly built and manipulated this growing image as the man who had brought protection to the nation. The myth, manufactured by Khan himself and perpetuated by Islamists and sections of the military, would prove vital in protecting Khan against scrutiny and also against action when his later activities emerged. Khan himself was growing boastful of his power and influence. A few weeks after Bhutto was ousted, speaking to an audience at a military institute in Rawalpindi, Khan bragged that he had repeatedly asked General Beg to remove Benazir because she was causing trouble for the nuclear program.[51]

In Washington the nuclear near miss in the spring of 1990 turned rumblings of discontent from the intelligence community into open rebellion. Analysts had been growing increasingly unhappy at the annual certification that Pakistan did not have the bomb when they knew it did. The 1990 crisis between India and Pakistan was the final straw. The notion that the United States could continue to certify there were no weapons when the country had nearly engaged in nuclear war made the whole exercise absurd. What if Pakistan had used the bomb? Whose head would be on the line for giving Congress and the American people the impression it didn't have that capability? Senior figures within the CIA's Directorate of Intelligence told the administration that if there was an attempt at re-certification they would no longer support it. Some in the Defense Department were unhappy with this move, hoping that the relationship could be preserved, not least to guarantee the major arms sales that were in the offing and were highly lucrative. But with the strategic motive of supporting the Afghan campaign gone, with the hopes for Benazir Bhutto to be the new face of a democratic Pakistan dashed, the commercial motive was not enough in itself to triumph over the stark truth.

And so the rupture finally came. Two months after the removal of Bhutto in October 1990, President George H.W. Bush finally invoked the Pressler Amendment and cut off American aid, saying he could no longer certify that Pakistan did not have the bomb. Overnight Pakistan went from being the third-largest recipient of military aid to getting nothing. The Cold War was over and Pakistan was far less interesting and useful to Washington's policymakers. Afghanistan too was forgotten by the United States despite control over the country remaining unresolved. With the U.S. aid tap turned off, Pakistan spent the 1990s teetering on the edge of bankruptcy. The sale of the F-16s was blocked although the United States still told Pakistan to pay for the planes.[52] Pakistan's military and scientists would have to look elsewhere for funds and friends. U.S.-Pakistan relations dipped precipitously with a sense of resentment from Pakistan at having been jilted so suddenly. In Pakistan the sanctions were seen somehow as another example of the fickle nature of U.S. friendship rather than a product of their own actions over nuclear weapons. "Pakistan had helped America sow the wind in Afghanistan, but when the time came to reap the whirlwind, it had to do it alone," writes Hassan Abbas, a former Pakistan official. "The abandonment of Pakistan by America left it more than 3 million Afghan refugees to care for; thousands of Madrasas (religious seminaries) funded by Saudi money to militarize the youth and convert them to the intolerant brand of Wahabbi Islam; a Kalashnikov culture such that one could rent an automatic gun in Karachi at less than two dollars an hour; and last not least—the drug trade."[53]

Through the 1990s U.S. relations with Islamabad would ebb and flow but were never close. At one point Washington nearly designated Pakistan a state sponsor of terrorism over Kashmir. The threat was staved off with the promise of a crackdown and the claim, echoed after 2001 with regards to Al Qaeda, that the militants were hiding in mountainous areas and so would be hard to find.[54] At another point there was an attempt to put Kahuta under international inspections but Pakistani politicians said taking such action would leave them too vulnerable to the military. There was some warming in the mid-1990s, but relations remained generally cool as

Pakistani domestic politics entered a messy period in which civilian governments came and went, one after another being dismissed (by the military rather than the electorate) for corruption. And through it all, Khan and his networks flourished. His power, influence, and autonomy had grown enormously whilst wider strategic interests had held his opponents at bay. Through most of the 1980s, the U.S. relationship would protect him as he built his bomb and his network. The shattering of that strategic relationship would then unleash him and provide him with free reign to sell the expertise he had built. He was now given freer license to seek out new partners and to move in his own directions. Khan had begun to embark on a new path, turning his knowledge and global network from import to export—from domestic procurement to international proliferation.

NATANZ

February 2003

AFTER MONTHS OF WRANGLING, PROTESTS, AND DELAYS, the International Atomic Energy Agency's (IAEA) inspectors were finally inside Iran. The team of three top officials had declined the offer of a helicopter ride, choosing instead to drive through hundreds of miles of dusty countryside. Their destination was Natanz. Surrounded by mountains, Natanz had previously only been known for its orchards of juicy pears but now it was alleged to be the secret site housing Iran's nuclear ambitions. Six months earlier, an Iranian opposition group had stunned the world by claiming that it was here that the Iranian government was constructing a clandestine enrichment facility. It was the first that many had heard about an active Iranian enrichment program and the possibility that Iran might be heading towards the bomb. A tough, tenacious IAEA inspector from Finland, Olli Heinonen, was leading the team. He had taken over as head of the group responsible for Iran only a few months earlier. Heinonen had been away from the Iran file for the previous five years and as he had leafed through the details to reacquaint himself, he had realized that there was much, much more information than the last time he'd opened it. He also had been pouring over satellite images of the site trying to discern what was going on but they revealed little of what was happening inside the series of buildings, sitting alone in a dusty landscape. The images only showed a facility that was being built deep underground in a well-protected bunker and surrounded by anti-aircraft batteries. The Iranians had claimed it was a center for agricultural research on preventing desertification.

The real truth was evident as soon as the inspectors arrived. Iranian officials escorted them through a hall full of pictures and exhibits detailing an Iranian centrifuge program. A single centrifuge sat in a glass box; elsewhere components were on parade. The display was designed to show touring Iranian political leaders that their money was being spent wisely, and it now gave the facility's international visitors a clear sense that this was not an insignificant operation. Heinonen hadn't been on an inspection in Iran for more than a decade and he was stunned by just how much the Iranians had accomplished in the meantime. The full extent of that progress dawned on him as he entered one large room inside the pilot facility. "The second I walked into the main room and saw the equipment, I thought 'Oh boy, this is a serious enterprise.' It was well organized." This was not a project at its inception but one already well under way.

In the pilot plant in which they were first taken, there was already a cascade of 160 centrifuges and room for a total of a thousand machines. Even more astonishing was a vast cavernous hall in another building. It was empty but the Iranians said a commercial plant was being constructed with room for fifty thousand centrifuges—enough to produce uranium for twenty to thirty weapons a year at full capacity. Heinonen asked his Iranian escort how they had managed to make such progress in developing centrifuges. "They said they started five years earlier from the Internet," recalls Heinonen. "I said this cannot be possible." The sophisticated equipment was beyond Iran's technical capacity. But for the coming months, the Iranians would stick to the implausible line that they'd made huge technical advances themselves. No one believed that for a second.

When British technical expert Trevor Edwards saw the centrifuges later, he instantly knew where the design had come from—they were almost identical to the URENCO design that Khan had stolen a quarter of a century earlier and which had been christened the P-1, the core of the Pakistan program for many years. Almost nothing had been changed from the model Edwards remembered from the time he had worked in URENCO in the 1970s. The specifications, the parts—everything was the same. What's more, some of the centrifuge parts had been used before and Iran's facilities would soon yield traces of highly enriched, weapons-grade uranium. The evidence seemed to point to one place and one man as the source for Iran's great leap forward. Initially, there was disbelief in many quarters that this could be possible. But despite that initial scepticism, a picture would slowly begin to emerge of A. Q. Khan's shadowy work and his long-standing, crucial support for Iran.

CHAPTER 3

Iran—From Import to Export

IN THE LATE 1980s Dubai in the United Arab Emirates was not yet a glistening business and tourist hub, but it was a focal point for Khan's activities and the place where he would take his first steps towards not only buying but also selling nuclear technology. From the late 1970s Khan had begun to use the city as a site for both meeting with suppliers and as a transit point for sending material to Pakistan. Its central location between East and West and its emphasis on business with no questions asked made it ideal for his purposes. Khan had become an unusually well-known figure in the usually shadowy world of proliferators. He was known as the man building Pakistan the bomb. He had the knowledge, and a model that other countries could emulate. And in Khan Research Laboratories he had a unique brand name he could exploit as he shifted his business towards export. It was in an office in Dubai in 1987 that the Khan network made its first deal. The network was meeting with representatives from Iran, a country whose nuclear ambitions had just begun to grow and which was desperate to get its hands on the latest technology.

In a meeting earlier that year in Switzerland where some of the suppliers were based, the Khan network had provided the Iranians with an item-by-item price list and the Iranians now returned with their shopping list. Representing the network in the Iran deal was S. M. Farouq. Farouq was a squat acerbic figure; originally from India, he was a bully to those below him and obsequious and fawning to those above him. He had become a close associate of Khan. Now based in Dubai, Farouq was a key player in the rapidly expanding business. Much of it was run out of his eighth floor, three-bedroom apartment-cum-office in the city. The deal with the Iranians would be concluded in a hotel.

Payment for the deal with Iran was by check in Swiss francs—the price was around three million dollars. Farouq went to the bank with an Iranian to deposit the check while other members of the Iranian team and members of the Khan network waited nervously in the hotel room across the city. In a briefcase owned by one of Khan's suppliers were the drawings and designs that the Iranians so desperately wanted. There was mistrust and nervousness on both sides. At the bank Farouq waited until the check was approved before he made a call back to the hotel room. The deal was on. The information could be passed over. With that, Iran had taken a huge leap forward in its nuclear ambitions.

Iran's nuclear aspirations had deep roots. They predated the 1979 Iranian Revolution that brought the current theocratic government to power, originating in the critical period of the mid-1970s. Flush with oil money, the Shah of Iran publicly declared that he wanted to move forward with an ambitious nuclear energy program. In 1976 Iran signed a deal with a German company to build nuclear reactors at Bushehr, on a sandy peninsula in the South East of Iran, on the coast of the Persian Gulf. Though the plant in Bushehr would ostensibly be devoted to nuclear power, U.S. intelligence suspected that the Shah also had a modest clandestine weapons development program or was at least keeping that option open through research work. As the same enrichment plants and reactors can be used for either purpose, it is difficult to tell whether facilities are for civilian purposes or for nuclear weapons. For the Shah, as with Iranian leaders decades later, nuclear technology was not just a means of delivering security but also a matter of prestige, a means of restoring status to the proud Persian people who had once ruled an empire.

Whatever the Shah's real intent, his decision in turn led Saddam Hussein in Iraq to press his own officials to move forward with a nuclear program to balance that of neighboring Iran, a typical domino effect created by nuclear ambitions. Iran's move was a "triggering factor," explains Iraqi nuclear chief Jafar Dhia Jafar as Saddam purchased a reactor from France.[1] Iran and Iraq were conscious of living in a dangerous neighborhood and were wary of each other's ambitions. Each was fearful of being outpaced by the other. The smallest suspicion of a nuclear program on the part of a neighbor was enough to drive the other forward. Each would maintain the story that it was only nuclear power they were after not the bomb, but both knew that the same technology could easily be used for both.

Iran's drive for nuclear technology in the 1970s under the Shah sent many young Iranians abroad to acquire scientific expertise.[2] But after the revolution in 1979 and the overthrow of the Shah, the nuclear program fizzled—Iran's new leader Ayatollah Khomenei rejected contact with the West, including in science and technology, and saw nuclear weapons as the work of the devil and un-Islamic. The Shah's half built facilities began to rust. The contracts for nuclear technology and construction were cancelled and a brain drain began, as educated professionals and scientists headed to the West. Before 1979 the Atomic Energy Organization of Iran was estimated to have employed more than forty-five hundred scientists, but soon after the revolution that figure was down to only eight hundred.

Sensing the new regime's weakness, Iraq's leader Saddam Hussein launched an attack on Iran in September 1980, beginning a long and bloody conflict. The destruction of Iraq's nuclear reactor in a bombing raid by Israel in 1981 took away any imminent nuclear threat, but even so the Iraqis proved to be a deadly foe. After its initial invasion stalled, Iraq began to deploy chemical weapons (manufactured with materials supplied from the West). At first Iraq's attempts were largely ineffective, often dropping its chemical bombs from too great a height or when the wind was blowing back in the direction of their own troops. But by March 1984 the on-slaughts became more deadly as Iraq became the first country to use a nerve agent on the battlefield. Iranian troops, defending positions on the Manjoon Islands, saw four Iraqi fighter-bombers appear and drop a dozen bombs. Rather than explode, the bombs thumped into the ground and released a white-colored vapour that engulfed the Iranian troops. The soldiers began struggling to breathe and fell to the ground, wracked with violent spasms.[3] In all, Iraq would use more than one hundred thousand bombs, rockets, and shells armed with chemicals during the eight-year war.[4] In response, Iran began to develop its own chemical weapons program. And at the same time, it began to look once more at the nuclear option.

From 1984 nuclear research in Iran had begun to pick up under the Speaker of Parliament (and later President) Hashemi Rafsanjani. Rafsanjani was a wily, enigmatic politician who would become a key proponent of developing Iranian nuclear capability. His task would not be easy: the 1979 revolution had left Iran with a paltry scientific and technological base with which to develop its own program. Thousands of students were sent abroad again and Iran even tried to lure former scientists back to the country but this was largely unsuccessful.[5]

With little sign of achieving a domestic breakthrough, Iran was forced to look abroad for foreign help in rejuvenating its program. After he became president in 1989, Rafsanjani began to seek allies and technology from amongst the web of states willing to trade illicit technology—countries such as Pakistan, China, North Korea, Libya, and others. From North Korea in the 1980s came a five-hundred-million-dollar deal with Pyongyang for missiles and other hardware as well as help in mining uranium. In January 1993 President Rafsanjani went to North Korea for further help on missiles. The two best-known sources of help on the nuclear side were China and Russia. However, the narrow focus on these two led Western diplomats to overlook another more important and more secret foreign supplier.

China's cooperation with Iran began in the mid-1980s in the field of missile technology. The first nuclear agreement came in 1989. In 1991 a major nuclear deal was signed when a senior Chinese official visited Iran, touring around facilities near the ancient city of Esfahan, one of Iran's most historic sites situated south of Tehran. Secretly that year, China provided Iran with three cylinders, one large and two small, containing 1.8 tons of Uranium ore, a deal that Iran did not report to the IAEA. This allowed the Iranians to carry out experiments in the 1990s without the IAEA noticing any diversion of existing material that the agency had been monitoring. China also agreed to build the Iranians a complete uranium conversion plant at Isfahan. As the decade wore on, China grew warier of Iran's intentions and the United States began to exert more and more pressure on China to halt its support. Eventually, a 1997 deal with the United States led China to cut off remaining assistance. But Iran already had the plans and continued to build the conversion facility at Esfahan using the Chinese designs.

Through the 1990s as China's support waned, Russia was perceived as the main facilitator of any Iranian nuclear program. In 1995, in the face of U.S. opposition, Russia signed a deal with Iran to rebuild the Bushehr reactor, which the Iraqis had bombed during the Iran-Iraq War. Russian motivation was as much commercial as it was strategic; Moscow hoped to make use of the former Soviet Union's scientific and technical expertise and bring in hard currency (between eight hundred million and one billion dollars).[6] The deal initiated a wide-scale training program for Iranian scientists, which gave the Iranians a useful foothold in the Russian military research infrastructure. This was used by Iran to gather intelligence (until a number of Iranian intelligence operatives were expelled and export controls tightened) as well as to try and find Russian scientists who might be willing to be recruited to work for Iran—not a difficult proposition when the Russian Atomic Energy Ministry (MINATOM) was desperately short of cash. In the mid-1990s Russian engineers and scientists were literally bumping into each other in the streets of Tehran.[7] Then the CIA managed to get hold of a copy of a January protocol of intent signed by MINATOM with Tehran to negotiate construction of an entire enrichment plant in breach of Nuclear Supplier Group regulations. State Department official Robert Einhorn went to Moscow to confront the Russians and the Foreign Ministry cancelled the deal quickly.[8] The United States put in enormous amounts of diplomatic time and energy during the 1990s to try and prevent Russia and China from passing on technology to Iran in the field of both missile and nuclear technology. But while Russian and Chinese help was useful to the Iranians, there was another secret partner. Iran, just like Pakistan in the 1970s, had realized that the plutonium reprocessing route to the bomb was highly visible and thus subject to diplomatic pressure, but enrichment could be much easier to conceal. It was to be the enrichment route pioneered in Pakistan by A. Q. Khan and then exported to Iran that would bring Iran closest to the bomb. In many ways, the Iranian path would be a close parallel to that of Pakistan.

In 1985 the Iranian leadership made the decision to begin work on its own enrichment program. Researchers were told to scour through publicly available technical literature for any clues on how to master the complex technology. But the Iranians would find that it was far easier to buy in outside help than do all the difficult research themselves. They knew that

Pakistan was developing the bomb and that Khan was the man who was working on it and so discreet inquiries began. It was under President Zia's watch that the first contacts were made between Pakistan and Iran in the nuclear field and these were on an official state-to-state level.

Even though they were secret, some of the contacts were at the highest level between the two states. Iran-Pakistan relations had been difficult in the early 1980s as Pakistan was closer to Saudi Arabia who in turn was backing Iran's enemy in its war, Iraq. But relations began to improve from around 1983. By 1986 economic and technical cooperation was increasing as Pakistan began importing Iranian oil. The Iranian president, Ali Khamenei, who would later become the country's supreme leader, was a long-time proponent of the nuclear option and paid a visit to Pakistan in February 1986. That year there were official but secret contacts between Iran and Pakistan on the nuclear field. Iran was looking for help and some Iranian scientists went over to Pakistan.[9] In 1987 a secret technical cooperation agreement was signed covering military and nuclear cooperation at a secret meeting in Vienna between heads of the two countries Atomic Energy Commissions.[10] This official but clandestine deal between the two countries would help provide the channels of contact for Khan's own work. Scientists began to travel back and forth between the two countries and the Iranians started to inquire about "non-peaceful nuclear matters."[11] On the official state level, limited cooperation between Pakistan and Iran continued into the early 1990s. But an even more clandestine and murky set of contacts, centred on Khan, began to spring up.

The moment of first contact between Khan and the Iranians is still unclear. Indian intelligence believe it came after a top Iranian scientist visited Pakistan in 1984.[12] It has also been reported that Khan secretly visited Iran to see the damage at the Bushehr reactor (which had been repeatedly bombed by Iraq) in February 1986 for the first of a number of visits. Some reports claim that in January 1987, Khan was flown on a private jet from Islamabad to Tehran to meet with top Iranian officials at an intelligence ministry guesthouse in Parchin, south of Tehran, and that during this visit he pushed the idea of pursuing uranium enrichment as a viable option.[13] The official 1987 nuclear deal would have facilitated and legitimized contacts with Khan, providing him with cover to do his work and for the Iranians to start asking what more Pakistan and Khan could provide to them.

Ultimately though, the deal would be driven as much by his network as by Khan himself.

Khan himself did not attend the crucial sales meeting in Dubai in 1987 but key members of his own supply network were present in force. S. M. Farouq played the lead role, and his nephew, a twenty eight year old named B. S. Tahir, also appeared for the first time at the meeting. Farouq's family, originally from India, had moved to Sri Lanka and then to Dubai in 1980. Farouq's brother, Tahir's father, started a successful import business in the city but then died suddenly in 1985. Farouq took over and began to stamp his authority on the business and the family in a manner some recall as overbearing, even tyrannical. Tahir was kicked out of his own father's house so Farouq could move in. Tahir was a slight, shy young man with dark skin and curly black hair. He was keen to go to London to train in accountancy but was told he would stay and help his uncle. He was highly ambitious and in the early days he would sleep under a desk in the office. He would later attain his revenge on his uncle and rise to become a key figure in Khan's operations. But at the 1987 Iran meeting he was a quiet presence. Overshadowed by his powerful uncle, he served as "tea boy." There were also a number of Europeans present, including a German, Heinz Mebus. Mebus was an old college classmate of Khan and had been a supplier since the early days of Pakistan's program.[14] In the early 1980s Mebus had been targeted for supplying Iraq's program. A bomb, suspected of having been planted by Israel's intelligence service Mossad, blew up at his house, killing his dog. Mebus would continue his deals with Khan and die of natural causes in 1992. Another German is also believed to have been present at the deal.

The Iranians said they wanted help and the Khan network replied that it could provide it. Iranian opposition sources claim that the main Iranian interlocutor was a man called Mohammad Eslami who is now a senior commander in the Revolutionary Guards.[15] Investigators at the IAEA believe that the Iranians present at the 1987 meeting actually worked for a front company for the military, designed to mask its role in the nuclear deal and that a member of the Iranian vice-president's staff was the key official.[16]

After the initial meeting, the network submitted a formal offer to the Iranians. The remarkable document consists of a menu from which the

Iranian buyers could choose whatever they wanted—from a disassembled sample P-1 centrifuge machine (the Pakistani model based on URENCO's work) to drawings and specifications and plans for a complete centrifuge plant as well as materials for two thousand P-1 centrifuges.[17] Also on offer was the required auxiliary equipment such as vacuum and withdrawal systems, electrical drive equipment, workshops to make components, and plans for an entire two-thousand-machine centrifuge plant. The prices ranged from millions to hundreds of millions of dollars depending on whether the Iranians wanted a basic starter package or the full deal.[18] Iran initially claimed it only bought some of what was on offer—primarily the technical designs and samples for the P-1s, rather than large amounts of actual equipment. Later it admitted it also received more information, including fifteen pages of technical data on how to cast uranium metal into hemispherical forms—something vital in making the core of a bomb. Iran claimed it received these documents without having asked for them, which would be surprising given the existence of a price list.

After Farouq cleared the check in the Dubai bank, he distributed the money across the network. An unusual division of payment suggests that Khan was not necessarily the dominant partner in the commercial transactions and that the network around him was already playing an important role. The deal was worth around three million dollars, which seems high for what is known to have been provided. Khan himself did not get the highest proportion of the proceeds (he received less than a quarter); the European members of the business network actually received more. Why would businessmen get much more than the man who had originally supplied the centrifuge designs? One answer is that the full contours of the deal remain unseen. Another possibility is that it was the business network and not Khan who were driving the deal. They could have been selling on the designs that Khan had originally passed to them when he had been asking them to buy equipment for Pakistan's program. By 1987 Pakistan had bought what it needed from the businessmen and so those individuals who had previously supplied Pakistan were now looking for new customers, having learned how lucrative clandestine programs could be for them. They may have been the ones looking for clients and knew Khan's contacts could deliver more deals for them.

Despite the air of mystery surrounding the exact details of the exchange, Iran does seem to have opted for much less than the full deal that was offered. But it did purchase designs and parts, which meant it could short cut large parts of the process of research and development for centrifuges that would otherwise have taken years, perhaps decades. Khan was also selling a shopping list of what the Iranians needed and where certain items could be found. Rather than buying a whole facility, Iran worked out that it was cheaper to buy the designs and then try and buy the individual parts itself using its own procurement campaign. Iran's ultimate goal was to become self-sufficient in production of centrifuges and related equipment. So from 1987, Iran went shopping. In some cases it purchased through the Khan network, but in other cases it used its own existing military procurement networks or built up new ones using front companies. The Iranians operate perhaps the largest global network of front companies of any nation, far bigger even than Pakistan. These front companies pose as legitimate businesses trying to procure dual-use technology that might be legal when heading for one destination, like a university, but which in fact is heading for a weapons program. These networks would utilize the designs provided by Khan but sometimes undercut the asked-for prices of the Khan network. However at this stage, Iran didn't go flat out for the bomb— instead it seems to have done initial research to try and build a test centrifuge or cascade. But even in this, it found itself faced with numerous technical problems and poor-quality equipment. Progress was slow and erratic. The parts Khan sold them were old, most likely discarded from Kahuta. And some may not have been in very good condition.

In 1989 Iran's Supreme Leader Ayatollah Khomeini died. He had opposed nuclear weapons on theological grounds but the new Supreme Leader Ayatollah Khamenei (who had been president) and President Rafsanjani were more pragmatic and began to push harder on the nuclear front, reaching out to a number of countries for help. Iraq's surprising progress towards the bomb, revealed in 1991, also spurred those efforts. At this point, British and U.S. intelligence were aware of some kind of exchange between Pakistan and Iran but not of the exact details.[19] The new Iranian leadership had arrived just as Pakistan's relationship with the U.S. had begun to nosedive following the end of the joint Afghan campaign. There were strong suspicions that Pakistan might have supplied centrifuge drawings to Iran, although the evidence was sketchy apart from emerging patterns of Iranian procurement activity.[20]

From 1991 Western intelligence agencies began to see signs of an active Iranian procurement network, particularly in Germany, buying specialized equipment and materials, such as balancing machines, suggesting a possible experimental centrifuge program.[21] Questions began to be asked at the IAEA and in Western capitals about whether Iran might be developing a nuclear program. To try and kill the speculation, Iran allowed a top-level IAEA team to visit some of its facilities. The first visit, in February 1992, highlighted the enormous challenges the IAEA faced. Because the IAEA lacked any precise intelligence, the Iranians simply gave them a guided tour. The inspectors were taken to Bushehr on a chartered twin-engine passenger jet and then to Tehran, Yazd, and Isfahan. Finally, they were taken on an Iranian Air Force helicopter to a mountain North West of Tehran called Moallem Khalliya, which was alleged to be a weapons or enrichment site. The helicopter had trouble finding the site before setting down on a mountaintop where there was nothing apart from two small streams of fresh water from the mountain snow, a spring, a few small buildings still being built, and some temporary bunkhouses. The IAEA team returned home to controversy over whether they had in fact been taken to the right site. During this visit and another in 1994, they found minor irregularities but nothing so serious as to prevent them from giving Iran a clean bill of health.[22] Iran fell off the IAEA radar.

With the IAEA's visit out of the way and confident it would not be stopped, Iran took another major step forward in the early 1990s—again turning to the Khan network and this time signing an even bigger and more significant deal. After signing up for the limited package with Khan in 1987, Iran was struggling to manage by itself and realized it needed more help. So it went back for more. The initial meetings occurred between August and December 1993. It was now clear that Iran wanted to move beyond research and testing and build an operational enrichment facility.

According to the Iranian account of events, the initiative came from the Khan network when B. S. Tahir approached an Iranian company purchasing computers from his family company in Dubai. The Iranians say he surprised them by verbally offering them centrifuge designs and machines. Tahir had graduated from being the tea boy to becoming a major player. He was young, bright, and very ambitious and Khan appears to have appreciated the young man's business skills. As a result, he was rapidly becoming a pivotal right-hand man in Khan's burgeoning proliferation business, doing much of the face-to-face contact and negotiations with both customers and suppliers on Khan's behalf.

The Iranians passed on the message from Tahir and the issue then went right up to President Rafsanjani himself. After discussions, the Iranian leadership decided to see what Tahir had to offer. As a result, the Iranian vice president sent representatives to Dubai to meet with Tahir and his uncle Mohammed Farouq. The team went back and forth a few times. Two shipments went from Dubai to Bandar Abbas in Iran in March and May 1994 but the actual deal was only struck in October 1994. The Iranians checked the components and then handed over about three million dollars to Tahir who then distributed it around the network. The cash was brought in two briefcases by Iranian officials and left at a lavish apartment that was used as a guesthouse by Khan during his frequent trips to Dubai.[23] This was only one of a number of payments.

This time around Iran signed up for a bigger package from the Khan network comprising of P-1 designs, five hundred components for P-1 machines, as well as drawings for the more advanced P-2 centrifuge. The first deal provided designs and a shopping list, but this time the Iranians were getting more centrifuges and components, as well as designs for a much more efficient machine with which to enrich uranium. Following payment, these parts were delivered to Iran in two more consignments in late 1994 and early 1995. Tahir personally arranged for the transhipment of two containers of parts via Dubai using a merchant ship owned by an Iranian front company. Some components were shipped from storage in Dubai before payment was received, an unusual occurrence, making it possible that the network wanted to clear out the parts in a hurry from the warehouse in Dubai where they were stored, perhaps because they feared someone was on to them.

It is unclear why an Iranian computer company would act as the interlocutor on a nuclear deal and many aspects of the Iranian account of this deal do not add up. Members of the Khan network later claimed that they were simply following up on a direct deal between Khan and Iran. Khan is believed to have visited Iran a number of times, and may even have had a guest house on the Caspian Sea in Iran, but the details are murky. Iran's initial claims of the timing have also shifted under pressure. Documentation is lacking, perhaps, because officials were on the take and are now trying to hide this. The lack of honesty has heightened fears that not everything is known about this deal. Some suspect much more was given—perhaps even a nuclear weapons design at one of the meetings.

The centrifuges and components that Khan provided were secondhand cast-offs from the Pakistan program. It some ways, the deal looks almost like a "clear-out" sale from the warehouse run by the Khan network, offloading the bits and pieces no longer required that were stored in Dubai. This seems to be the case as there were odd numbers of components rather than a coherent set with the same quantities of each different part. It also explains why some of the material was shipped even before payment. Khan had been busy from the mid-1980s updating the centrifuges at Kahuta from the P-1 with its aluminium rotor to the more efficient P-2, which used maraging steel, leaving used machines and surplus components that could be sold.[24] These were supposed to be sent to a company in Pakistan to be scrapped and destroyed. Instead, they appear to have been sold in a hurry on this occasion.

The Iranians have tried to make out that its dealings with Khan were just a one-off sale completed between 1994 and 1996. But contact and supplies from the Khan network continued after 1996 with ten more meetings in the next three years. Members of the Khan network advised on technical issues and procurement although the Iranians say the meetings were largely to complain about the quality of what had been supplied. "They bought what they wanted to buy and unfortunately many of the things they bought were useless," said Ali Akbar Salehi, a former Iranian Ambassador to the IAEA.[25] The meetings appear to have stopped in June 1999, although no one is entirely sure why or even if that really is the case. One theory is that the Iranians were unhappy with the equipment and the costs but it is also possible that Iran had what it needed from Khan and had made the decision to move towards self-sufficiency in production of centrifuges. Iran began to diversify its procurement to try and evade detection and export controls, using Turkey and Eastern Europe rather than Western Europe to source the materials with which to make centrifuges, often exporting items first to Russia and China where it was hoped that they would be associated with existing nuclear programs in those countries. No one is sure that there were not more meetings with Khan than are currently known about or that more material wasn't transferred. There are reports that Khan could have made three further shipments in 1997, each of one advanced P-2 centrifuge, shipments which have never been admitted by the Iranians but no one is sure if these actually took place.[26] But from what is now known for sure, it is clear that Khan's support was critical to Iran's nuclear program and that Khan helped Iran overcome major technical hurdles. Both in the 1980s and 1990s, Khan helped jump start the Iranian program, allowing them to move much faster by providing plans, blueprints, technology, and advice.

With its help from the Khan network, the Iranian clandestine enrichment program stepped up a gear from 1995, moving from the more visible Tehran Nuclear Technology Center to the much more discreet cover of the Kalaye Electric Company in the suburbs of Tehran. This was a semi-state front company in a small building, clearly designed to be as hard to find as possible. The Iranians would later claim that it was simply a clock factory, but investigations would later reveal that it was the location at which P-1 centrifuges were produced and tested. It was here that uranium hexafluoride gas (UF6) was first fed into a centrifuge to be enriched in 1999 and into a cascade of nineteen machines in 2002 to test the process.[27] The first attempts to spin a centrifuge were met with failure. "In the early stages of our work we realized that our centrifuges had many malfunctions," commented Iranian nuclear chief Gholam Reza Aghazadeh years later. "After considerable effort, we noticed that when our experts assembled the centrifuges, they did not wear cloth gloves. We realized that if you assemble the centrifuges with bare hands, a little bit of sweat from between the fingers may transfer to the rotor and increase the mass. When the rotor spins, it becomes a problem, which completely unbalances the centrifuge causing it to explode. When I say that it exploded, it doesn't merely explode, but turns to powder."[28]

But slowly Iran began to master the complex technology. By 2000 Iran was ready to begin the construction of the two enrichment facilities at Natanz: the smaller pilot plant was to have one thousand centrifuges, the larger fifty thousand. This would provide the capacity to produce highly enriched uranium for twenty to thirty nuclear weapons each year. Natanz was carefully built with deep bunkers reinforced by triple layers or concrete and then covered with earth to hide their existence and to provide protection against any possible air strikes. A dummy building covered the vehicle entrance ramp and power lines were hidden. A building that housed the power supply was made to look like a cafeteria.

Iran continues to claim that it is building these plants because it wants nuclear power, not nuclear weapons. And it maintains that nuclear power—and the technology to have a homegrown nuclear fuel cycle—is its right under the Non-Proliferation Treaty (NPT). Opponents of the Iranian regime believe that even though so far no "smoking gun" has been found to prove Iran is seeking nuclear weapons, it is using the legal right to civilian technology as a cover to acquire the infrastructure for a bomb, manipulating the treaty's provisions. Critics point to Iran's duplicitous behaviour, its relationship with Khan, its history of concealment and deception, and the configuration of its program to argue that it is intent on weapons not just power. A broad national consensus has also emerged domestically that backs Iran's drive to acquire nuclear energy technology, partly because of reasons of national pride and self-perception as a regional power and partly because of the perceived security (not least against any U.S. plans for regime change) that having the capability to develop nuclear weapons might bring. That desire is heightened because Iran lives in a neighborhood where nearby states like Pakistan, India, Russia, and Israel are already nuclear.

The fear that Iran could be using the NPT as cover for a weapons program is heightened because it would be easy for Iran to develop a fuel cycle legitimately and then pull out of the treaty by giving ninety days notice. Once this had happened, enrichment plants could be quickly converted from producing low-enriched uranium for reactors to producing highly enriched uranium for bombs by rearranging the cascades—a so-called "breakout capacity." A stockpile of low-enriched fuel could be legitimately built up and then fed into centrifuges, reducing the amount of time required to produce weapons material by a factor of five.[29] This may well be the most attractive option for Tehran since it is technically legal and provides more diplomatic room for maneuvering than rushing headlong towards a bomb with all the consequences that this would entail. Retaining a nuclear weapons option just short of the bomb is a route that a number of other countries around the world have decided upon, although another possibility is the Israeli path of developing and deploying weapons but not saying so openly, retaining a level of diplomatic ambiguity. Another option that analysts believe Iran could be pursuing is creating a secret parallel program, for a so-called "sneak out" capacity. A large declared facility makes it much easier to run a parallel undeclared facility since it provides cover for research and procurement activities. The fear is that Iran may have pursued such an option based around the P-2 information (and possibly material) it received from Khan.

Thanks to Khan's help and Iran's skill at working around the gaps in the non-proliferation regime, Tehran has managed to travel a long way down the path, but just how far is unclear. Western intelligence officials still suspect that Iran may have another, still undiscovered, parallel nuclear program run by the military and based on Khan's help. This is a possibility that the IAEA does not rule out, although the evidence so far points to the parallel program being centered more on research than actual facilities.

As Khan became a seller, not just procurer of key nuclear materials, building a commercial network without parallel, a larger question arises of just how much the Pakistani government knew and sanctioned. Was this initial shift towards the commercialization of Pakistan's nuclear know-how a decision by Khan alone or the state as a whole? Looking at the broader strategic context as well as some of the individual personalities involved in the Iran deal provides some clues. There has been a welter of reports of official contacts on the nuclear issue and of the Iranians asking for help. These have fuelled speculation that the entire dealings were government-led with Khan acting as an intermediary. The reality is likely to be more complex. One reason is that Pakistan's relationship with Iran has been difficult and fluctuating. Rather than any fundamental similarity of inter-ests, it has largely been motivated by a belief that an unfriendly Iran on Pakistan's border would be a danger and so it was best to stay as close as possible. But would Pakistan really want to see a neighbor with nuclear weapons? A few individuals might but not the whole government over an extended period. In essence, it appears that Khan could have received tacit approval and support from a small number of senior individuals but he may have continued and deepened the relationship on his—or his network's—initiative.

Much of the evidence of possible complicity centers on certain crucial individuals. During the mid to late 1980s, when Pakistan and Iran were moving closer together and nuclear dealings began, General Mirza Aslam

Beg was first vice chief from 1987 and then from 1988 to 1991, chief of the army staff. Beg is a suave figure, with a shock of dark hair. He is also strongly Islamist and anti-Western in his outlook. As soon as he became vice chief, he was "made privy" to the nuclear program for the first time.[30] He supported a more overt nuclear policy and greater distancing from the United States and the West. According to his own writings, Beg thought in terms of "democratizing" the global nuclear non-proliferation order and moving to a multipolar world, which he believed would be safer than either a bipolar Cold War world or a unipolar world of American power. The spread of nuclear weapons could therefore be seen as a positive move to disperse power around the world. Beg, in a view echoed by Khan, claimed the nuclear proliferation system was deeply discriminatory, allowing Western countries to develop weapons and Israel to have its bombs but denying that same technology to the Muslim world.[31] "Some safety against extinction is the inalienable right of an individual or a nation," Beg has written. "'Oxygen' is basic to life, and one does not debate its desirability, the "nuclear deterrence" has assumed that life-saving property for Pakistan."[32] Nuclear weapons, in Beg's eyes, are not used "to win a war, but only to deter it." According to this view, nuclear weapons represented security and the more countries that had the bomb the less chance there would be of anyone actually going to war. Beg and Khan were close friends and political allies and shared many of the same views.

The same years as Beg led the Pakistani military, Robert Oakley was the U.S. ambassador to Islamabad. At the best of times, Oakley, a gaunt, experienced diplomat, enjoyed a testy relationship with Beg, but during 1990 relations with the United States were plunging rapidly as the old certainties dissipated, increasing the tension between the two men. The joint Afghan campaign was over and in October the United States imposed sanctions over the nuclear program, losing any remaining leverage and angering many in Islamabad who felt they were left to pick up the pieces of Afghanistan alone. The suspension emboldened hardliners in the army who argued that the United States could never be trusted. After Saddam Hussein's invasion of Kuwait in August 1990, tensions were also growing over U.S. plans to drive Iraq out. The 1990 invasion of Kuwait by Iraq was a tricky issue for Pakistan. New Prime Minister Nawaz Sharif was close to Saudi Arabia and visited King Fahd in November 1990 and offered five thousand troops to the kingdom in its defence against a possible Iraqi invasion.[33] Beg differed. He viewed the coming Gulf war as a means of covertly "control-ling the oil wealth of the Muslim world, destroying the military machine of Iraq for the sake of Israel."[34] He talked of the need for "strategic defiance" by countries like Iran and Pakistan, backed by China, a stance that would be supported by accelerating their nuclear programs.[35]

On one occasion, Oakley went to see Beg who had just returned from a visit to Tehran and believed that he could work very closely with the Iranians—and particularly with the Revolutionary Guards, whose leader he had met. "Beg had his own visions and I think the Iranians played him brilliantly. They were building it up—saying look at what we can do together. He was con-vinced the U.S. was going to run into terrible trouble if it should decide to push Iraq out of Kuwait," recalls Oakley.[36] "This was going to produce tremendous upheaval and eventually the Americans would come home and countries like Egypt and Saudi Arabia who were allies of U.S. would be discredited. Thereby Pakistan and Iran would be able to take the lead in the Muslim world. This was fantasy but nonetheless it was an idea he had." Iran offered support to Pakistan over Kashmir, as well as supplies of oil, but it wanted something in return. It wanted the bomb. Beg was quite open in his meeting with Oakley that he could see a real prospect for pro-viding assistance to Iran in the nuclear field. Worried by what he'd heard, Oakley cabled back to the State Department, and the United States com-plained to Pakistan. Beg would make similar remarks to other U.S. offi-cials, including General Norman Schwarzkopf. The Pakistani civilian leadership reassured the United States that there was no agreement with Iran and that whatever Beg had said had not been approved.

There was never any actual intelligence or evidence of a deal in 1990—just Beg's claims of a discussion with the Iranians. There have been claims that during one of his visits to Iran, Beg did come to an agreement with the Iranians for a military-to-military transfer but Beg has said that this and Oakley's claims are a "fabrication" and part of a "conspiracy against me by the Jewish lobby" and that no transfers took place with his knowledge.[37] The problem for Beg is that this is not the only report of Beg and parts of the army pushing to transfer technology, nor of the Iranians being keen to get their hands on it.

Benazir Bhutto has said that when she took over from Zia the issue of exporting technology was on the agenda. She says that in late 1989 she called in senior officials and imposed a ban on all exports at a meeting.[38] Other reports have surfaced that in 1989, President Rafsanjani spoke to Bhutto at a reception in Tehran and told her that her generals had made an offer to transfer the technology on a purely military-to-military basis. Rafsanjani wanted Bhutto's approval for the transfer of nuclear technology but she says she objected and prevented it.[39] She also says there were more discussions when she returned to office in 1993. "I was told that an offer had been made to the Iranians," and that there was a debate about providing more. "It was certainly their belief that they could earn tons of money if they did this. And it was something that I was disabusing them of . . . because if they chose to sell it, only three countries would buy it. It wasn't like McDonald's hamburgers that have a huge consumer market."

Similar proposals were being pushed forward when Nawaz Sharif was prime minister. Former Pakistani diplomats claim that Beg and Inter-Services Intelligence Agency (ISI) Chief Durrani approached President Ghulam Ishaq Khan with a proposal to sell nuclear technology in order to finance ISI operations that were ongoing in Afghanistan (but now without U.S. financial support) and just starting up in Kashmir.[40] Sensing the potential political dangers, the president, however, passed the issue onto Prime Minister Nawaz Sharif who declined the proposal.[41] A finance minister under Sharif would later claim that Beg told Prime Minister Sharif that a friendly state, believed to be the Iranians, were willing to pay twelve billion dollars for nuclear technology transfers (other reports say eight billion dollars). The former minister said that other military officers along with Beg put pressure on the civilian government to agree. And in December 1994 a Pakistani newspaper reported that the head of the ISI, Lieutenant General Durrani received an offer of $3.2 billion in return for technology around 1992.[42]

Khan himself is alleged to have implicated Beg in approving the transfers of centrifuges and components to Iran and there are reports that Beg was at least told of Khan's transfers. Khan claimed the technology wouldn't be good enough to do any actual enrichment.[43] Beg denies all the allegations. He would later give his explanation for what happened. "We all protected him [Khan], right from Mr. Bhutto to General Pervez Musharraf. We protected him in his efforts to acquire instruments and materials to enrich uranium. . . . My apprehension is that Iranians, maybe Libyans and North Koreans, would have known that Pakistan was stealing, buying and smuggling all the items which are needed for developing nuclear capability. So, they must have approached these scientists. And what they might have done is told them to go to certain companies for the equipment they needed. Now is that a crime? How can these scientists be penalized simply for identifying their sources?" [44]

So was this a private deal between Khan's network and Iran or an official deal between Islamabad and Tehran? As noted earlier, the intermediaries in the two deals were members of Khan's network rather than Khan himself or the Pakistan government. However, it is clear that a number of senior officials in Pakistan were supportive of the idea of passing on technology and of Iran getting the bomb at around the same time. This, of course, could have been sheer coincidence. It also seems possible that someone could have given Khan a green light, although it may not have been Beg alone. Beg took over as chief of army staff in 1988 and boasted of his Iranian contacts in 1990–91 but the Khan network had been selling to Iran in 1987. Other deals would also be concluded in 1994 long after Beg had gone. Some reports claim that Zia himself in 1987 secretly approved a standing request from Iran for nuclear weapons help. One senior former scientist told the *Washington Post* that the Zia "asked me to play around but not to yield anything substantial at any cost." [45] Zia may have wanted some limited help to appease the Iranians but is unlikely to have wanted to give them the bomb on a platter. Following Iranian entreaties resulting from the 1987 official, but secret, nuclear deal, Khan may have gotten a nod from Beg, Zia, or another figure to begin more clandestine contact in the mid to late 1980s. But Khan may have continued without any authorization from the government and used his enormous autonomy to go about enriching himself and his business partners (who seemed to be driving the 1987 deal in particular). The Iranians may have gotten a taste from Khan and his network but then wanted the full package from the government and pressed for it in their meetings with various officials.

It is almost impossible to prove any direct order was given for Khan's activity. Khan himself boasted that he had direct access to the army chief, president, and prime minister and could see any of them anytime he wanted. Only the chief of army staff and one or two officers around him were privy to all the secrets of the nuclear program. Because of this personality-oriented command-and-control system, if there was encouragement from an army chief to deal with Iran, almost no one else would have known. The essence of Khan's role was clandestine. He was given license to do whatever it took, meet whoever he had to meet, engage with whatever shady characters he had to engage, in order to deliver Pakistan the bomb. No one had to—or perhaps wanted to—approve any specific deal in which he was engaged. He was also encouraged to develop and then sell new conventional weapons technologies to generate funds rather than rely on a relatively poor state. This provided Khan and his associates with the freedom to travel to other countries and meet with foreign officials to negotiate deals. This could have provided him with the ability to act alone. If there were a wink and a nod from senior officials for Khan there would be no paper trail or way of proving this. Pakistani military and intelligence officials certainly knew that Khan was traveling to Iran but did they know what he was up to? "Some elements of the Pakistan government were probably aware of and supported the transfers to Iran, but others were either ignorant of it or actually opposed it," believes Gary Samore, senior director for non-proliferation in the White House in the late 1990s.

Khan's dealings would almost certainly have grown or continued without official approval into the mid to late 1990s and have become more purely commercial and designed to enrich Khan and his network. Through the 1990s Pakistan's relations with Iran deteriorated as the two countries clashed over control of Afghanistan, relations with the United States and India, and over alleged support for sectarianism by Iran within Pakistan. This makes it highly unlikely that by the mid to late 1990s the transfer of technology was state policy. By this time a nuclear-armed Iran doesn't appear in Pakistan's strategic interests, given Sunni-Shia tension within Pakistan, Afghanistan, and regionally.

Whatever the exact details, the volume of conversations points to a wider reality: a number of senior people in Pakistan felt that the bomb was something that could, maybe even should, be shared around other, primarily Islamic, nations. Some former officials believe there was a "lackadaisical attitude" towards the nuclear weapons in Pakistan in this period in which the bomb was not valued as something to be tightly controlled by the nation but instead could be traded and used for wider interests or sold to fund other covert activity. It may also have appeared, briefly, in Pakistan's national interest for more countries to have bombs, thereby making it more acceptable and reducing the power of the United States and the pressure on Pakistan and its nuclear weapons program. Khan himself seems to have believed this.

The revelations over Iran's progress that began with allegations by an Iranian opposition group in August 2002 and were confirmed by the IAEA visit to Natanz in February 2003—including Tehran's relationship with Pakistan—were not as much of a surprise as is often assumed. The late-1980s contacts between Iran and Pakistan were known about in a limited way by Western intelligence agencies. However, their significance was not appreciated, either in terms of what it said about the Iranian program or about Khan's transition to an international salesman. The belief at the time in London and Washington was that these contacts were state-to-state deals between Pakistan and Iran and not overly significant. In London, any transfer was seen as having occurred under a military government and it was believed that as Pakistan moved towards a civilian government it became less pro-Iranian and therefore there was less chance of anything significant happening. In Washington, the view was that any Pakistani/Khan transfers to Iran were a single, isolated instance and the relationship hadn't endured. "In the late 1980s we were concerned that Pakistan might help Iran," says Robert Einhorn, a senior non-proliferation official at the State Department until 2001, "and I remember during the 1990s it was the belief in the U.S. government that Iran had received some centrifuge equipment from A. Q. Khan but it was our assumption through the 90s that Iran didn't see this as a promising basis for a program. It was our impression that Iran considered the equipment to be out of date and not very effective. It was our assumption that by the early to mid-90s that Pakistani-Iranian cooperation was not a significant factor. We believed through the 1990s that Iran was looking elsewhere—Russia and China for instance. We spent a lot of time in the 90s trying to turn off Russia and Chinese connections to Iran but Pakistan was not on our radar screen." A late-1991 U.S. National Intelligence Estimate judged that Iran was committed to developing nuclear weapons.[46] This was based on a U.S. assumption of Chinese help and Iranian procurement patterns. But it was seen as being at an early stage. The efforts to block procurement and to persuade Russia and China not to assist Iran seemed to be bearing fruit and so, by the mid-1990s, U.S. intelligence actually became more optimistic about containing Iran's ambitions and lowered its estimate of Iranian nuclear capability.

The problem was that the scale and persistence of the contacts between Khan and Iran and particularly the large mid-1990s deals were missed (there were some rumors but no more). In the mid-1990s, just as the Iranian program was actually picking up a gear and becoming more secret, the expansion was missed, a failure that would have major consequences. U.S. intelligence on Iran became weaker with fewer sources. It was only at the end of the 1990s that there would be some signs of renewed Iranian activity. This was based around procurement patterns as European states began to report that dual-use technology, in other words technology that could be used for civilian or military purposes, was being sent to Tehran. British and American intelligence officials following Iran's program had been aware that Iran was conducting research in both enrichment and reprocessing and was trying to buy components and materials. In the late 1990s some technical analysts in Britain warned that if Iran had enough fissile material, they judged the country would be able to build a bomb, perhaps, even a relatively advanced implosion device. However, at the time policymakers were trying to take advantage of the election of the moderate Mohammed Khatami as Iranian president in 1997, and there was resistance in pushing such views higher up the intelligence chain. Around 2000 the CIA also tried to pass on flawed information on the triggering mechanism for a nuclear weapon to the Iranians through a Russian agent, another indicator of the level of awareness and concern over the Iranian program long before it became public.[47] The Iranians may have uncovered that operation but U.S. and Israeli intelligence are also believed to have tried to pass other flawed machinery and equipment to Iran to disrupt its program and cause technical difficulties.

Beginning in 2000 intelligence analysts in London and Washington watched Natanz being built. Every day they scoured satellite photography of the site they noted how the Iranians were clearly aware of the points at which satellites were not overhead to carry out certain work, leaving discrepancies between sequences of images (a trick they had apparently learned from the Indians in their 1998 test). The evidence of what was going on at the site was limited and no one was sure what was going on inside. There was some debate over what to do with the knowledge. Should it be made public? Should it be provided to the IAEA? But it was pointed out that building an enrichment site secretly did not actually break any of Iran's international agreements, only the introduction of uranium and the carrying out of enrichment without notification would violate agreements and there was no proof yet of this kind of activity.

Every site that was revealed by the Iranian opposition in 2002 was already known to the British and American intelligence, but they had chosen not to show their hand. "It was not publicly known as it was secret information but it was shared among the close allies that work on this issue," says Gary Samore who was in charge of non-proliferation in the White House until the start of 2001.[48] But it was not appreciated just how far the Iranians had gone. Nor was Khan's pivotal role in the Iranian program appreciated until it was too late. It was only after February 2003 when Olli Heinonen and the IAEA entered Natanz that a more complete picture began to emerge and with it the evidence of just how central Khan had been and how he had helped the Iranians move far faster than anyone suspected. Even now, much is still unknown about the scale of his assistance. In 2003, as a result of the Natanz inspection, the revelations over Khan's handiwork would begin to leak out and put pressure on him in Pakistan. But by then, he had already been a busy salesman. Many other deals had already been made.

CHAGAI HILLS

May 28th, 1998

THE DAY WAS CLEAR AND SUNNY. Prayers were offered as the equipment was checked. A helicopter carried dignitaries including A. Q. Khan, to the site. At 3:16 P.M., a scientist recited "All praise to Allah" and pushed a button. There were an agonizing few seconds of silence as the firing sequence went through its motions, then the grey mountain shook and cast off a cover of dust against the blue sky. Cries of "God is great" echoed out again and again from observers. Pakistan had become a nuclear power.

India and Pakistan had spent the previous part of the decade possessing nuclear weapons but declining to make that possession public for fear of repercussions. But that year a new, assertive Hindu nationalist government had come to power in New Delhi and it was determined to make a show of national pride and strength. Tension had begun to rise in the spring after Pakistan tested its Ghauri missile, developed by Khan, on April 6—it was a missile that could reach a significant number of Indian cities. On May 11, the Indian Prime Minister stunned the world when he announced that his country had tested a nuclear weapon that day. Clinton administration officials only learned about the Indian tests from the media.[1] The vast U.S. intelligence community had failed to spot the preparations despite numerous warning signs, including heavy hints in the incoming government's election manifesto.[2] "Since one of the CIA's jobs is not to be fooled, it was in fact a very serious intelligence failure," reckons Strobe Talbott, who was the deputy secretary of state.[3]

All eyes then turned to Pakistan. There was an intense diplomatic effort to try and persuade Pakistan to take the moral high ground. In one of four calls, President Clinton telephoned Prime Minister Sharif on May 13 asking him to "resist the temptation" to test, but Sharif told the president he was under tremendous pressure to respond.[4] Sharif had his doubts—and was worried over the economic impact—but the military was always in the driving seat. Sharif would give visiting U.S. officials the clear impression that if he didn't test he wouldn't survive in office and his replacement "would be a fundamentalist who has a long beard."[5] Huge rallies by Pakistan's Islamist parties demanded a test. The United States looked at repealing the Pressler Amendment and delivering the F-16 fighters as well as more aid as an incentive not to test. However, at the same time Saudi Arabia was encouraging its fellow Muslim state to test. Saudi Arabia offered Nawaz Sharif fifty thousand barrels of oil a day to overcome the impact of any Western sanctions that resulted from testing.[6] Sharif was close to the Saudis and felt that the Saudi promises of money for testing were more likely to materialize than American promises of money not to test.

A meeting was called of the Cabinet Defence Committee on May 15 in Islamabad to discuss what to do. At the meeting, the rivalry between Khan and the Pakistan Atomic Energy Commission (PAEC) was all too evident.[7] The new PAEC Chair Ishfaq Ahmed was away in North America and so Dr. Samar Mubarakmand briefed the committee on the options. The debate was firstly whether to test and secondly whether it should be led by PAEC or Khan Research Laboratories (KRL). There were some voices of restraint, particularly from the civilian side with fears of the effect of economic sanctions on the country's fragile economy. However the failure of the international community to take any really tough action against India meant there was little disincentive. At the meeting, Dr. Mubarakmand said that PAEC was capable of testing within ten days. A. Q. Khan countered that KRL was also capable of testing within ten days and said it should be given the honor of carrying out the first tests. However, since PAEC had control over the testing sites and had carried out more cold tests, it was given the go ahead.[8] Khan protested to Chief of Army Staff General Karamat, who discussed the subject with the prime minister. He agreed that KRL staff could assist PAEC. Khan was not pleased.

As early as 1976, a group of PAEC scientists flying over rugged territory in a helicopter had identified a granite mountain in Baluchistan as a possible test site. Once it was confirmed that the mountain was able to withstand a detonation, tunnels and facilities had been constructed and by the end of 1979 the military closed the area the public.[9] Two Boeing 737 flights shuttled engineers to Chagai on May 19 while the nuclear devices were taken semi-assembled on board two flights of a Pakistan Air Force C-130. They were escorted by four F-16s who had been given orders to shoot down the planes if they were hijacked or flew out of Pakistani airspace. Once the devices were assembled, the tunnels were sealed with six thousand bags of cement. By the end of May 27 the prime minister was told that Pakistan was ready to test. President Clinton made a twenty-five minute phone call, described by U.S. officials as "intense," to once again try and defer the test.

The evening before the tests, reports came out of Pakistan's Army Headquarters that Israeli fighter jets might be trying to launch a pre-emptive strike.[10] Prime Minister Sharif personally called President Clinton and Tony Blair to say Israeli planes were on the way and the Pakistani ambassador to the United Nations appeared on CNN to raise the alarm. Pakistan claims that all this activity led to the attack being called off. However, it's thought possible that the whole incident could have been concocted by the military to put pressure on Prime Minister Sharif and prevent him backing down.

With the detonations at Chagai, the rest of the world now had to deal with two nuclear powers, who had a history of going to war, facing each other with the flashpoint of Kashmir in between. But in Pakistan the test was a cause of huge national pride. For all the poverty, the corruption, the sectarian divisions, the bitter disappointments domestically and internationally, over the years, Pakistan was now the first Muslim country to have the bomb. Enormous, flood-lit, fiber-glass models of the Chagai hills would be placed in every town centre. Other Muslim countries celebrated as if the bomb was their own. The Iranian foreign minister arrived a few days later to congratulate Pakistan and said now Muslims can "feel confident, because a fellow Islamic nation possesses the know-how to build nuclear weapons."[11]

The long-running feud between PAEC and KRL burst out into the open as the tests triggered a full-scale media war between the two organizations. Khan was angry at the way the government was building up Samar Mubarakmand as a hero. That PAEC had conducted the weaponization and not his labs threatened Khan's self-image, which he promoted so avidly, and directly challenged the notion that he was personally responsible for the program. Khan was furious and his supporters immediately called the TV networks to complain about coverage and organized interviews for Khan. Mubarakmand then briefed against him in return, saying Khan was only an "invited guest" who turned up a few minutes before the test.[12] "We invited Dr. A. Q. Khan to the Chagai test site to show him what a nuclear test explosion looks like," Mubarakmand said.[13]

In the end, through some careful spinning Khan managed to preserve, even enlarge, his public image. Khan's role in Pakistan's tests may not have been as extensive as he and his promoters like to claim, but the myth was born and perpetuated that he was the "father of the Islamic bomb." His status rose to something many likened to a "demi-god." Khan would often joke that the King Faisal Mosque in Islamabad, one of the largest in the world, which could hold seventy thousand worshippers, took longer to build than it did for him to give Pakistan the bomb. Khan's popularity was reaching stellar proportions, which would provide him with protection against those who had suspicions about his work. But few at that time realized that Khan had been doing far more than simply helping Pakistan along the way to becoming a nuclear power and had begun to direct his ability outwards. At exactly the same time that Pakistan was testing its bomb, Khan was offering the experience he had gained working for Pakistan to others.

CHAPTER 4

North Korea—Pyongyang and Back

THERE WAS A VAST, COLORFUL AND PERFECTLY ORCHESTRATED CROWD to greet Benazir Bhutto when she stepped off her plane. It was a bitterly cold late December day in 1993, but the welcome in North Korea was predictably warm if carefully stage-managed. Benazir Bhutto had just returned to power for the second time and thousands lined the streets as her car made its way through the streets of Pyongyang. That night, the banquet held in the Kumsusan Assembly Hall was lavish. The leaders of the two nations entered to music and applause. Kim Il-Sung, the leader of North Korea, spoke first, and for a long time. Although it was their first meeting in person, Kim Il-Sung said Benazir Bhutto was "following the road of friendship pioneered seventeen years ago by your beloved father" who had established full diplomatic relations between the two countries. Kim went on to give a long tribute to Zulfikar Ali Bhutto speaking of the "high esteem" in which he was held and the work he had done to build relations between the two countries. The "technical know-how acquired by the Asian people" was an important guarantee for the independence and prosperity of the continent based on co-operation, he stated. Benazir replied that she was deeply moved by the remarks and agreed "Asian countries should cooperate with each other to develop their potentials." "Pakistan firmly holds the view," she continued, "that nuclear non-proliferation should not be made a pretext for preventing states from exercising fully their right to acquire and develop nuclear technology for peaceful purposes."[1]

Beneath the veneer of diplomatic niceties, there was an ulterior motive for the visit. During her short stay, Benazir Bhutto struck an important deal for Pakistan. Her plane also departed with a precious cargo—either dismantled parts to a North Korean Nodong missile or blueprints of the missile held on computer discs, according to different accounts. These would open the door for Khan's dealings with the hermit kingdom.[2] North Korea is one of the most secretive nations in the world and its program—and dealings with Khan—are shrouded in layer upon layer of mystery and speculation. But it was Khan who paved the way for Bhutto's visit and Khan who would be at the center of Pakistan's relationship with Pyongyang on the nuclear front. The North Korean deal also opens a window on to the much broader networks of illicit proliferation between key states in which Khan was just one of many players and in which the lines between the actions of states and those of individuals blur.

The acquisition and spread of nuclear weapons technology and of ballistic missile technology is closely and intimately intertwined, both in the case of A. Q. Khan and globally. For states, as opposed to terrorists, having the bomb by itself is not enough, you need a reliable way to deliver it. Aircraft are one possibility but ballistic missiles offer a longer range and a better chance of getting through enemy defensess. They can also be kept in hardened bunkers or on mobile launchers making them less vulnerable to the possibility of a pre-emptive strike. In themselves, missiles have also become a source of prestige for states, something that can be paraded through the streets and change the strategic balance in a region.

Because of this, programs to develop and procure nuclear weapons almost always go hand in hand with efforts to acquire ballistic missile capability. The latter can be nearly as expensive and time consuming as developing nuclear weapons and so it is hardly worthwhile doing so if all you plan on putting on top of a missile is a conventional explosive. Weaponizing a nuclear bomb and working out how to miniaturize it in order to make it compact enough to fit onto a missile is another major technical challenge. Because of this, missile development patterns can be a good indicator of intent to develop nuclear weapons.

In the 1970s the CIA was reassured by the fact that it saw Pakistan as "extremely limited in delivery capabilities for many years to come. It presently has no capability for indigenous production of either aircraft or missiles." The

CIA believed it would take Pakistan years to develop a warhead that could be delivered by ballistic missile.[3] In the 1980s, Pakistan set its sights on American F-16 aircraft as a primary delivery mechanism while it tried to develop missile technology, but the 1990 sanctions scotched those hopes, resulting in an even greater urgency in the search for missiles. Cut adrift from U.S. military assistance, Pakistan's gaze turned from West to East and towards the two most active exporters of ballistic missile technology: China and North Korea.

In the early 1990s satellite photos revealed that the Chinese had supplied M-11 missiles to Pakistan, the result of a suspected 1987 deal, but these were left in their crates at an air force base west of Lahore to try and avoid sanctions and growing international pressure on China's activities. China also helped Pakistan build an M-11 factory near Rawalpindi. In the mid-1990s, when the intelligence leaked publicly, there were calls from Congress to sanction either China or Pakistan but the Clinton administration was desperate to avoid taking such action as it was trying to improve relations with both countries. The failure to sanction led to deep disquiet amongst senior non-proliferation officials at the CIA who viewed the administration as placing too much pressure on intelligence to shape its judgements to fit policy. Policy-makers had used "almost any measure" to block judgements that would have led automatically to sanctions, said Gordon Oehler who ran the CIA Non-Proliferation Center until 1997.[4] But China itself was nervous about going too far and risking U.S. wrath and so Beijing began to edge away from its active role in missile proliferation.

So Pakistan was left looking elsewhere for a missile with a longer range and which could carry a larger payload. The North Korean Nodong fit the bill. North Korea was also more likely to be a reliable vendor of ballistic missile technology. It had provided extensive help to Iran during the 1980s and was known to be willing to sell pretty much anything for hard cash, of which it was desperately short. North Korea has sold missile technology to Pakistan, Iran, Egypt, Iraq, Libya, Syria, and Yemen—most of it based on reverse engineering of Scud-B missiles that it acquired from Egypt in the 1970s, which in turn came from the Soviet Union. The double-act of Khan providing the bomb and North Korea providing the means to deliver it to countries like Libya and Iran would be a particularly worrisome development to those trying to prevent proliferation. North Korea and Pakistan had been involved in conventional arms transfers back to 1971 when Zulfikar Bhutto approached Pyongyang for help replenishing the country's depleted arsenal. And their relationship had become closer in the 1980s as they both provided support to Iran. Pakistani and North Korean engineers first had contact as joint advisers on Iranian missile program.[5]

The bureaucratic rivalry in Pakistan's nuclear program between the Pakistan Atomic Energy Commission (PAEC) and Khan Research Laboratories (KRL) also played a part as each had their own missile program. The Chinese M-11 deal was run by PAEC but Khan wanted to develop his own rival missile system for reasons of prestige, status and also the huge funding that would come with it. But through the 1980s he was struggling. As a result, he became a key driver in developing relations with North Korea and he began making contacts and traveling to Pyongyang to try and get hold of their technology and forge a deeper relationship. In 1992 Pakistani officials went to North Korea to view a Nodong prototype and in 1993 Pakistani and Iranian specialists were thought to have been present in North Korea for a May test of the Nodong missile.

Both the Pakistani military and KRL were desperate for the Nodong because of its longer range which provided the ability to hit more targets in India. So they enlisted Benazir Bhutto, who had good relations with Pyongyang thanks to the family name, for help. Learning the lessons from her first, aborted tenure as prime minister, Benazir began her second term by staying closer to the army and the Inter-Services Intelligence Agency (ISI). She has also described herself as the "mother of the missile program" in the way her father, Zulfikar, had been the "father" of the nuclear program. In terms of the 1993 deal to get the Nodong, Benazir Bhutto is adamant that the deal with the North Koreans was for cash, paid out of a secret account. "When I went to North Korea, A. Q. Khan told me we can get their [missile] technology [so] that we can compare to our own. So I took [it] up with Kim Il Sung. . . . December '93 I talked to him, he agreed. . . . and it was cash, they needed money and so it was done for cash."[6] "It was a cash transaction, no exchange of nuclear technology. Exchanging nuclear technology for missiles was never even discussed during my visit."[7]

As a result of the deal Khan got his Nodong and rechristened it the Ghauri, named after a twelfth century Muslim warrior who fought the Hindus. In a three-hundred-thousand square-meter production complex in

Kahuta, his team began work adapting it; although, Khan would always claim the Ghauri was entirely his own work.[8] In the years after Benazir Bhutto's visit, scientists and military officers went back and forth between North Korean and Pakistan, and also Iran, to work on missile designs. The main transfers seem to have begun at the start of 1997. Between January of that year and March 1998, North Korea exported twelve Nodong missile components to Pakistan which were believed to have been transported in eleven special flights of Pakistan C-130 aircraft. In April 1998, Khan finally tested the Ghauri. It was an important moment for him. As well as a warning to India, the test also publicly demonstrating that his contribution to Pakistan's security extended far beyond simply enriching uranium and at the same time it allowed him to show his value by beating PAEC on the race to deliver a longer range missile.

The money for the missiles was paid in installments, under the cover of conventional arms purchases. It has been estimated the Nodongs would have cost at least three billion dollars.[9] But by 1997, cash was getting harder to come by for the Pakistani government with foreign reserves nosediving to critically low levels. Could they have looked for an alternative form of payment? The circumstantial evidence points to a deal in which Khan provided enrichment technology in return for missile assistance.

The notion of such an exchange makes sense because by the mid-1990s North Korea was looking for help with a clandestine enrichment program. During the 1980s, U.S. satellites had tracked the worrying emergence of a North Korean program taking the plutonium route. In 1989 Pyongyang shut down its Yongbyon reactor and was thought to have removed enough fuel rods to produce plutonium for one or two bombs. By the early 1990s concern was growing rapidly about North Korea's activities and its resistance to full inspections. The IAEA's ability to monitor activities began to degrade with surveillance equipment running out of power and film and in 1993 North Korea said it planned to withdraw from the Non-Proliferation Treaty (NPT). At a U.S. National Security Council meeting, Secretary of Defense William Perry presented senior officials with three options, including military strikes. He laid out satellite photos of the North Korean installations but also made clear that there were concerns that the intelligence wasn't necessarily good enough to be sure that all facilities could be targeted successfully. But halfway through the meeting a call came into the

White House from former President Jimmy Carter who had traveled to Pyongyang and said a deal might be possible. His freelancing was not well received in the White House. After intense diplomatic activity in October a deal was struck. The 1994 Agreed Framework involved a monitored freeze of North Korean nuclear facilities in exchange for a package including the provision of oil, help building light-water nuclear reactors (which are believed to be less useful for producing weapons) and also broader diplomatic engagement. From 1994 North Korea's nuclear ambitions appeared to be on hold.

But as with so many other countries, while public attention was on reprocessing, the uranium-enrichment route could be pursued largely below the radar and with outside help. North Korea believed it had to get the bomb and would explore every path. Robert Gallucci was a chief negotiator of the 1994 deal. He remembers that survival seemed to be the priority for the North Koreans. "You wish to strangle us," he was told by one of his North Korean counterparts, who, like others, seemed to believe that nuclear weapons were the only means by which to preserve their regime against the threat of American power.[10] Gallucci was aware of the danger in the deal he'd struck but hoped it could at least stop plutonium production for a while. When he was discussing the agreement with Congress shortly after it was signed, members who were angry about the deal asked him if he thought the North Koreans could cheat. "I said—yes they could cheat. I don't know if they will but they could. And if they do they will cheat in centrifuge technology. They said 'why?' I said I'd crawled over the Iraqi program and watched Pakistan and there are good technical reasons that's what they'd try and do because it is more clandestine."[11]

Gallucci was right and the North Koreans would cheat. It is not clear when exactly North Korea's enrichment program began. There are some indications that a clandestine enrichment program dated from the late 1980s and some defectors have claimed that by 1987 there was already some kind of enrichment research starting up.[12] It is possible that, as with Iran, there was some initial activity and even perhaps some initial contact with Khan in the late 1980s. Khan reportedly admitted that he began dealing with North Korea over enrichment in the late 1980s, although major shipments only arrived in the late 1990s. There is also evidence of North Korean enrichment purchases in the late 1980s, such as dual-use equipment from a German company, which was a long-time supplier of the Khan net-work.[13] But defectors have claimed that by 1992, the nascent enrichment program had ground to a halt due to cash shortages.[14]

Whatever the early origins, in the mid- to late 1990s there was a new surge forward in activity and determination, most likely as a means of evad-ing the restrictions of the Agreed Framework.[15] In 1997 Hwang Jang-yop became the highest-ranking defector from North Korea. A former aide to Kim Il-Sung, he testified that in the summer of 1996 there was a deal to trade long-range missiles for enrichment technology with Pakistan after a technical delegation from Pakistan visited North Korea.[16]

By 1996–97, Pakistan was running low on hard currency as its foreign reserves hit the danger point, putting the country on the edge of default. It began to trade food, machinery and oil. And at exactly the same time, traffic increased between A. Q. Khan and Islamabad and Pyongyang, and transport planes visited North Korea more frequently. A barter was in the interest of both countries, as each had technology the other desperately wanted and neither had the cash to pay for it. By 1998 there were nine flights per month, following high-level visits of North Korean officials to Pakistan and a higher volume of Nodongs and their components was traveling over.[17] In December 1997 Chief of the Army Staff General Karamat traveled to Pyongyang. And at this same point, there were signs that North Korea's uranium enrichment program began to move forward more rapidly. Although there's no direct evidence, this seems to be the point at which a barter began—enrichment technology in exchange for ballistic missile technology.

In all, Khan is thought to have visited North Korea at least thirteen times from 1997 (as well as having made more visits earlier), sometimes traveling alone and sometimes as part of a larger delegation. Khan's planes were arriving as late as July 2002, long after the timeframe initially ac-knowledged by Islamabad and while Pervez Musharraf was chief of the army staff and later president.

Eventually, after years of denial, President Musharraf admitted that "prob-ably a dozen" centrifuges were sent to North Korea during this period—both parts and complete devices (on another occasions he uses the number twenty). More importantly, blueprints and designs were also passed over. Musharraf also said that Khan had sent uranium hexafluoride to North Korea and also designs for facilities, but he said that there was no proof of the transfer of the Chinese weapons design.[18] A dozen centrifuges are clearly not enough to run an enrichment program but are enough to conduct the kind of research and experimentation to lay the foundations for designing one. Khan also provided his "shopping list" that he had given to the Iranians in 1987 of what to buy and where, which would prove a useful clue for intelligence agencies. The centrifuges most likely went between 1997 and 1999 with technical advice and follow up provided after. However, this is simply what is known or admitted to have been transferred. Given the number of flights—and the scale of Khan's deals with other countries— much more material could have gone to Pyongyang.

The degree of intimacy between the North Korean and Pakistani programs was evident when Pakistan tested its bomb in 1998. One Western diplomat who was in Pyongyang at the time of the test recalls witnessing an odd celebration. "I was in the Foreign Ministry. About 10 minutes into our meeting the North Korean diplomat we were seeing broke into a big smile and pointed with pride to the tests. They were all elated," the diplomat told the *New York Times*.[19] Was this simply pride at seeing a fellow developing-world state get the bomb or was it a sign of some other unknown cooperation? Theories abound that not only were North Koreans present at the Pakistani tests but the Pakistanis may have actually tested a North Korean device for them in addition to their own. This may have been the sixth and final test, which took place at a different location and had a different signature, including traces of plutonium when the other bombs were thought to be only uranium.[20] This could have been done for the North Koreans to provide the confidence of a validated weapons design without increasing diplomatic pressure and is similar to a rumor that China tested for Pakistan and South Africa for Israel. The evidence is inconclusive and it could simply have been a more limited form of technical assistance from Pyongyang. But even if it was not a North Korean test, the North Korean and Pakistani nuclear programs were close, with test data, centrifuges, missiles, and even uranium hexafluoride going back and forth, a far deeper relationship than a simple one-off barter of missiles for centrifuges. The top Pakistani diplomats in Pyongyang are almost always former senior member of the ISI or army. Around 1998 the relationship was at its most intense with North Korean planes delivering missile components to Pakistan twice a month.

Just over a week after the tests came another mysterious episode when the wife of a North Korean diplomat was shot dead at point-blank range at a home in Islamabad. The shooting took place within yards of A. Q. Khan's house, possibly even in his guesthouse. Government officials claimed it was an accidental shooting by a neighbor's cook, but rumors soon emerged that she might have been killed for being a suspected spy who had been in contact with Western diplomats and could be passing on information about contacts between Islamabad and Pyongyang. Her husband was officially an economic counselor but secretly a key figure in the arms deals between the two countries—and particularly in deals with Khan Research Labs. He was also thought to have been one of those who had personally witnessed Pakistan's nuclear tests. KRL technicians were frequent visitors at his house. The killing was swiftly covered up by Pakistani authorities.[21] Three days after being shot, the woman's body was flown back to North Korea. A military official told Japanese TV that he was on board the Pakistan Air Force Boeing 707 detailed to return the body. Just before departure he learned that A. Q. Khan would be traveling on the same flight and with him were five crates of luggage, two of them large, which no one was allowed to check. Khan's presence was authorized by the military.[22] In a macabre twist, it has been claimed that on board with the woman's remains were P-1 and P-2 centrifuges as well as drawings and technical data and even uranium hexafluoride.[23]

Khan's visits to North Korea were known about within the Pakistani military and intelligence community. His travels were closely watched by intelligence agencies, largely for his own security. Even if a member of Khan's family had to travel outside the city, they had to get permission because Khan was a security asset whom it was feared others might try and kidnap to get hold of Pakistan's deepest secrets. So how much would the military have known about Khan's provision of enrichment technology? One crucial question is how Khan was able to transfer centrifuges on military planes. The planes were chartered through official channels in the defense procurement agency in Pakistan's defense ministry. The rationale was that, as well as cooperation over the Ghauri, KRL was involved in major conventional arms deals with North Korea, which at one point was Pakistan's main supplier of weaponry. This gave Khan the freedom to go back and forth and it is not clear that pilots or other officials linked with transport would necessarily recognize a centrifuge as distinct from say, a missile part. There was never any accountability or records over the movement of weapons and material in and out of Pakistan, a product of fighting covert wars in the 1980s in Afghanistan and in the 1990s in Kashmir as well as running a clandestine procurement program. Covert activity had become an integral part of the Pakistani state and meant Khan could go about his business with minimal oversight, whether acting on his own or not.

KRL was subject to tight security but Pakistani officials say that this did not mean they knew what Khan was up to. The security was orientated towards shielding the lab and its scientists from external threats rather than keeping check on their activities. From the beginning, the whole rationale of security was to protect the nuclear program from the web of international non-proliferation controls, to ensure that external procurement networks went undetected by foreign intelligence agencies and that knowledge of them was restricted to those who needed to know. "The idea was to protect the national laboratories and national strategic organizations from all external threats," says Feroz Khan who was involved in that security.[24] "The key purpose was to provide them the space they needed to work rather than control them. They were not in anybody's oversight . . . They were not seeing what packages were going and what was inside the packages."[25] The same was true of the budgetary and financial aspects of KRL's work—their aim was to facilitate not to check up on Khan's activity. Military officers were assigned to run his security detail amid fears that he might be kidnapped by a foreign intelligence agency to reveal Pakistan's secrets. But the security officers at KRL were actually paid by Khan himself not by the government. They were often retired officers or officers approaching the end of their career whose loyalty could be pliable. Military figures inevitably have claimed that this autonomy explains why Khan could have sold material without any state knowledge. "[The] Pakistan army, if they deputized a person to be responsible at the site about the security of the project or the program, they were made responsible to the boss, that is Khan," argues General Beg. "They were not responsible to the army chief—not before, not after me, or to another army chief. They reported directly to the KRL and its director, Khan. And it has come out they were getting paid by him. So [the] army as such was involved in decision-making policy—but not directly responsible for all that was happening within the Kahuta lab."[26] The head of security at KRL Brigade General Mohammed Iqbal Tajwar was amongst Khan's closest confidants, traveling with him on his shopping and selling trips. Tajwar was one of those detained in late 2003 when Pakistan finally acted against Khan. He told interrogators that he had no idea what was going on.

As well as autonomy, Khan also had his protectors. The ISI and other organizations tried to keep tabs on Khan and his travels. This was reported to top officials. Why they chose not to act is the awkward question for them. The first known case of this came in 1989, when Lieutenant General Hamid Gul, the head of the ISI, delivered a report to the President of Pakistan, G. I. Khan. In it, Gul warned that there was evidence that A. Q. Khan was meeting with suspicious characters in Dubai. There might be a problem. According to reports, the president summoned Khan to his office but rather than question him, he warned him that the ISI were investigating him and that he should be careful.

Of all the deals, the North Korean is the least likely to have been carried out without wider complicity of the Pakistani military since it involved key strategic concerns like missile purchases. Khan is reported to have said that generals Karamat, Waheed, and also Musharraf, the chiefs of army staff through the mid-to-late 1990s, knew not only of the missile dealings but also the provision of nuclear technology as a barter. Pakistani military officials maintain that they did not authorize the transfer of nuclear technology and that Khan was acting purely on the basis of internal competition with PAEC. They argue that Khan was so desperate for continued help in developing his missiles that he was willing to trade nuclear secrets on a private basis for assistance.

The extent of North Korea and Pakistan's nuclear cooperation remains unclear, as does the precise degree to which it revolved around Khan's own private deals or broader state transfers of technology. The same murkiness applies to Khan's relationships with a number of other states. In May 1999 Shaykh Abdullah bin Zayed Al-Nahyan, the minister of information for the United Arab Emirates, paid a visit to Kahut and to KRL, an unusual event given the secrecy surrounding the facility. Khan welcomed his distinguished guest and provided him with a detailed briefing about the organization. But that wasn't all. "The Prince Abdullah bin Zayed also asked Dr. Qadeer Khan what help he could give them. Dr. Qadeer replied that

Pakistan would not present the atomic bomb or a missile on a platter but could train UAE manpower," according to reports in a local paper.[27] That same month saw an even more important visitor to Kahuta. Traffic was suspended for four hours on the road into the facility for Saudi Arabia's Defense Minister Prince Sultan. Prince Sultan—a powerful prince with control over procurement—was given a guided tour by Khan, accompanied by Nawaz Sharif (possibly the first time a Pakistani Prime Minister had been allowed into the site). Prince Sultan later said he only went to the outer entrances and not the "secret parts."[28] But when word leaked out and U.S. officials asked what the purpose was, the response from both Pakistan and Saudi Arabia was evasive, adding to the alarm.[29] U.S. officials hoped that Saudi Arabia was just interested in buying Pakistan's missiles rather than nuclear material, but no one was sure. Concern had grown over Saudi Arabia's possible interest in unconventional weapons after it emerged that in the late 1980s, Saudi Arabia had secretly purchased dozens of intercontinental CSS-2 ballistic missiles directly from China's operational nuclear force inventories. Because of their relative inaccuracy, the missiles are almost useless for carrying conventional explosives but are ideal for delivering unconventional warheads.[30] The man who arranged the deal, Prince Khaled, son of the defense minister, repeatedly made reference to 'deterrence' in explaining the purchase, saying Saudi Arabia needed "a weapon [that] would make an enemy think twice before attacking us" and that could deliver "a painful and decisive blow."[31] Some former intelligence officials believe that this could refer to a Saudi chemical weapons program rather than nuclear. The triangle of relations between Saudi Arabia, China, and Pakistan has always been watched closely, not least in the field of missile and nuclear technology, and Khan's close relationship with Saudi Arabia and its close support for Pakistan's nuclear program has always been a concern in some quarters.

As Khan expanded his operations through the 1990s, his freedom was enhanced because of a lack of understanding in the West of just how ambitious he had become. Khan had always been on the radar of U.S. and European intelligence agencies and was understood to be a key player in Pakistan's own nuclear program but his role as a salesman was underappreciated. In the mid-1990s, intelligence agencies saw a constellation of individuals, groups, organizations and states involved in proliferation. In

1996 the IAEA counted twelve nations being involved in the illegal nuclear business. Different networks overlapped with each other, two different states would often use the same middlemen and the same companies to supply them. Sometimes one country would approach multiple networks to try and shop around for the best price. Disentangling who was actually running a sale was not easy. When one middleman's activity was traced back it might lead to a plethora of both suppliers and buyers. In one corner of this confusing galaxy was Khan, perhaps the brightest star. But was he a customer of the various networks or a supplier? A master or a servant? It would not be clear for many years that Khan was actually at the centre of a web pulling the strings behind so many of the deals that would occasionally emerge into the light. It would not be clear until near the end that Khan and his network had risen to become preeminent in the world of proliferation.

After an initial flurry of hints and signs in the late 1980s and early 1990s, the trails went cold on Khan. U.S. attention focused on Russian and Chinese support to Iran whilst North Korea was seen as less of a worry due to the Agreed Framework deal. In the 1980s, U.S. intelligence had deeply penetrated the Pakistani program to the point of being able to mock up the Pakistani warhead design. But through the 1990s U.S. intelligence on Pakistan's nuclear program becoming less informative and less revealing, policymakers say. By 1996, the CIA and ISI, once such close partners, were estranged as the ties that bound the United States and Pakistan atrophied. "The liaison between the CIA's Islamabad station and Pakistani intelligence—the spine of American covert action and intelligence collection in the region for fifteen years—had cracked," according to author Steve Coll.[32] The ISI had sprawled out of control, sponsoring the Taliban's rise to power in Afghanistan as well as militant groups fighting in Kashmir, running training camps, and providing support. Its officers were even meeting with Osama bin Laden. Thanks to the reliance on the past relationship with the ISI, there were few independent CIA assets left in Pakistan, including in the nuclear program. "I don't think we ever had a feel for what they were doing and certainly didn't before their test," says William Milam who was ambassador to Islamabad in 1998. "I don't think we ever really knew what was going on within those programs."[33]

It was only at the every end of the 1990s that Washington picked up signs of a possible North Korean enrichment program based on evidence of suspicious procurement patterns. In 1999 the Department of Energy raised concerns after hearing of an attempted purchase in Japan of frequency converters that could be used for centrifuges.[34] In early 2000, South Korean intelligence passed on information about North Korean procurement attempts that appeared to be based on Khan's URENCO designs. In some cases, businesses and middlemen who were part of the broader Khan network had been contacted. In 2001 North Korea began seeking centrifuge-related materials in large quantities as well as equipment for uranium feed and withdrawal. The evidence of a link to Khan and Pakistan were now growing. In November 2001 a classified U.S. intelligence report stated that North Korea was building a centrifuge plant somewhere in the country.[35] A mixture of human intelligence and technical intelligence combined with procurement patterns was slowly raising suspicions over North Korean activity and in turn, as the threads were later unravelled, they would point back to Khan.

More confirmation of North Korea's enrichment activities and the role of Pakistan came in April 2002 when the French cargo ship the *Ville de Virgo* was stopped in the Suez Canal. Germany had been a favorite location for North Korean procurement activities for sometime, and authorities had become suspicious about an order from a German company for two hundred metric tons of aluminium tubing. On the surface the order was from a Chinese aircraft company to be used in fuel tanks but investigators soon discovered that the real customer was North Korea. In November a URENCO official testified in a German court that the tubes were exactly the type required for casings in a URENCO centrifuge—down to the millimetre. They were also exactly the same specifications of the tubes as those being made for Libya at the same time.[36] The order would have provided enough aluminium tubing for up to four thousand centrifuges.[37] The order provided some of the strongest evidence yet of the scale of the North Korean enrichment program and of it using Khan's plans and network.

By late 2002 the U.S. government began to go public with its concerns over a secret North Korean enrichment program. A CIA report said: "The United States has remained suspicious that North Korea has been working on uranium enrichment for several years. However, we did not obtain clear evidence indicating that North Korea had begun constructing a centrifuge facility until recently. North Korea's goal appears to be a plant that could produce enough weapons-grade uranium for two or more nuclear weapons per year when fully operational."[38] The CIA estimate was alarming— the plant could produce enough uranium for two weapons a year and could be fully operational by 2005. However, the confidence of that estimate was problematic, not least because of the danger of assuming that procuring the right items automatically means a country has the ability to put them together in a working whole.

The big question is how successfully the North Koreans cheated on the 1994 deal. Some feel that the evidence is less conclusive than suggested by Bush administration officials; others say it was clear by mid-2002 that North Korea had indeed acquired the material for a facility.[39] Intelligence on North Korea is even harder to come by than it was on Saddam's Iraq because of the hermetically sealed nature of the regime. Recruiting human spies has proved a near impossibility because there are so few contacts with Pyongyang on a business, personal, or diplomatic level, so there's a reliance on technical intelligence like satellites and environmental sampling to try and piece together what might be happening. But the North Koreans are aware of this and have become the world's leading experts at building military installations underground or within mountains (including constructing an aircraft hanger and runway inside a mountain to protect it from air strikes). The defector Hwang believed that the secret enrichment plant was based in a series of caves at Kumchangri, one hundred miles north of the capital. In 1998 satellite imagery and other intelligence revealed activity at the site, which was not far from North Korea's nuclear reactor.[40] It seemed to show a huge underground complex being built by fifteen thousand workers. International experts visited the caves in 1999 but found them empty. Some of them retained suspicions that nuclear related activity might take place there, partly because it was so well secured. Not knowing what facilities or capability North Korea really has makes negotiations with the North Koreans highly difficult. It also makes military options deeply unattractive, since any strike would have little guarantee of being able to destroy the capability and could well lead to a retaliatory attack in which the South Korean capital Seoul might well be obliterated.

In January 2004 North Korea invited a former head of the Los Alamos Lab in the United States, Siegfried Hecker for an unusual tour of its nuclear facility at Yongbyon. As he was escorted around the storage pool, reactor, and reprocessing facility, the plant reminded him of a Soviet-style operation or Los Alamos in the early 1950s, when he started working there. It was clean and tidy but much of the technology was clearly decades old, especially when it came to electronics. Rather than modern computers, there were strip-chart recorders that had been phased out in the United States in the 1960s. But what he was shown was also clearly more than adequate to do the job for which it was required. Around a conference table, the North Koreans slid open a wooden box and revealed two glass marmalade jars with screws on tops. Inside was what appeared to be plutonium. The North Koreans technicians were smiling with quiet pride. They were clearly trying to pass on the message that they were a force to be reckoned—and therefore negotiated—with and that they did indeed have nuclear material. Inviting in Siegfried Hecker was a way of showing this without having to actually conduct a test with all the repercussions that might involve.

But while its plutonium program is a bargaining chip, the enrichment program backed by Khan remains a mystery and an important one. No one knows for sure where any facility is or how advanced it is or whether it has already started working. Detecting clandestine enrichment sites is particularly hard since they do not have the size or power needs of a reprocessing plant, which provide telltale signs for satellite intelligence and other forms of sampling. North Korea with its love of tunnelling will make it even harder to find a plant than perhaps anywhere else in the world. Without Khan, the North Koreans would still have had nuclear material from their more advanced plutonium work. But Khan's dealings with North Korea remain amongst the most shadowy and worrying, since without knowing what North Korea received and what it has done with the assistance, any negotiations risk being irrelevant as the North Koreans could simply repeat their previous performance and agree to a deal on the plutonium program while continuing down the clandestine enrichment path. No one is sure how far the North Koreans have actually been able to turn the nuclear material they have into a weapon and, as with Iran, there are questions over whether Khan has provided weapons design information that would short circuit that process. "It is a very important question as to whether they have that design and the additional information on manufacturing," says Hecker. But as one U.S. official starkly told a journalist: "While they had the world focused on Yongbyon, they were out developing a separate path to nuclear weapons. And we don't know where the uranium-enrichment facilities are; we don't know how big they are; we don't how long they've been engaged in actually doing the enrichment; we don't know how much weapons grade uranium they have; we don't know whether they've made it into weapons; we don't know anything about it."[41]

JORDAN

August 7, 1995

A FLEET OF BLACK LIMOUSINES PULLED INTO THE FORECOURT OF THE HOTEL in Jordan's capital Amman. When the doors opened, a party of unusual fugitives stepped nervously out—Iraqi President Saddam Hussein's daughters, their children, and their two husbands. Two of the most powerful men in Baghdad had fled to Jordan to defect after falling out with Saddam's brutal sons, Uday and Qusay, who were emerging as the new favorites of their father. One of the husbands, Hussein Kamel, was particularly significant. Over the coming months, senior British and American intelligence officers debriefed him extensively because he had run the Military Industrial Commission in charge of the development of weapons of mass destruction in Iraq. Later, Hussein Kamel made the bizarre decision to return to Iraq; he would be promptly murdered by Saddam's sons. But his short defection had opened up many avenues of inquiry including an intriguing insight into A. Q. Khan's work.

In Baghdad Iraqi officials had realized they were in trouble and led UN weapons inspectors to a chicken farm owned by Hussein Kamel. Hidden in a large shed were hundreds of thousands of documents on paper and microfiche relating to Iraqi's secret activities. Within the haul was a memo from Iraqi intelligence officials dated October 6, 1990. Titled "Top Secret Personal," it details a meeting between intelligence officials and an intermediary for Khan.[1] "We have enclosed for you the following proposal from Pakistani scientist Dr. Abd-el-Qadeer Khan regarding the possibility of helping Iraq establish a project to enrich uranium and manufacture a nuclear weapons . . . He is prepared to give us project designs for a nuclear bomb. Ensure any requirements or materials from Western European countries via a company he owns in Dubayy. . . . [and] request a preliminary technical meeting to consult on the documents that he will present to us. . . . The motive behind this proposal is gaining profits for him and the intermediary." It ends with a request for the unnamed superior to "review and make suggestions."[2] Another document lists the items for sale with a price tag of five million dollars—as well as 10 percent commission on all procurement details. Notes and signatures on documents from the Iraqis asked officials to follow it up and explore further. The one-page ten-line offer seems to have similarities to the 1987 offer to Iran—although of course the Iranians claim that the weapons design was not offered—as well as the initial offer to Libya. As with the Iranian offer, Khan does not appear to have gone directly to the Iraqis but worked through an intermediary of the network who got in touch with Iraq's intelligence service. In this case, the offer appears unsolicited. Khan was peddling his wares to whoever might be interested. The fact that Khan was quite happy to supply both Iran and Iraq—two bitter enemies—says much about his motivation. As well as pointing towards greed rather than any strategic interests, it also shows the way in which Khan's business could become self-generating. The more countries that acquired nuclear technology, the more demand in the marketplace would be stimulated, leading others to follow suit and turn to the best-known supplier.

Iraq had been developing a nuclear weapons program in the late 1970s, until the Israelis bombed the Osirak reactor. After the attack, Saddam pushed the program forward but on a clandestine level. In the wake of the bombing, he summoned the urbane, British-educated nuclear expert Jafar Dhia Jafar from a jail cell and was explicit that he wanted a bomb and wanted Jafar to build it for him. When inspectors arrived after the 1991 Gulf War, they were shocked at how much further Iraq had moved than anyone had estimated. Iraq had run a successful covert, international procurement program to obtain nuclear technology, very similar to that of Pakistan (even getting hold of URENCO designs but from a different source). What's more, some of the same companies and individuals in Europe, especially in Germany and Switzerland who supplied Pakistan, were also approached by Iraq.[3] By 1991 Iraq had a single machine working in a test stand and was building a facility for a small cascade.[4] The whole system had been developed under the supposedly watchful eye of the IAEA and the realization that it had missed the program rocked the organization and the entire non-proliferation regime.

International inspectors scratched their heads when they examined the document detailing Khan's offer after it emerged from the chicken farm in 1995. They questioned Iraqi officials who told them they had rejected the offer because they suspected it was a sting operation by Western intelligence agencies, although the intervention of the Gulf War may have been the real reason why it did not progress. "We pushed the Iraqis every possible way but everything ended up in impasses," says Jacques Baute, a senior IAEA inspector on Iraq. Pakistan was also questioned but it swore it was not possible for any deal to have been offered, much less to have actually taken place. It was only a decade later when Jacques Baute arrived in Libya that he suddenly realized that the Iraqi offer was no fake and that Khan really was willing to follow through. But for the time being, the Iraqi documents proved another missed opportunity. Khan was able to prosper, bringing in more deals and expanding his network.

CHAPTER 5

The Network Expands—
The Libya Deal

IN JUNE 1998, KHAN'S NETWORK of global suppliers assembled in one place for perhaps the only time. The event was a grand society wedding at which the lynchpin of the network, B. S. Tahir, was to marry a well-connected Malaysian woman, the daughter of a former diplomat. Khan's suppliers had their airfare and hotel bills paid for and found large black limousines waiting for them at the airport when they arrived. The limousines were available for them during their entire stay. The opulent wedding festivities went on for three days. The main celebration took place at the Sheraton hotel with a sumptuous banquet, but the street on which Tahir had a house was also closed for an outdoor party. "It was the who's who of KRL and the suppliers," remembers one of the attendees. An inner core of members of the network sat on one table with Khan. They had much to celebrate because Khan was in the process of negotiating a deal on a scale previously unseen and which promised them riches far beyond what they had already accumulated. The network, set up originally to supply Pakistan, was about to take a major step towards becoming an independent private-sector operation.

Khan had become a globe-trotting salesman, peddling his wares on the clandestine market. From as far back as the late 1970s, he had been a well-known figure within the shadowy world of proliferators. Word was out that he was a man who had the goods. From the late 1980s, Khan began traveling to or meeting with officials from almost every country in an arc stretching from North Africa across the Middle East, perhaps into Asia, talking to anybody and everybody who had an even peripheral interest in buying banned nuclear technology. Sometimes officials talked to him but didn't bite on a deal, wary of the risks of getting caught and unsure of the benefits. Others went further.

The longer he went without getting caught, the bolder Khan became. Khan had never been shy about telling the world what he was doing, occasionally writing in technical journals to boast what marvels he had achieved and using the articles as a form of free advertising for the technology that he could provide. But by the end of the 1990s, he went even further. Khan Research Laboratories was setting up booths at arms fairs around the world and advertising its willingness to sell both conventional weapons and centrifuge technology. Brochures were being handed around that bore a proud seal saying "Government of Pakistan." Catalogues listed everything you needed for a nuclear program even "complete ultracentrifuge machines." Those who inquired were told that there would be no problem selling items to foreigners.[1]

The Pakistani government also got in on the act. An advertisement appeared in local Pakistani newspapers in 2000 offering specific nuclear expertise and material, raising more questions about the government's attitude towards the spread of the technology. "It's not a secret. It was a full one-page ad given by the government of Pakistan," said General Mirza Aslam Beg, former chief of the army staff. "Pakistan had all those items, which were offered for sale, which are not banned. And all the requirements were met for any one who wanted to see. So what was wrong with it?"[2] KRL also produced a half-hour promotional video boasting of its achievements. Tantalizing shots of the inside of Kahuta are interspersed with the father of the Pakistani bomb sitting in an armchair and explaining his accomplishments. The video was handed around to potential clients.[3]

Many of Khan's contacts are opaque. But in the mid-1990s (and possibly even earlier), a country that twenty years earlier had been involved in the start of the Pakistan nuclear program got back in touch. In 1995 Khan began what would be a series of five meetings with the Libyans, who appear to have approached Khan, aware of his reputation. Khan himself attended the key meetings, along with his loyal lieutenant B. S. Tahir. According to Tahir's account, they met two Libyan officials: a man called Karim and

Matuq Mohamad Matuq—a revolutionary with a hazy past who eventually became a deputy prime minister and ran the nuclear program.[4] The Libyans wanted a nuclear capability and wanted to know if Khan could provide it. Meetings continued sporadically between the group over the next five years to hammer out the details, once in Casablanca and many times in Dubai.[5]

Colonel Gadaffi's interest in acquiring nuclear technology had been longstanding, initially part of his self-image as a leader in Arab and African affairs and later as a deterrent and means to protect his regime against the United States. For a while in the 1970s, Zulfikar Bhutto seemed the answer to Gadaffi's nuclear aspirations and Libya began importing uranium from Niger in preparation. The Bhutto relationship proved less fruitful than Gadaffi hoped, yet he never relinquished his ambitions. In the 1980s Libya was under sanctions over its support for terrorism and so looked to the black market. It bought items haphazardly, buying what it could, when it could. But Libya wasn't any closer to having a bomb as a result of their shopping and the nuclear program was plagued by technical problems. Libya simply did not have the indigenous expertise and the market was too fragmented to provide the kind of capability it needed. Amongst their 1984 purchases was a uranium conversion facility, which arrived without instructions for assembly and operation and was left in storage for years. After ten years of work, Libya had failed to construct a single working centrifuge.

In July 1995 Gadaffi made a strategic decision to try again. This time he would get much further. Khan's great innovation had been to act as a broker, integrating a complex marketplace into something much simpler. A country such as Libya could cut a deal with Khan alone. Khan would then source them with the right materials using his knowledge, experience, and network. Rather than purchase piecemeal, a country would be offered everything on a platter—but at a price. By 1997 the first tranche of equipment arrived—twenty assembled P-1 centrifuges and parts for two hundred more, enough for the Libyans to begin research.

In an Istanbul café in mid-1997, Tahir and Khan met with Matuq again. Khan sat with Matuq while Tahir was at a nearby table.[6] The Libyans said that the initial parts and centrifuges were useful but not nearly enough to run a program. And they didn't have the capacity or the desire to try and start up their own production line based on the samples. They wanted

Khan and his network to provide an entire centrifuge facility. Discussion focused on the more advanced P-2 centrifuge. Two sample models arrived in Libya in September 2000. This set the scene for a massive order for ten thousand P-2 centrifuges, enough to produce fissile material for up to ten bombs a year. Also included were designs for a plant, twenty tons of UF6 and almost all the associated equipment. There would also be the offer of training sessions around the world (as there had been with Iran and North Korea) and ongoing consultations about using the equipment. It was the full service.

This was a deal of a different scale from those with Iran and North Korea. Those countries had a fair degree of technological expertise but needed help. However, the Libyans wanted the works—an entire nuclear weapons capability from start to finish. With Iran and North Korea, Khan could simply sell off the leftover parts from Pakistan as it upgraded or else draw from a stockpile he'd built up from over-ordering for Pakistan's own program. But Libya was purchasing a turnkey program that it would simply have to assemble. Not only that, but it was also being supplied with equipment to manufacture its own centrifuge parts. This would potentially provide even more capacity than the ten thousand machines supplied by the network.[7] The workshops were actually the big money spinner for the network because as well as being expensive pieces of equipment they also took large commissions on the purchases. The magnitude of the deal was enormous—potentially the network's biggest and most lucrative contract.

Because the size and scope of this order broke new ground, it would require a refocusing of the Khan network to a full-service, private sector model—a logical fruition of Khan's activities. It presented new challenges in terms of sourcing the materials and producing the components. But the new, expanded network driven by the Libya deal would still have its roots in the same business and personal relationships that Khan had utilized for the previous two decades.

The relatively young B. S. Tahir would be the key figure in running the operation. He had risen fast and had a nearly familial relationship with Khan. "Dr. Khan used to treat him as a son—the son he never had," recalls British businessman Peter Griffin, who knew both for decades.[8] Khan would often stay with Tahir when he was in Dubai. The businessmen were the board of the network and Khan was the founder and chairman, the dealmaker who brought in the business. But it was Tahir who was the CEO, the man who got things done. He would organize transhipments of material and move the money around the world. When Khan gave the order, it was Tahir who would tap other members of the network to carry it out, or recruit new individuals who could best help with a particular project.

Tahir had risen fast. In September 1997 the soft-spoken young man had ousted his uncle from control of the family business, SMB Group, in a bitter and acrimonious struggle that ended up involving lawyers. Tahir became managing director of SMB Group, as well as running a number of more obscure businesses with at least two warehouses attached. Tahir had no particular technical skills but was good at fixing things and making connections. Dubai was his business hub, but he had also developed strong links to Malaysia where he had arrived in 1994 and built up extensive and varied business interests (including in expensive chocolate). Tahir's marriage provided him with permanent residency in Malaysia and he began to build high-level business and political contacts in Malaysian society. He was a flamboyant character who wore the best suits and enjoyed driving a Lexus and a BMW. People remember that he "took care to cultivate prominent individuals."[9] In Malaysia, neighbors said he was rarely at home as he traveled frequently, including to Dubai and Turkey. Later, Malaysian authorities would detain Tahir and details of his interrogation form the basis for much of what is known of the business network behind the Libyan deal.

Apart from Tahir's wedding, the loose collection of businessmen from around the world who made up the Khan network rarely gathered in one place. A few network members would bump into each other when their stays at Khan's spacious eight-bedroom guesthouse next to his residence in Islamabad overlapped. In some cases, there was tension, especially in the 1990s when the business that Khan brought in appeared to be drying up. There were fights over the diminishing spoils that Khan was providing. Relations between the different parties were sometimes uneasy and scarred by competition. For Griffin, the supplier of many items to Khan through legal channels, even the description of a network is misleading. "It was never a network, a network implies that people are working together. It was intensely competitive. I would compete against, for instance, Slebos. Sometimes I'd send a quotation over for some equipment and when I asked 'when are you going to place the order' I was sometimes told that they had decided not to proceed but later I'd find out that someone had passed my quotation to Slebos who had come in 5 percent or so cheaper and therefore got the order." In one case, one individual believed that another had tried to set him up with his country's authorities in order to take him out of the picture and leave more of the pot for himself. There were frequent clashes over money. On one occasion, Peter Griffin was in Tahir's office and witnessed a row between German supplier Gotthard Lerch and Tahir's uncle, Mohammed Farouq. "Lerch was shouting angrily over a considerable amount of money that he had given to Farouq. Lerch was asking for it back, but it had already been spent by Farouq," according to Griffin. Even with the Libya deal, it appears that different projects were put out to tender within the network with different members submitting their own costings and offers from which Tahir and Khan chose.

Should the growth of the network have been spotted earlier? Asking why the United States did not stop Khan risks over-focusing on the head and ignoring the body of the problem. Khan's network was largely European (although with some individuals based outside of Europe and with the important exception of B. S. Tahir). The scale of the buying and selling was huge. One European middleman received enough orders for equipment in the mid-1990s to organize air shipments to Pakistan every week. Given the sprawl of Khan's operations in Europe, the responsibility lies with European governments as much as the United States for not appreciating the danger that Khan represented. The reality is that European countries were well aware that a number of their own citizens were playing a role in supplying Pakistan, yet the authorities never really managed to put any of those involved out of business or even watch them closely enough to realize that Khan was also selling on to other countries rather than just buying for Pakistan. The European end was also tricky for the United States. American diplomats occasionally got into rows with allies when they discovered that the United States had been spying on European citizens or businesses involved in proliferation in the 1990s.

The lack of effective export control laws (and the wiliness of proliferators) meant that convictions were hard to come by. Hank Slebos was sentenced in the Netherlands to twelve months in 1985 for selling an oscilloscope to Pakistan but never served any time and the arrest certainly was not enough to deter his involvement in the network. In 1998 five shipments from his company Slebos Research and another company were intercepted by Dutch authorities carrying sensitive dual-use goods heading to Pakistan. The Swiss authorities investigated Friedrich Tinner in 1996 for his exports to Iraq but they found that none of the country's export laws had been broken. German suppliers Otto Heilingbrunner and Gotthard Lerch were also both investigated by their government in the 1980s for sales to Pakistan but not prosecuted.[10] As late as 2003 Slebos sponsored a conference at KRL in Pakistan, according to KRL's own website, which was attended by European businessmen and academics, one of whom has admitted working for Dutch intelligence.

Britain was always a major base of operations and transhipment for the network and the Pakistan diplomatic mission in London was a hub of activity. When one of Khan's workers was arrested, orders came from Khan telling senior diplomats to do everything it could to secure his release. In a later incident in October 2001, a businessman Abu Bakr Siddiqui was convicted in a British court for exporting a number of nuclear-related items to KRL as well as knowingly trying to evade export restrictions. He claimed that he had failed to check whether certain materials needed a license for shipment as he was too busy. Prosecutors said orders came directly from Khan. Siddiqui had been trading with KRL for around a decade, often sending materials through Dubai. Over a number of years, he had sent a five-ton gantry crane, a twelve-ton furnace, and sophisticated measuring machines to Pakistan and was only caught by UK customs when trying to sell sensitive aluminium. British corporate records from 1999 show that Siddiqui was a business partner with B. S. Tahir in a European branch of Tahir's Dubai-based SMB computers. SMB Europe was dissolved in April 2001, just before Siddiqui's conviction. Siddiqui was given only a twelve-month suspended sentence because the judge said that even though Siddiqui knew he was dealing with A. Q. Khan he did not know of Khan's role in Pakistan's nuclear program (U.S. officials were said to be unhappy with the leniency of the sentence).[11]

The identities of key members of the network were well known to intelligence and customs officers in the United States and Europe. These businessmen also had their phones and other communications tapped for decades, but the spies preferred to monitor the individuals involved and keep them in business. The rationale was that this way the intelligence agencies could see what was heading to Kahuta and gain some insight into

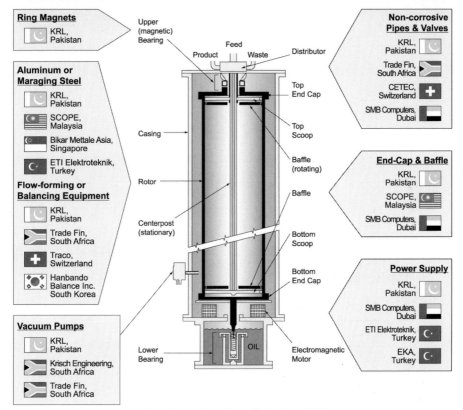

COMPANIES REPORTED TO HAVE SOLD OR ATTEMPTED TO SELL LIBYA GAS CENTRIFUGE COMPONENTS

Ring Magnets
- KRL, Pakistan

Aluminum or Maraging Steel
- KRL, Pakistan
- SCOPE, Malaysia
- Bikar Mettale Asia, Singapore
- ETI Elektroteknik, Turkey

Flow-forming or Balancing Equipment
- KRL, Pakistan
- Trade Fin, South Africa
- Traco, Switzerland
- Hanbando Balance Inc. South Korea

Vacuum Pumps
- KRL, Pakistan
- Krisch Engineering, South Africa
- Trade Fin, South Africa

Non-corrosive Pipes & Valves
- KRL, Pakistan
- Trade Fin, South Africa
- CETEC, Switzerland
- SMB Computers, Dubai

End-Cap & Baffle
- KRL, Pakistan
- SCOPE, Malaysia
- SMB Computers, Dubai

Power Supply
- KRL, Pakistan
- SMB Computers, Dubai
- ETI Elektroteknik, Turkey
- EKA, Turkey

Labels on diagram: Upper (magnetic) Bearing, Feed, Product, Waste, Distributor, Top End Cap, Top Scoop, Casing, Baffle (rotating), Baffle, Rotor, Centerpost (stationary), Bottom Scoop, Bottom End Cap, Lower Bearing, OIL, Electromagnetic Motor

Source: Center for Nonproliferation Studies, January 2005

Graphic representation of the number of countries involved—generally without their knowledge—in the Libya nuclear weapons program. Information for this chart was taken from open press sources and unclassified government documents (Center for Nonproliferation Studies).

KHAN'S TRAVELS

KAZAKHSTAN

TUNISIA

SYRIA
• Damascus

AFGHAN-
ISTAN

MOROCCO

IRAN

PAKISTAN

EGYPT

SAUDI
ARABIA

Riyadh•

Dubai•

Inset

MAURITANIA

MALI
• Timbuktu

NIGER

UNITED
ARAB
EMIRATES

SENEGAL

•Naimey

Khartoum•

IVORY
COAST

NIGERIA

SUDAN

• Lagos

KENYA

INDIAN

ATLANTIC
OCEAN

Countries to which Khan travelled shortly before
his detention (specific cities visited are noted
when known)

0   1000   2000 Miles
0   1000   2000 Kilometers

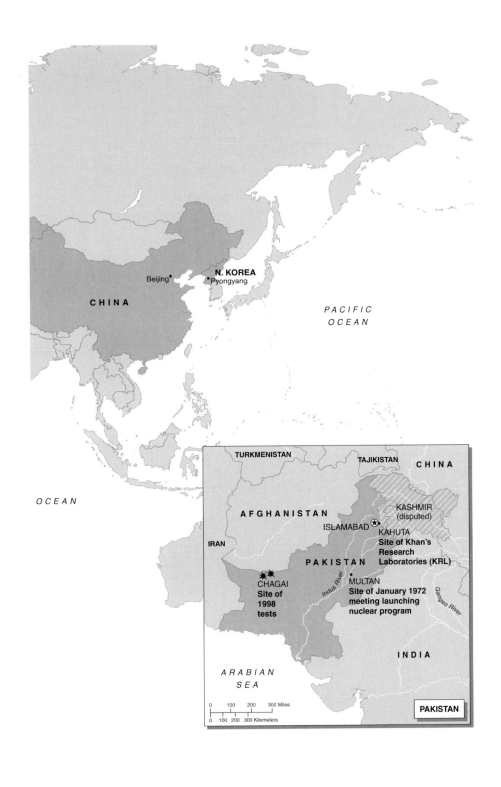

CHINA

Beijing

N. KOREA
Pyongyang

PACIFIC
OCEAN

OCEAN

TURKMENISTAN

TAJIKISTAN

CHINA

AFGHANISTAN

KASHMIR
(disputed)

ISLAMABAD

KAHUTA
Site of Khan's
Research
Laboratories (KRL)

IRAN

PAKISTAN

CHAGAI
Site of
1998
tests

MULTAN
Site of January 1972
meeting launching
nuclear program

Indus River

Ganges River

INDIA

ARABIAN
SEA

0   100   200   300 Miles

0   100   200   300 Kilometers

PAKISTAN

Below: U.S. President Eisenhower's "Atoms for Peace" address before the United Nations General Assembly on December 8, 1953 (The United Nations / Dwight D. Eisenhower Library).

Right: A cascade of centrifuges (Piketon, Ohio) (DOE Photo).

Lieutenant Lt. General A.A.K. 'Tiger' Niazi (R), Commander of the Pakistan Army in the East surrenders to India's Lt. General Jagjit Singh Aurora on December 16, 1971 at Dhaka (AP Photo).

Zulfikar Ali Bhutto (1928–1979), former Pakistani President (1971–1973) and Prime Minister (1973–1977) (Keystone/Getty Images).

Abdul Qadeer Khan addresses a gathering after inaugurating the model of the country's surface-to-surface Ghauri-II missile in Islamabad on May 28, 1999. Pakistan tested Ghauri-II on April 14, 1999 (Usman Khan/AFP/Getty Images).

Right: Pakistani President Pervez Musharraf (R) and Abdul Qadeer Khan (L) in Rawalpindi on February 4, 2004. Khan accepted full responsibility for the transfer of nuclear technology and sought clemency from the President (AP Photo/Press Information Department).

Colonel Gadaffi has been the leader of Libya since 1969 (Audiovisual Library of the European Commission).

General Aslam Beg
(B.K.Bangash/AP Photo).

B.S. Tahir (AP Photo).

IAEA Director General Dr. Mohamed ElBaradei (Dean Calma/IAEA).

Aerial view of Natanz, Iran's Gas Centrifuge Uranium Enrichment Plant
(DigitalGlobe).

Pakistan's own nuclear program. Yet, initially they never watched these individuals closely enough to realize that Khan was doing much more than simply importing into Pakistan; he had also begun selling the equipment onwards to other countries.

To fulfill the Libya deal, the network would now expand significantly and develop entirely new tentacles: it is estimated that up to thirty companies in twelve countries would be involved in some way, with half a dozen workshops scattered over three continents.[12] After the final deal was agreed with Libya in 2000, Tahir appears to have looked around for the best place to site the different aspects of the manufacturing process. What locations would be furthest from the prying eyes of Western intelligence agencies? The plan was for different parts to come from all over the world only to be finally assembled in Libya itself, thereby reducing the chance of being spotted.

For the more straightforward aluminium components, Tahir turned to Malaysia. The country offered a number of advantages. Countries with existing nuclear programs or histories of supplying other nations with parts were closely watched and part of the non-proliferation regime, including bodies like the Nuclear Suppliers Group. But a state like Malaysia with no nuclear program was essentially off the radar and had virtually no export laws against the manufacture of components that could be used in a nuclear program. What's more, Tahir had cultivated some influential relationships that he may have hoped would protect him. He turned first to a well-connected company called SCOMI, which was largely owned by an investment vehicle called Kaspadu.[13] One of Kaspadu's controlling shareholders was Kamaluddin Abdullah, who was the son of the Malaysian prime minister. Tahir himself was a director and his wife an investor in Kaspadu from December 2000 until February 2003.[14] His wife's connections may have been useful but there is no evidence that other investors in Kaspadu, including the prime minister's son, had any knowledge of Tahir's other involvements or the deal with Libya.

According to Tahir's story, the deal was made in the name of another company Gulf Technical Industries (GTI), a Dubai company run by Peter Griffin that had been set up in June 2000. SCOMI says that it signed a two-year $3.5-million contract with GTI in December 2001 for fourteen types of aluminium centrifuge components such as casings, end caps, and baffles—although not the key parts, the actual rotors.[15] Peter Griffin denies making the order. According to Griffin, Tahir photocopied and mocked up GTI company letterhead and forged signatures, letterhead, and documentation in order to make it appear that the legally registered GTI was making the deal instead of Tahir's bogus GTI company. Griffin had left Dubai permanently in August 2001 and had previously refused to allow Tahir to import items through his company. He says that Tahir ignored him when he issued the order and continued to do so, culminating in the 2001 forgery.

The SCOMI umbrella would be a useful cover for Tahir, but he also wanted it to be under his control. To meet the Libya order, Tahir helped set up SCOMI Precision Engineering—known as SCOPE on December 4, 2001. SCOPE based itself in a nondescript thirty-three-thousand-square-foot factory in a large industrial plant fifteen miles north of Kuala Lumpur in a town called Shah Alam. The factory had about thirty staff. They were under the impression that the parts that they were manufacturing were intended for the petroleum and gas industry in Dubai. It was an audacious move by the Khan network. No longer would they simply act as middlemen and brokers. Rather the network was setting up its own production facility dedicated to producing custom-made equipment for its clients. Once established, the factory could churn out parts for other customers at a startling rate.

According to a press release from Malaysian police based on his questioning, Tahir then hired Urs Tinner in April 2002 as a technical consultant. Urs Tinner was the son of Freidrich Tinner who had supplied Khan as far back as the mid-1970s when he was an export manager for the Swiss Company VAT. Friedrich Tinner says he last met Khan in Dubai in 2000 with Tahir present.[16] Urs Tinner says he never knew what was being manufactured or that the destination for the products was Libya.[17]

To make the components, SCOPE bought equipment from around the world, including three hundred tons of aluminium, chosen carefully because was it not on an export control list, from a German company through its Singapore subsidiary. According to information from Tahir, Urs Tinner's job was initially to import and set up the machines in the Shah Alam factory, which he did in conjunction with his father and brother, importing machines from around the world. He was also given the job of ensuring that the manufactured end product matched the designs he'd been given. The highly sensitive designs for each part of the centrifuge were enormously valuable to the network. Staff at SCOPE remember that Tinner was careful to always take back component drawings when they had finished work, telling them he had to safeguard trade secrets. Staff also noticed that Tinner would erase all the technical drawings on his computer at the factory. In October 2003 after the parts were finished and shipped and his contract was over, he left taking with him the hard drive of his computer and also removing his personnel file from the company records. He gave the impression that he didn't want to leave behind any record of his time there and didn't want there to be any chance of any of the technical drawings being discovered. He has denied knowingly assisting a Lybian nuclear program.

At the factory the aluminium was machined into its fourteen different components. Tahir also organized for Libyans to visit the site and train on the machines. Nothing was sent directly to Libya. Instead components were sent in four stages to Dubai between December 2002 and August 2003 through a number of dummy trading companies that used post-office boxes. It was the August consignment that would be tracked by the CIA and Britain's Secret Intelligence Service (MI6) as the crates eventually ended up on the *BBC China*.

Turkey was another production site. Khan and Pakistan had procured components from there from as far back as the 1970s, leading to intermittent U.S. demarches. It was in Turkey that the electrical parts for the centrifuges were made. Many of these were more complex than the items made in Malaysia. The actual parts were imported from Europe before being assembled in Turkey and then sent on to Dubai. According to Tahir, Gunes Cire, a fair-haired Turk who once worked for the German firm Siemens, was one major supplier of equipment. Another Turk, Selim Alguadis, was alleged by Tahir to have supplied other items through a firm called Elektronik Kontrol Aletleri (EKA). Alguadis has said he had no idea that the parts were destined for Libya or for a nuclear weapons program. He admitted to having met Khan a number of times but has said the relationship was "purely social" and that "the only Tahir I know in Dubai is a gentlemen who owns computer shops and two to three years ago I bought myself a laptop from his store."[18] He would later claim that while his company did make frequency converters, it had not exported any to Dubai in 2003 and didn't make motors. In another illustration of the global breadth of the network, four balancing machines (costing $190,000 each) that were used to minimize the vibrations of spinning centrifuges came all the way from South Korea, arriving in Libya in June 2002. The money from Libya was laundered through different companies, and moved across banks in six countries in the Middle East and

Europe. Account holders would take a commission for allowing their accounts to be used for passing on the money.

Tahir organized another center of production at a meeting in Dubai in July 1999.[19] This project is alleged to have involved Gotthard Lerch. In the 1970s and early 1980s, Lerch had worked for Leybold, a German company that supplied material to the nuclear programs of Iraq, Iran, South Africa, and Pakistan before the company's management and sales policy changed. In 1987 Lerch along with another Leybold employee, Otto Heilingbrunner, were investigated by German authorities regarding the passing of URENCO blueprints for handling UF6 that were suspected to have ended up in Pakistan via Switzerland. No charges were pressed.[20] It has been alleged in a German court that Lerch received $34 million to set up his end of the Libyan deal. Nearly half of that promised to be profit.[21] Lerch denies the allegations.

At a Dubai dinner party Tahir and Lerch met Gerhard Wisser. Wisser was a German national who had been a supplier for the South African clandestine program during the 1980s (during which time he'd met Lerch) and had remained in South Africa. At the meeting, according to South African court documents, Tahir allegedly asked for Wisser's help in supplying the vast piping and feed systems used to pump UF6 gas into the centrifuges and to extract it following enrichment. This was the structure into which the actual centrifuges would be placed. Wisser says he believed it was piping for a refinery in the UAE. Wisser told Tahir that he could find someone who could help out.[22]

South Africa was an attractive choice to base production since the country had its own clandestine nuclear weapons program until the early 1990s. Even though the weapons had been dismantled and South Africa had joined the non-proliferation system, it retained a reservoir of both technical expertise and manufacturing infrastructure that could be put to nefarious uses. What happens to nuclear scientists and businessmen who have supplied a nuclear program after it is terminated has long worried non-proliferation experts, and South Africa is a worrying case study in what can occur. From the mid-1980s, South African suppliers began selling to Pakistan and then further afield.

Wisser is alleged to have gotten in touch with Johan Meyer, another contact from the South African program, who ran a manufacturing company called Tradefin Engineering based in Vanderbiljpark. Wisser returned to Dubai in April 2001, this time bringing Meyer. Meyer says he was never told the destination of any material. According to a South African indictment, Meyer opened a Swiss bank account in order to receive payments, including from Libya. He referred to his task as "Project X." Daniel Geiges, a Swiss national based in South Africa who had worked for Wisser, was allegedly brought on board to help. Geiges was another veteran of South African clandestine procurement in the 1980s. Meyer began working on the facility in 2000 and by May 2003, it was complete. Once tested, it was taken apart and put in eleven forty-foot containers ready for shipping. All marks and labels on the equipment were removed. In June 2002, two Libyans, "Abdul" and "Ali," are also alleged to have inspected the plant.

One mystery has always surrounded where the most sensitive part of the centrifuge—the rotors—were to be produced. Production of rotors requires a specialist machine called a flow-forming lathe, which shapes the metal into a cylinder with the necessary precision. Two lathes were legally acquired by Peter Griffin in Spain and exported to Dubai in accordance with export regulations. According to Griffin, they were then handed over to Tahir who paid for them and told Griffin that they were for the Libyan National Oil Company repair shop being set up in Dubai. Tahir shipped one to South Africa in November 2000. But the South African end of the network apparently declined to be involved with the making of the rotors and said it could not obtain the right type of maraging steel. As a result, the lathes were shipped back to Dubai in November 2001. After that, one lathe went to Malaysia and one to Libya. The original lathes as purchased would not have been able to make rotors of sufficient quality, so questions arise as to how and where they would have been modified. In the end, the decision seems to have been made to provide Libya with the manufacturing capability of producing its own centrifuge components and rotors.

For all these different activities spanning the globe, Dubai had become the hub. Raw material would be bought in one country, manufactured or assembled in another, and then taken to Dubai ready to be shipped. Parts from eight different countries were sent to the city. This was not new for Khan—his deals had been routed through the city from the late 1970s onwards, and Dubai has been a center for illicit activity not just for years but decades and even back to the nineteenth century. By the late 1990s,

Sheikh Zayed Road—where some of the network's front companies were based—had been transformed from a dusty road in the desert to a traffic-jammed thoroughfare lined by skyscrapers, a symbol of Dubai's emergence as a major trading point. Khan's offers, negotiations, and deals with Iran, Libya, and also others like Iraq, all took place here. One of Khan's sponsors, a rich Pakistani businessman, was also based in the city. When Khan arrived at the airport he would be ushered through the VIP channel.

According to intelligence services based in the Gulf, Khan made forty-four visits to Dubai over a four-year period, after it became his base of operations around 1999. With only a few miles of water to separate them, Dubai was well placed for dealings with Iran and became a key point of contact between Iran and the outside world. Scores of Iranian front companies litter the city, procuring for military programs. Khan made twenty trips from Dubai, often accompanied by Mohammed Farooq (a key Pakistani from KRL, not Tahir's uncle of a similar name) to fulfil the Iranian deal. For the Libya deal, Dubai was also very helpful because of its role as a re-exporter of goods. Dubai has deliberately marketed itself as a hub for transhipment with minimal hassle. Established in 1980, the Jebal Ali Free Trade Zone covers 750 acres of what was once desert. No duty is paid on anything imported and then exported from the zone.

The Libya deal was ambitious in scale and global in reach. How was the network able to evade global export controls so easily and trade the world's most dangerous materials? Khan's activities exposed a deeply flawed system for controlling the spread of technology. Khan did not run a black-market network involving illegal smuggling so much as he did a "grey-market" network—working through the holes in the existing export control regime and using a variety of techniques to disguise the use or final destination of dual-use items.[23] Dual-use goods require a certificate stating where an item will end up. Proliferators either fake these or put false end users on genuine certificates and assume (often rightly) that they will not be checked. They use front companies to import material and then re-export them to countries of concern, often using incorrect declarations on the manifest. It has been estimated that at least two-thirds of the Khan network was entirely legitimate, breaking no law. With the lack of a comprehensive multilateral export regime, it is easy for proliferators to find new gaps as quickly as countries try to plug existing holes.

Given that there were no export control laws in Malaysia and that it was not a member of the Nuclear Suppliers Group, SCOPE wasn't breaking any laws when it shipped goods in and out of the country. The same goes for much of the activity within Dubai where there are few restrictions on what comes in and out, especially of the free trade zones. Turkey also had lax free trade zones. Globalization has meant a rapid growth in trade, and attempts to facilitate and expedite this as much as possible have been a blessing for those involved in proliferation. Essentially, the Khan network was highly skilled at exploiting the realities of globalization in which production—even of relatively advanced components—can now be sited anywhere around the world. Components can be designed in one country, manufactured in a second, shipped through a third, assembled in a fourth, and put to use in a fifth. It is simply a case of picking places which have not been used before, where people are unlikely to look and which have weak laws. Globalization means that it has recently become possible to outsource even the more technically advanced manufacturing processes to other countries that have no track record of nuclear activity. A related problem is the arrival of the latest computer-controlled machinery. In the early days, centrifuges were virtually handmade, a task requiring an exceptional degree of precision and skill. But now the latest computer-controlled lathes can simply be programmed to produce components with a dramatically lower failure rate and far lower cost. The pre-programmed lathes can then be placed anywhere in the world.

The dissonance of attitudes between nuclear states and non-nuclear states also contributes to the problem. The entire export control system is viewed in many parts of the world as a closed cartel that is used to deny technology to those on the outside. Critics argue that nuclear technology suppliers have formed cartels that in turn force countries seeking weapons to develop clandestine programs to produce components. The view from Pakistan and states outside the nuclear club is that the export control system has become its own worst enemy—by denying countries legitimate nuclear technology, it drives countries to the black market and to individuals like Khan who offer weapons as well as civilian power.

Although the Libya deal showcased a major role for his network, Khan himself remained intimately involved in the Libya deal throughout. He personally sent centrifuge components on government-chartered cargo flights direct from Pakistan. As with North Korea, Khan's use of government chartered C-130s to transfer enrichment technology to Libya raises questions. How much did the government know? At the very least, Khan had cover to use when chartering planes because of an authorized conventional weapons deal between KRL and Libya, the product of a visit to Libya by Musharraf in 2000. When they were later examined, the inventories of the plane stated that the cargo was filled with anti-tank missiles.

Khan was also sending out far more dangerous material. In September 2000 he sent actual nuclear material—two small cylinders of uranium hexafluoride (UF6), meaning the Libyans would not have to go through the difficult process of converting raw uranium in order to test their enrichment cascades. The precious material transited through Dubai (and may even have been transported in the back of a car by a member of Tahir's family). In February 2001 Khan sent a further consignment. This consisted of a much larger 5m-by-1m cylinder containing 1.7 metric tons of UF6 gas. It was sent to Libya on a flight from Pakistan with a manifest masking its true contents. It had been enriched to about 1 percent and was enough material for one bomb and to test the centrifuges. Twenty more tons were due to be delivered at a later date. The origin of this material would later become the focus of investigation, controversy, and uncertainty. With all this help, Libya began to make some progress. A centrifuge was successfully tested in October 2000. By 2002, Libya had constructed three cascades but only a small one with nine centrifuges was operational.[24] Finally, and most worrisome, in late 2001 or early 2002, Libya received a set of documents that included a tested design for a working nuclear bomb and details of how to make all the required components.

By 2003, the material for Libya's larger facility was starting to come together. For this expansive, dangerous package, the rewards for the network were vast. Western officials say at least $100 million was spent on the program, members of the network have offered figures between $85 million and $140 million.

Some believe that it is possible that Pakistani officials, including perhaps Khan, felt that Colonel Gadaffi was somehow owed something of the Pakistani program thanks to his extensive funding in the early 1970s. But on the whole, the Libya deal looks much more like a money-making enterprise than a strategic decision. There is far less evidence of any Pakistani government involvement than in the case of North Korea or even Iran and there appears a much larger role for the businessmen around Khan (although that's not to say that some in Pakistan didn't know what Khan was up to). The Libya deal represents the ultimate fruition of Khan's move into the private sector. He now had a global business empire able to manufacture material largely independent of Pakistan and state control. It had been put together for Libya and could now be used for any other customers he could find.

How had the young scientist sitting in the Netherlands in the early 1970s eager to help his homeland been transformed into this globe-trotting merchant of shadowy technology? Simple greed is the easiest response. It is undoubtedly the answer for the business members of his network who stood to gain millions in kickbacks, commissions, and contracts. With only a dozen or so individuals involved at the highest level, each deal was incredibly lucrative. Khan himself was also wealthy. He built up an extensive network of properties in Pakistan and also in Dubai, London, and other cities around the world. He had interests in hotels, restaurants, and even a nightclub. He reportedly spent a million dollars on the weddings of his two daughters.

But does greed explain everything? In his daily life, Khan was not particularly ostentatious. Those who visited him in Pakistan remember his abode being a relatively modest, standard Islamabad house with few obvious signs of extravagance, apart from an array of trinkets from his travels. In many ways, he came across as a middle-class bourgeois figure. His most notable eccentricity was his love of animals. He virtually ran his own pet sanctuary out of his house and was known for the care he bestowed on any stray cat, dog, or bird that wandered across his path. Friends recall that he treated these animals almost like family.

Greed was clearly a major motivation but it doesn't quite work as an all-encompassing explanation. After all, Khan could have become filthy rich through the everyday corruption of Pakistan in which military men on meager salaries would frequently retire as millionaires. There would have been plenty of opportunities to make his millions on kickbacks of his procurement activity for Pakistan's own program without the need to risk everything by selling on nuclear technology.

A complex concoction of religion, nationalism, and internationalism provides more of the answer. There's no doubt that Khan was firstly a fervent Pakistani patriot or nationalist, motivated by a deep-seated dislike of India. A huge painting depicting flames and the last train to Pakistan at the time of partition sat on his study wall.[25] Serving his country was his first priority. But Khan's work in delivering the bomb to his own country also helped instil a wider sense of grievance against the West, particularly on behalf of Muslim nations. Khan talked of "efforts to curtail the development of the Muslim world which the Western powers unjustifiably see as a potential threat to their monopoly. Development made by certain Muslim states in the restricted technologies does not trickle down to others because of international pressure and lack of coordination and cooperation among the Muslim countries."[26]

Khan was a Pakistani patriot first and a Muslim internationalist second who resented the power and influence of the West and who had found a means of challenging it. Khan was religious but he wasn't a fanatic. He didn't drink but there was always plenty of alcohol in his guesthouse for visitors from Europe. He was also intensely superstitious, regularly employing fortune-tellers (on one occasion a relative and business partner paid a fortune-teller to try and convince Khan that business should come their way). For him, spreading technology to other Muslim countries was a way of sticking up two fingers at the West and at its exclusive and exclusionary nuclear cartel. And, of course, the more countries that had the bomb, the more the despised non-proliferation system would creak under the weight and the less pressure there would be on Pakistan over its ownership of the weapon. In this way, it could be argued that proliferating helped secure Pakistan's grip on its own bomb by distributing the strain of the international non-proliferation system more broadly whilst at the same time undermining it.

Despite his Western education and Dutch-South African wife, Hendrina, Khan was explicit in his resentment and his anti-Western feelings. "I want to question the bloody holier-than-thou attitudes of the Americans and the British. These bastards are God-appointed guardians of the world to stockpile hundreds of thousands of nuclear warheads and have the God-given authority of carrying out explosions every month. But if we start a modest program, we are the Satans, the devils," he wrote as early as 1979 in a letter to the German magazine *Der Spiegel*.[27] Some of his friends and business partners felt the same. "Who is determining what is illegal?" replied Hank Slebos when asked about helping Pakistan. "The countries that have the bomb. If you say: You are not allowed to take part in this nuclear business, then you should also close down the Almelo plant. Then you should give up all nuclear technologies."[28] For Khan and his supporters, the bomb represented security not danger and there was no reason why more countries should not have it. The only obstacle was the way in which the West jealously guarded the technology. The solution was greater cooperation amongst Muslim states.

Khan's anti-Western attitudes developed as early as the 1970s in tandem with the attempts to stop him and Pakistan. "Western countries had never imagined that a poor and backward country like Pakistan would finish their monopoly (on uranium) in such a short time," he told a Pakistani journalist in 1984. "As soon as they realized that Pakistan had dashed their dreams, they pounced on Pakistan like hungry jackals and began attacking us with all kinds of accusations and falsehood. You see yourself . . . how could they tolerate a Muslim country becoming their equal in this field?"[29] Khan always disliked the picture painted of him in the Western media as some kind of "evil mastermind," unhinged and bent on the world's destruction. "I am not a madman or a nut," he told one interviewer. "They dislike me and accuse me of all kinds of unsubstantiated and fabricated lies because I disturbed all their strategic plans, the balance of power and blackmailing potential in this part of the world."[30]

Over time, Khan began to see Pakistan as the center of the Muslim world, largely thanks to "his bomb." Khan saw Pakistan's nuclear capability symbolically as an Islamic bomb that, if not owned by the wider Islamic community, was at least a sign of its scientific prowess. The rest of the Muslim world would be protected under the nuclear umbrella he had provided to Pakistan and was now extending outwards. "His desire is to see the Islamic world rise above other nations, and for Pakistan to occupy the top position in the Islamic world," wrote Khan's biographer and close associate, Zahid Malik.[31]

This viewpoint is often emphasized by Khan's supporters because it bolsters his position across the Islamic world and undermines the damaging notion that he acted on the basis of something so petty as greed. "I,

myself, have seen Dr. Khan almost in tears when he used to see the Pales-
tinians, the poor ladies, the children, the old people, harmless people being killed by Israelis," says his biographer Malik. "Sometimes now I realize
when I ponder over the whole episode that perhaps Dr. Khan was hurt,
you see as a true Muslim . . . perhaps he might have thought that if any
country, maybe Egypt or Lebanon or Syria or Saudi Arabia or Iraq, Iran, or
any country around Israel, develops its nuclear program it will be good. If
that was the case then it has ideological contours, you see, it was not for
the lust of money, it was something higher—something sublime . . . If
Israel has the right to develop this program, why not Palestine, why not
Egypt, why not Iran for that matter?"[32] But why, after all, if he was such a
Muslim nationalist was he willing to help North Korea, clearly not a Muslim state? And North Korea was also not a country that had much cash to
hand out. Clearly, Khan's motivations are complex and may also have
changed over time, from decade to decade from deal to deal, but perhaps
the one constant through is the power of his ego.

From being a middle-ranking engineer in Holland, Khan was suddenly
at the centre of a billion-dollar program with all the allure, glamour, and
secrecy that went with it. He was also given unprecedented control and
power. That power fed both his ego and his bank balance and helped turn
a patriotic nationalist into someone who began to enjoy the power and the
money—and especially the glory—that came with his unique role. Khan
became increasingly corrupted over time, corrupted by his own power and
his own status. Status, in particular, was an important motivator, according to friends, especially from the 1990s onwards. He made everyone stand
when he entered a room. He was fiercely protective of his reputation, often
writing letters to Western journalists and newspapers and complaining of
their coverage. He also paid out large amounts to Pakistani journalists to
secure favorable coverage. While he tried to maintain the impression of
humility, he often couldn't help but boast of his fame to interviewers. "I
can't even stop by the roadside at a small hut to drink chai without someone paying for me. People go out of their way to show love and respect for
me. It is very gratifying."[33] "Once, I was leaving the VIP lounge at an airport, and the security guard asked to see my VIP lounge card. I didn't
scream and wave my arms and say 'Don't you know who I am? I'm Qadeer
Khan!' I just took my card out of my pocket and showed it to him, that

man was just doing his job, and that wasn't a problem for me at all. His supervisor did come and yell at him though, he waved his arms and said 'Don't you know who this is? This is Dr. Qadeer Khan!'"[34]

The glory bestowed upon him by the Pakistani state and civil society fuelled his ego. A cricket team—the Dr. Abdul Qadeer Khan Eleven—was named after him as well as schools and other institutions. Stamps were issued to commemorate the 1998 tests featuring his official portrait and he was given his nation's highest honors. Khan claimed that he was a descendant of the thirteenth-century Muslim hero Ghauri. He named a missile after Ghauri and spent a large amount of money refurbishing a monument to him. It was even reported that he wanted a city named Qadeerabad. In a TV interview, Khan proclaimed, "Who made the atom bomb? I made it. Who made the missiles? I made them for you."[35]

His reputation made him feel impregnable and able to do things that others would have considered madness. Khan's displays of power, fuelled by the adulation and acclaim heaped on him, became increasingly ostentatious and reckless. Perhaps because he had gotten away with so much for so long, he became a man who believed he could get away with anything. This was evident in his life in Pakistan as much as in salesmanship around the world. On the shores of the Rawal Lake, in Rawalpindi, he built a palatial house in flagrant violation of local planning laws that spewed sewage into the lake that provided public drinking water—a visible symbol of a man who felt he was above the law. When a bulldozer came to demolish the house on the orders of local authorities, one of Khan's bodyguards shot the driver and the house remained standing. Khan himself kept a gun in his car and in his house for his own security; he also employed bodyguards. On December 10, 2002, Khan summoned together a group of accomplices, which included some of his cronies from KRL, as well as a number of armed men. They went to a building on some prized land that housed the Institute of Behavioral Sciences in Karachi. It was a busy time of the day and about forty mental health patients were waiting for examination. According to court documents, Khan's group confronted the security guards, pushed them aside, and adopted positions "in a somewhat dramatic battle order." Khan summoned officials from the institute and told them that the building had been taken over and there was a change of administration. In court, Khan's lawyers would defend his actions with reference to his status.

"The plaintiff is a national hero. He is singularly responsible for facilitating the requisition of nuclear technology for Pakistan. . . . It is pertinent to point out that the plaintiff deserves great respect and trust in society."[36] Even in Pakistan's often-corrupt society in which elites enrich themselves, Khan's self-aggrandizement caused disgust. It was, one journalist wrote, the depths of degradation. Who could stop him from doing what he wanted? Greed, power, competition, nationalism, frustration, and pride all drove Khan onwards, heightening an ambition and a belief in his own imperviousness that would ultimately bring him down.

Part 2

FALL

CHAPTER 6

Picking Up the Trail

As HE STOOD AT THE FOOT OF THE DUSTY CHAGAI HILLS on that clear, bright day in May 1998 watching the cloud of smoke drift from the mountain, Khan appeared to be a man at the peak of his powers. Witnessing Pakistan's test and its entry into the nuclear age, he was an idol to his nation. His side trade as a nuclear salesman was also reaching a crescendo. The deal with Iran had been done, the barter with North Korea was ongoing and a new customer, Libya, was being lined up with the hope of many more on the way. But those present also remember Khan cutting a strange isolated figure, uncomfortable and not quite sure of his place. He was already encountering resistance at home and, as his nefarious activities grew in scope, they were beginning to garner attention abroad. Out of his frightening ambition would come his downfall.

During most of the 1990s, Western intelligence agencies had lost track of Khan. There had been early hints that he was selling his wares to Iran in the late 1980s. Germany also believed that Iraq and possibly Iran and North Korea had received some kind of enrichment assistance from Pakistan because it saw dual-use equipment going over to these countries in the late 1980s. But Khan was viewed essentially as one performer within a broader web of actors, all acting as agents of their government. "There were a lot of proliferators that were active," remembers Richard J. Kerr, a former director of intelligence at the CIA, "North Korea, China, the Russians—there were a lot of people providing assistance and he [Khan] was seen at that point in time as one of the players in that. It was also known that he was providing information out. I think the view was that it was going both ways. I think people knew he was a player in the larger field of proliferation as well as in Pakistan but I don't think they knew it to the extent that was later revealed."[1] The notion of Khan as an actor within a national program was the dominant mindset during this period. The idea of an individual transcending this role to become a semi-independent, international sales-man was not yet appreciated. "We had an image that there were a lot of national programs and the countries would barter with each other, so if Pakistan wanted missiles it would do a deal with the North Koreans and get the Nodong," explains one former British intelligence official. "What we didn't realize was that A. Q. Khan was running a global corporation which transcended the national boundaries."

This analytic mindset that focused on Khan as primarily a state actor and customer rather than as a salesman led to some missed signals in the mid to late 1990s. The CIA saw the network over ordering parts and won-dered why? The obvious answer was that perhaps Pakistan had an alter-nate, still unknown nuclear facility somewhere in the country. In an era when Al Qaeda was still largely unknown even within the CIA, the whole notion of transnational networks had yet to come into vogue and be treated with the seriousness of later years. Intelligence analysts who were monitor-ing faxes and communications saw sensitive orders being placed by Khan Research Laboratories (KRL) through the network—for instance for flow-forming lathes—but the paperwork made it look like it was for Pakistan's own program. That the machines were actually for Khan's other customers simply didn't occur to those watching at first. Even when material went out of Pakistan to Dubai it was thought that it was being sent abroad to vendors for repair. Khan had many tricks, one of them was to disguise orders for a small number of sensitive parts within a much larger request for largely useless items, hoping to confuse or overwhelm those trying to track him.[2] A vast array of companies, institutions, and universities was used to disguise Khan's hyperactive acquisitions of sensitive materials.

In the 1990s, the key period when Khan's activities were growing, the U.S. intelligence community hit a difficult patch. Having been designed primarily to focus on one target, the Soviet Union, the 1990s saw a decade of turmoil as the intelligence community struggled to adapt to the departure of its principal opponent and the beginnings of a new, more complex environment of overlapping, emerging crises and threats. Cuts had a real impact on capabilities. Human intelligence in particular suffered as money continued to go into technical collection methods like new satellite technology. Technical intelligence can be highly useful in watching plants being built and detecting emissions. But understanding a country's intent is vital to unlocking nuclear, chemical, and biological programs, especially when a nation is purchasing dual-use equipment whose purpose is ambiguous. And intent can often only be judged on the basis of human intelligence, not on satellite photography to which the bulk of resources and effort were being directed.

In the mid-1990s, only about a dozen officers a year were being trained for the CIA's clandestine service and analytic resources were stretched so thin that they were close to a meltdown.[3] The result was a series of poor performances by the U.S. intelligence machinery—it was wrong in Iraq, both underestimating the danger before the 1991 Gulf War and overestimating it afterwards. The buildup to the Indian tests was missed, as was Khan's shift from procurement into sales and the emergence of a North Korean enrichment program.

The notion that Khan might be aggressively peddling his wares to others was not fully appreciated until his career as a salesman was well under way and much damage had been done already. The originality of what Khan was doing made understanding his role harder. And when it was appreciated, there was the even more difficult question of how exactly to stop him. His unique semiautonomous status within a country that had its own strategic importance to the United States complicated matters enormously.

In the late 1990s, Khan's trail would be picked up again by British and American intelligence officials. One of the signs that drew attention was his unusual and extensive travel around the world. Deep in the bowels of Britain's Ministry of Defence, members of the Defence Intelligence Staff began drawing to their superior's attention the fact that Khan was going regularly to some pretty strange places. Historically, Khan's wide-ranging travel itinerary was seen primarily as a function of his role as a purchaser and importer for Pakistan's nuclear and missile program (and to some extent as an exporter of conventional arms). Though Khan had always been a prodigious traveler, his routes were looking increasingly suspicious. According to one list, in the five years leading up to 2004 he traveled to Afghanistan, Egypt, Iran, Ivory Coast, Kazakhstan, Kenya, Mali, Mauritania, Morocco, Niger, Nigeria, North Korea, Saudi Arabia, Senegal, Sudan, Syria, Tunisia, the United Arab Emirates, and China.[4] In the late 1990s, alarm bells over travel were also beginning to ring within the CIA. "There were hints," says Gary Schroen, CIA chief of station in Islamabad. "We knew he had offices in Dubai and that he was running around the world."[5]

The trips that caught the attention of intelligence officers were reports of Khan's travels around Africa. "He was taking some very strange trips," remembers William Milam, ambassador to Islamabad from 1998. "The ones I found strange were to Timbuktu."[6] That particular set of travels by Khan led to much scratching of heads at Langley and Vauxhall Cross, the headquarters of Britain's Secret Intelligence Service.

The details of three trips to Africa between 1998 and 2000 have emerged in an unusual way. Before his proliferation activities were well known, one of Khan's friends, Abdul Siddiqui, a London-based accountant, wrote a memoir-cum-travelogue that reveals unique details of where Khan went and who accompanied him—although not every detail of why he went.[7] Siddiqui is the father of Abu Bakr Siddiqui who was Tahir's business partner and who was convicted in the UK in 2001 of illegally exporting items to Pakistan. According to translations of the memoir that have emerged in the press, in February 1998, Siddiqui says he received a call from B. S. Tahir, "a dear friend of mine and a very close associate of Dr. Khan. He said that A. Q. Khan is planning a visit to Timbuktu and you are invited to join him." Siddiqui arrived in Dubai on February 19 to meet Khan. With him was "Mr. Hanks, a Dutch businessman dealing in air filtration, solar energy, metallurgical machinery and materials"—an apparent reference to Henk Slebos. Also present for the trip were Lieutenant General Dr. Chauhan, former surgeon general of the Pakistan Army and then the director general of the Medical Services Division of KRL, and Brigadier Sajawal Khan, director general of the maintenance and general services division of KRL. Brigadier Sajawal Khan had been with Khan since the building of Kahuta in 1977. Some individuals in the group, including Sajawal had also traveled to North Korea for the deals there.[8] This traveling party was to become a core group of friends and accomplices. Khan told Siddiqui that they would fly to Timbuktu via Casablanca in Morocco and Bamako, the capital of

Mali. The trip was by no means secret. At many stops they were given full diplomatic welcomes befitting a guest of Khan's stature. In Casablanca, the first secretary of the Pakistan Embassy received the group and the honorary consul-general of Pakistan in Morocco gave a dinner in honor of Khan, which was also attended by the ambassador. The next day, they took a Royal Morocco Airline flight for Bamako where a plane was chartered for four thousand dollars for Timbuktu. "We had only a few hours at Timbuktu, which we spent in sight-seeing. We returned to Dubai by the same route." Whether their mission had another, less harmless purpose, Siddiqui does not mention.

Siddiqui's next meeting with Khan came on June 28 in Kuala Lumpur at B. S. Tahir's wedding, a key gathering for the network. "It was decided there to make another trip to Timbuktu because the last visit was short and we could not see much of the city," writes Siddiqui. Siddiqui made his way to Dubai on February 19 the following year to meet Khan along with the previous travelers and also some new arrivals: Dr. Fakhrul Hasan Hashmi, chief scientific adviser to Khan, Brigadier Tajwar, director general of security at KRL, and Dr. Nazir Ahmed, director general of the science and technology division at KRL. "Dr. Khan told us that this time we would take a different route to Timbuktu. We will fly there via Sudan and Nigeria."

This group flew from Dubai to Sudan's capital Khartoum on February 21 where they were met by the education minister and put up at a state guesthouse. By February 24, the party was in Timbuktu. After a few days in which Khan's movements are not outlined by Siddiqui, the group went first to the capital of Niger, Niamey, and then to the capital of Chad, N'Djamena, before going back to Khartoum. Intriguingly, after attending "some business," Siddiqui says that the group visited the Sudanese factory that had been destroyed in August 1998 in a controversial U.S. cruise missile strike in retaliation for the bombings of two U.S. embassies in Africa. Khan then met the president of Sudan before the group returned to Dubai on February 28. In February 2000 the group again went from Khartoum to Niamey in Niger where Nawaz Sharif's former military secretary welcomed the group before they passed on to Timbuktu. The party returned to Dubai at the end of February having visited ten African countries.

Why these elaborate African travels? According to Siddiqui, they were sight-seeing trips in order to see the heritage of Mali, which was once the center of Islamic publishing. But Khan was traveling with KRL officials and key members of his proliferation network with business meetings as part of the itinerary. He was also welcomed by Pakistani diplomats indicating the visits must have been widely known about, including back in Islamabad. Uranium could be one answer. The only hint that Siddiqui gives of a nuclear aspect to the trips comes in a single line. "Niger has big uranium deposits." Niger only sells one major commodity and it makes up three quarters of its exports. And both Libya and Pakistan (through the Libyans) received yellowcake from Niger in 1978.[9] Other countries, including Japan, also received illicit supplies of uranium into the 1980s direct from Niger. Could Khan have been looking for supplies for the network as part of his plans to offer a full-spectrum service? Or to broker a deal with the Libyans for Niger's uranium from which he would take a cut?

As the first signs of Khan's suspicious travel emerged in 1999, the CIA decided to investigate further. It sent out Joe Wilson, a former U.S. ambassador to Gabon who had served in Niger, to investigate reports of Khan's presence using his extensive contacts. This trip came after Wilson's wife who worked for the CIA's non-proliferation division told her supervisors that her husband was planning a business trip to Niger in the near future and had good contacts. Wilson toured around the dusty streets and asked around the relatively small community in Niamey if anyone had seen a party traveling through. Wilson talked to local politicians, taxi drivers, and anyone else who might have spotted the group. But the trip turned up a blank and no CIA report was written based on it.[10] A later visit by Joe Wilson back to Niger in 2002 to look into claims that Iraq tried to buy uranium would end up generating enormous controversy. The Iraqi ambassador to the Vatican had visited Niger in February 1999 (the same month as Khan), a trip noted by British intelligence as well as local press and the U.S. Embassy. Following his 2002 investigative trip, Wilson argued that Niger had not sold uranium on its own since the mid-1980s but operated through an international consortium led by the French and any sales moving large amounts of uranium would have left a vast paper trail that simply wasn't there.[11] There remains disagreement between officials in the United States and UK over whether a side trade of uranium could have occurred out of abandoned or operating mines; whether the French would have been aware of such a trade and over whether Niger could have been looking for new sources of revenue as an existing contract came to an end.

But Niger was only one stop. Another curiosity is that Khan helped finance a two-storey hotel on a dusty street in Timbuktu owned by a local guide; the hotel was named after Khan's wife, not exactly the sign of some- one trying to keep his role secret. By 2000 the Hotel Hendrina Khan was open for business boasting two suites and twenty-four rooms. Locals gos- siped that the hotel was built for missionaries "with Al Qaeda money" and that there were lots of "Saudis passing through."[12] Hotel records show that Khan paid another visit to Timbuktu in February 2002. Reporters exam- ined the guest list and found he was still traveling with senior members of staff.[13] Signing into the hotel on February 16, 2002, were many of Khan's standard traveling party, like Dr. Chauhan, Dr. Nazir Ahmad, and Briga- dier Sajawal Khan. This seems to have been an annual jaunt for Khan and his friends but few believe it was purely pleasure. "That man always had business on his mind," one of Khan's network would later comment when asked by international investigators about these travels.[14]

Could the series of visits have been sales trips? Some of the countries like Sudan could have been approached with offers to sell but many of the others are simply too poor. Also in cases like Sudan there was an existing conventional weapons deal with KRL for anti-tank weapons (although Khan often piggybacked his nuclear proliferation activities onto the authorized conventional weapons transfers). The 1999 trip included a stop in Nigeria at a time when the country was seeking fuel for a Chinese-built research reactor in the northern city of Zaria. There have been concerns that Nigeria could have embarked on a weapons program and in May 2004, following a visit by a senior Pakistani general, the Nigerian Defence Ministry issued a surprise announcement that it was working with Pakistan to strengthen its military capability and to acquire nuclear power. The statement was quickly retracted, however, as a "mistake," as was a previous statement from the vice president's office released a few weeks earlier that said North Korea would help with missile technology.[15]

Business could easily be combined with pleasure. After being received by a head of state or senior minister over a pleasant dinner, Khan could easily sidle up and inquire whether it might be worth thinking about buy- ing some nuclear technology. Some may have been interested but most likely lacked the money or confidence to seal a deal. It is also possible that the trips involved looking for places to outsource production or retransfer components for the Libya deal, further from the gaze of the West. There has been increasing evidence in recent years of advanced dual-use machine tools and equipment being imported into Sudan for which the country has no conceivable use. A large amount was imported just before 2001, but has gone missing. It is possible that the country was being used as a base for Khan to house equipment destined for other customers.[16]

There is likely to be more than one valid explanation for the trips. But the most important one is that the visits were, in all likelihood, closely related to the Libya deal.[17] B. S. Tahir would later admit that he and Khan met with the Libyans in Casablanca in 1998 and several times in Dubai from 1997–2000. The Casablanca meeting looks to have taken place in February 1998 during a stop over on the Mali trip when the group was staying at the Sheraton hotel in Casablanca. Some Libyan nuclear experts are suspected to have met with the network in Timbuktu as well.

The hotel in Timbuktu also seems to have served as a useful cover for the transport of items to Libya. When investigators from Pakistan started to look into the travel, they discovered that a Pakistan Air Force C-130 was used in 2000 to transport carved rosewood, brass-inlaid furniture from Pakistan to the hotel. They then found that "because of landing problems," the cargo was offloaded in the Tripoli, the Libyan capital and taken to Mali by road. Even more surprisingly, Dr. Mohammed Farooq, a top centrifuge expert at KRL, was detailed to accompany the furniture on the plane.[18] Farooq was of course the intermediary on the Libya nuclear deal and had a habit of traveling with lots of large containers when he went abroad. Enormous effort was put into tracking Khan's travel by British and American intelligence—they even recovered his airline tickets and hotel reservations—but the evidence was ultimately inconclusive about what exactly he was up to. But it was clear that he was up to something.

Alongside his unusual travel, there were other important warning signs that a large deal was going through. The Khan supplier network was being reactivated and ordering materials in quantities far larger than those needed for Pakistan's own program. The sheer scale of the Libyan deal necessitated a level of activity within the network (as well as its expansion to new suppliers) that inevitably began to spark curiosity. Britain's Secret Intelligence Service also began to see what looked to them like board meetings of the Khan network as key members turned up in Dubai at the same time. Something was happening, it was clear. Crucially, the first hints were also coming in from Libya, separate from the Khan network, that there was some kind of unusual activity going on in Tripoli and that there might be an attempt to rejuvenate the nuclear program. By the start of 1999, Russia was becoming concerned about nuclear cooperation between Iran, North Korea, and Pakistan. The head of the non-proliferation directorate of the Russian Foreign Intelligence Service warned that intelligence services in the three countries had been "obtaining classified technology and materials from secret, mostly military related sources," sharing it almost immediately between them.[19]

The North Korean linkup was, alongside the travel and business activity, the other major sign of Khan's possible salesmanship. When Pakistan tested its Ghauri missile in April 1998, it was immediately clear to intelligence analysts that Pakistan had received extensive help from North Korea because the Pakistani missile was almost identical to the Nodong. Given that both countries were out of cash, the suspicion immediately arose that there might have been some kind of barter. "There were at least indications that North Korea was pursuing an enrichment program and therefore people judged that Pakistan might very well have been the source of that program, especially as we knew about North Korea's transfer of Nodong missiles," remembers Gary Samore.[20] U.S. intelligence officials began watching the military planes go back and forth between the two capitals and wondered, with increasing concern, what they were carrying. At this point, there was almost no hard evidence but they knew Khan had only one thing to offer.

The United States immediately expressed its concern to Islamabad. The first to do so was Bill Richardson, the U.S. ambassador to the United Nations, during a visit immediately in the wake of the Ghauri test. In the subsequent years, U.S. concerns over Khan's activities with North Korea were raised to the highest and most classified level, often bypassing the U.S. Embassy in Islamabad. President Clinton would raise the subject each time he met with Pakistan's leaders. U.S. officials had almost no details of the deal at that point beyond a general belief that something was going on, but they hoped that the warnings would encourage the Pakistani government to investigate or act. These warnings were always communicated in a way that reflected the White House's belief that Khan was acting as an agent of the Pakistani state and not as a rogue actor, not least because he seemed to be working through official channels and using military aircraft and because the nuclear and missile program were both judged to be under the control of the military leadership. But the evidence of actual nuclear technology transfer was scant, based more on supposition than fact, and so the warnings were opaque.

The problem for the United States was that it had neither the evidence nor the leverage with which to push Pakistan to act and stop Khan. Since the imposition of sanctions in 1990, many of their old pressure points had been lost. At this point, there was almost no aid or military cooperation that could be cut. Lifting sanctions would require congressional approval, which wasn't on the cards. As a result, there were neither healthy carrots nor strong sticks to put to use. And finally, the issue of proliferation had to jostle for space with a series of other major policy concerns with Pakistan. Tensions between Pakistan and India were on the rise over Kashmir and August 1998 saw a new issue catapulted to the top of the agenda when Al Qaeda attacked two U.S. embassies in Africa. Since Al Qaeda was being hosted by the Taliban and the Taliban was being sponsored, at least in part, by Pakistani intelligence, the new drive to fight terrorism was already requiring the United States to place heavy pressure on Islamabad. Things did not get off to a good start when a U.S. general told his Pakistani counterpart over a dinner that U.S. missiles had just flown over Pakistan to strike Afghan training camps. The United States had not trusted Pakistan enough to be able to warn them in advance and the missiles killed Pakistani intelligence agents involved in training militants in the camps.

When Pakistan's prime minister, Nawaz Sharif, came to Washington in December 1998, dealing with Kashmir and also bringing Osama bin Laden to justice were the discussion topics over lunch. But when Clinton and Sharif moved into the restricted session with only one or two other officials present, the latest intelligence on nuclear proliferation pushed Khan to the top of the agenda, leading to some frustration from those at the CIA and elsewhere who wanted to prioritize the hunt for Bin Laden. "That went right to the head of the class for the discussion between the two leaders," says Karl Inderfurth who was assistant secretary of state for South Asia. "The result was an expression by Nawaz Sharif that he certainly was not aware of such activity but would look into it on his return to Islamabad and take appropriate steps." Khan's work continued.

In July 1999 a nervous Nawaz Sharif was back in Washington, D.C. A. Q. Khan and proliferation were again raised to the most classified level but this time talks at the official guest residence for visiting dignitaries, Blair House, focused on a serious crisis with India. Preventing imminent nuclear war rather than future proliferation was the overriding priority. Pakistani troops had crossed the line of control with India at a town called Kargil at the dizzying height of seventeen thousand feet. The events surrounding Kargil are an interesting example of how far the Pakistani Army was willing and able to take major decisions outside of any significant civilian control in the 1990s. The operation had been planned by Sharif's new Chief of the Army Staff, General Pervez Musharraf, with little input from the civilian leadership until the late stages. Up until that point, Musharraf had been a relatively low-key figure. Smart and smooth talking, he kept his cards close to his chest and retained an enigmatic, chameleon-like ability to present different faces in different situations. But beneath the relatively Westernized and liberal exterior was a fierce nationalist temperament. He had been deeply affected by the 1971 partition of Pakistan and had later told a group of officers that Pakistan needed to recover both the territory and honour it had forfeited in that defeat.[21] Kargil was to be his moment. But rather than create a fait accompli that the Indians would be forced to accept, the operation quickly threatened to escalate into a full-scale war with India. The developing peace dialogue between India and Pakistan was shattered, President Clinton was furious, and a nervous Sharif was in a tight corner when he flew to Washington. Sharif feared the possibility of being toppled by a military coup as his relationship with the army was deteriorating rapidly; he was unsure how much negotiating room he actually had. When U.S. officials heard he was bringing his family with him, some thought he might be seeking asylum. On the eve of his visit, U.S. intelligence picked up signs that that Pakistan might be preparing to escalate towards using nuclear weapons. President Clinton berated Sharif for bringing the continent to the brink of nuclear war, although Sharif appeared taken aback when he was told that his own military was apparently preparing nuclear missiles.[22] The prime minister was forced to back down from the standoff with India. The debacle would only heighten already deep tensions between the Pakistani Army and Sharif.

Those tensions would reach the boiling point in October as a plane carrying Musharraf began to run out of fuel on its journey back from Sri Lanka. In an attempt to relieve Musharraf of his command, Sharif had given orders that the plane carrying his army chief should not be allowed to land in Pakistan. Disaster seemed imminent but Musharraf managed to contact his supporters and the plane landed safely. Musharraf, thanks to the support of key figures in the military, toppled the prime minister and took over the country, sending Sharif to exile in Saudi Arabia. Now, there was a further complicating factor in U.S.-Pakistan relations to add to the list of competing problems—the return to democracy. In the seventy-two hours after Musharraf's seizure of power, the U.S. administration deliberately avoided using the word "coup" in the knowledge that its use would trigger a new round of congressionally mandated sanctions, complicating diplomacy. The United States hoped that Musharraf might somehow make moves to avoid that conclusion. In January 2000 Assistant Secretary of State for South Asia Karl Inderfurth traveled to Islamabad and for the first time took with him not a proliferation official as he had done in the past, but a counterterrorism coordinator, reflecting the new priorities.

In March 2000 President Clinton's motorcade swept through a city that looked eerily deserted. Islamabad's streets had been emptied for security. Intelligence that Al Qaeda had planned an assassination attempt also meant that the Secret Service first asked the president not to go to Pakistan and then made him travel on an unmarked dummy aircraft. Some U.S. officials had argued that the president should not go to Islamabad as a visit with Pakistan's new military leader would be seen as legitimizing a military ruler who only six months earlier had overthrown a democratically elected prime minister in a coup. It was the first presidential trip for decades, but the tight security and speed of the visit left an unpleasant taste in the mouths of Pakistanis. The whole experience seemed to be more humiliating than anything else, especially since the president had spent five days in India and only five hours in Pakistan.

On March 25, for the third time under the Clinton administration, a North Korea–Khan linkup was raised to the highest level. At the restricted session, National Security Adviser Sandy Berger and Secretary of State Madeleine Albright raised the issue of a possible quid pro quo between Pyongyang and Islamabad, although now the primary issue between the countries was democratization, pushing proliferation as well as Kashmir and Osama bin Laden down the agenda.[23] But after meeting Musharraf, President Clinton made a TV address that was broadcast live because of concerns it would be edited. Within the address was a coded warning: "I ask Pakistan to be a leader in non-proliferation in your own self-interest," the president said, "and to help us prevent dangerous technologies spreading to those who might have no reservations at all about using them."[24] Musharraf has acknowledged that the first he heard that Khan might be sharing information with other countries was in early 2000, although he has claimed the information was not specific enough to act upon and gave no hint of the scale of activities that would eventually be revealed. "We were getting this information in trickles," he'd later explain.[25]

Other officials had also raised the issue of Khan and North Korea when they visited Islamabad. Deputy Secretary of State Strobe Talbott was told by Sharif that any illicit activity would be stopped but that other conventional dealings would proceed. Robert Einhorn, assistant secretary of state for non-proliferation, also brought up Khan with both Sharif and senior military figures during a number of visits to Pakistan. "We kept pressing to stop these interactions between Pakistani and North Korean specialists. We mentioned specifically our concerns about KRL and scientists. When I would mention KRL and what it was up to there was a kind of pained expression on the faces of people I was dealing with. The impression I got was that perhaps we knew things about what Khan was up to that they didn't know. I had a sense this was embarrassing."[26]

The UK also expressed concern over Khan in a general sense as part of a wider laundry list of concerns ranging from Kashmir to narcotics. They always got the same deadpan and weary answer: Pakistan would never, ever do anything to foster proliferation, and the rest of the world could be sure that his activities were under the closest watch and control. Do let us know if you have anything more specific, they would add. The Pakistani reply that there was a lack of specificity to complaints was not just used over Khan but over all issues such as support for the Taliban, for training camps in Kashmir and problems over the line of control with India. British diplomats felt the argument was used whenever Pakistani knew what the problem was but wanted deniability to continue pursuing something considered to be in the national interest. From 1998, Japan also began to complain about Khan as did China.

The man on the receiving end of the barrage of day-to-day protests was Feroz Khan, a senior military officer at the Combat Development Directorate, which was designed to keep watch over the nuclear establishment, a tricky task. "They did talk to us," he recalls. "But they never had any specificity. It was very general concerns."[27] The lack of specific evidence was the crucial problem. At first the reaction to the complaints was to ask where the leak was in Pakistan. When the United States placed KRL under sanctions for missile cooperation with North Korea in 1998 there was a realization that the problem could get embarrassing. The Combat Development Directorate had begun to try coordinating the feuding Khan Research Laboratories and Pakistan Atomic Energy Commission (PAEC) from the early 1990s. Trying to place them too tightly under military control, however, might have been seen as an attack on the president or prime minister's authority because the military, prime minister, and president were all at loggerheads and competing for control over the state. The jockeying for power at the highest level made it harder to develop any formal institutions to supervise the nuclear program and make it answerable to anyone. The increasingly bitter conflict made dealing with Khan a low priority, especially given the scientist's power base and supporters in different places.

As U.S. complaints continued, Khan was questioned about his activities at several meetings, both formally and informally. Khan would always deny transferring enrichment technology; any authorization for Khan's activity by the military would only have been known at the highest levels. "We were saying this North Korea connection is going to be counterproductive because it will make three countries angry—U.S., Japan, China," remembers Feroz Khan, who was present at some of the meetings. "It is becoming too risky," Khan was told. Khan was authorized to deal with the North Koreans in conventional technology including the Ghauri missile. But it was questioned why the Ghauri, which was a volatile liquid fuel missile, was needed when there were more reliable solid fuel Shaheen missiles being developed by PAEC and when the economic and diplomatic costs of A. Q. Khan's work were so high. But when it was Khan's turn to speak up at a meeting, everyone else would stop and listen. He did not speak as a man with a guilty conscience but as a man conscious of his own aura of power and mystery. Khan coolly and rationally explained why working with North Korea was vital for the nation's security and claimed that "others" were out to stop him and hurt the nation. He said that his Ghauri missile needed more tests and more work. He insisted on maintaining contact with North Korea to make technical adjustments to the missile because certain problems had become apparent in the April 1998 test. Because of this he would have to continue to meet with North Korean technicians in both Kahuta and Pyongyang.

The arguments were fierce and couched in the bitter bureaucratic politics of Pakistan and its nuclear program. Anyone who criticized A. Q. Khan was said to be a supporter of PAEC. From the late 1980s, Munir Khan and his allies raised the alarm over Khan's possible sales activities and warned that it could become embarrassing, but because PAEC were under stricter oversight than Khan, it often sounded like sour grapes and merely part of the long-running feud. The debate also became subsumed within broader issues. At the same time that Khan was being criticized, there was a dispute within Pakistan's national security elite about whether the country's support for the Taliban in Afghanistan was also creating too many problems in its relations with the United States and the outside world. Some voices around the table argued that the Inter-Services Intelligence Agency (ISI) and religious hardliners' support of the Taliban was endangering the nuclear deterrent by drawing too much criticism of Pakistan and that links should be cut. Those who supported the Taliban tended to be the same as those who supported A. Q. Khan, partly around the historic alliance of hard-line nationalists and Islamists. They had the stronger voice and would only be silenced after September 11, 2001.

From 1998 the Pakistani government knew something might be amiss with Khan because of intelligence supplied by the United States. Judging from public comments, it would appear as if Khan's activities came as a total shock to the Pakistani government when they were finally revealed. But in fact, the possibility that he was passing on technology had been known for years inside the country, at least as far back as the late 1980s. Khan was even investigated but what little was done to stop his work proved ineffective. Khan was too powerful. Appearing too critical of Khan's activities was dangerous for anyone. "Nobody questions beyond their authority on nuclear matters. If you probe too much you will be under suspicion," explains

Feroz Khan. The sad truth is that A. Q. Khan is perhaps the only person since Jinnah, the founding father of the country, who was seen as a national hero in Pakistan. In a country with no national heroes, he was made into one. Only the highest officials could risk challenging him, and even then at some considerable risk.

But after the 1998 tests, Khan's protected position within Pakistan began to erode. The growing U.S. pressure began to take its toll. There were also internal changes within Pakistan's nuclear program. With the May 1998 tests complete, the program moved from covert and clandestine to declared and open. With that came the pressure to become a more responsible nuclear power and to implement the command and control and security functions that had been lacking up to this point. Slowly an infrastructure began to emerge of military supervision that would look after security and development across all parts of the program. This was designed to ensure Pakistan's arsenal was secure from both internal strife and from external proliferation. The plan for a new National Command Authority (NCA) to oversee the entire nuclear complex first emerged under Nawaz Sharif, but it became tied up with the bitter wrangling between the him and the military leading up to his removal in October 1999. In February 2000 the NCA, chaired by Musharraf, was officially inaugurated (an NCA had technically existed since the 1970s but it had no real teeth). Under it were a series of bodies that were supposed to bring coherence and accountability to nuclear policy, development, and control. Both KRL and PAEC were supposed to report to the NCA and to no one else. The idea was to have control over accounting and auditing procedures, over foreign travel, over security, including the screening of personnel by the intelligence agencies, and even over media access since journalists could easily approach figures like Khan without any authorization, allowing him to fight his turf wars in the press. Quickly though, problems appeared. "PAEC had no problem. There were only problems with one organization," says Feroz Khan who worked in the NCA. Khan refused to provide full details of his travels or meetings. "They kept on resisting despite the formal announcement that you are under command. They would not send financial reports. . . . Then there would be intelligence reports that he [Khan] has moved without authorization."[28] Khan and Musharraf began to clash more openly. The two never got on well personally, and Khan would complain to journalists that

Musharraf was weak and selling out Pakistan's security. It became clear that bringing KRL into line would be impossible while Khan was still in charge.

From 2000 the weight of both internal and external pressure began to make Khan's life increasingly difficult. There were also deeper investigations into Khan. Khan had first been investigated by the ISI in the late 1980s but the report had been ignored by Pakistan's top officials. "We had piles of files on A. Q. Khan but nobody was interested," one former senior officer told the *Financial Times*.[29] Another investigation was started in 1996 under Army Chief Jehingar Karamat who asked KRL and PAEC for details of where its procurement money was going. But the inquiry met with considerable resistance. U.S. officials in 2000 passed on intelligence that Khan had been depositing tens of thousands of dollars in the personal bank accounts of KRL scientists.[30] Some scientists within KRL, probably a new younger generation less in thrall to Khan, were also worried about his activities even before 1998 and were warning government officials of suspicious activities.[31]

Around 1998–99, under Nawaz Sharif, the ISI began a new, comprehensive investigation of Khan's finances. This may have been ordered to check out U.S. claims that were beginning to be passed on. The ISI pulled together hundreds of pages on his assets and bank accounts. Initially nothing was done with this. However, President Musharraf may have sensed an opportunity in 2000, soon after he had come to power. Fighting corruption was a central plank of his claim to legitimacy. He argued that the previous civilian administrations of Benazir Bhutto and Nawaz Sharif had been venal and that he would clean out the system. As a result, he established the National Accountability Bureau (NAB) to investigate corruption and take individuals to task. An aggressive campaign was a potentially useful way of winning critics over to the concept of a military government. The NAB in turn represented a possible way of cutting A. Q. Khan down to size.

Immediately after President Clinton had visited in March 2000 and warned the Pakistanis of Khan's activities, Musharraf personally asked the head of the NAB, Lieutenant General Syed Mohammed Amjad, to look into Khan quickly. Rather than conduct a fresh investigation, Amjad handed over the dossier prepared by the ISI in 1998–99 to NAB investigators. They were told by Amjad to randomly check aspects of it—for instance, seeing if it was correct in its assertions that Khan owned a particular house in

Islamabad. NAB had access to all records, including bank accounts and looked into about 10 percent of the Khan file. It found it essentially and worryingly accurate. Khan appeared to have eight million dollars stashed in various bank accounts and to own multiple properties in Pakistan purchased with money apparently raked off from his KRL work. The report also showed Khan was buying too much material for Pakistan's own program.[32] And it included the claim that Khan had given a house to General Beg and was paying off numerous Pakistani journalists and even funding a newspaper. It was hard for investigators to make out what part of the money was personal funds and what came from KRL since money would flow through so many dummy accounts in the procurement process. General Beg admitted that KRL had at its disposal funds that were not subject to auditing but defended the findings. "Dr. A. Q. Khan and his scientists have given this country a credible deterrent for a paltry sum of money," he said. "What they have in their accounts is what I call gold dust—they have not taken the government's money. If a scientist is given 10 million dollars to get the equipment, how would he do it? He will not carry the money in his bag. He will put the money in a foreign bank account in somebody's name. The money lies in the account for some time, and the mark-up that it fetches may probably have gone into his account. It is a fringe benefit."[33]

The NAB report was highly secret and never openly discussed in meetings of the bureau. The file had no numbers, making it untraceable, and it was not allowed out of the office. By the autumn of 2000 the investigation was complete. But at a subsequent meeting the investigators and General Amjad concluded that Khan was simply too big a fish to try and net. Soon after Amjad left the job and the NAB went into decline, becoming a political tool. Details of the Khan file would surface only years later.

Meanwhile, Khan's travel and transport were drawing concern within Pakistan as well as internationally. "There was some suspicious movements," President Musharraf would later explain. "There were special handling of cargo, special handling of anything that had to do with KRL . . . And in that special handling we were getting suspicious. That in under the garb of the special handling, maybe there is some proliferation activity, some underhand proliferation activity going on."[34] As they dug deeper, investigators found more and more and began to inform the nuclear oversight officials about front companies and more movements. Although the actual evidence was circumstantial, within the NCA there was growing concern that they were technically responsible for KRL's activities but didn't really know what Khan was up to. That could be dangerous. Could the NCA end up taking the fall if it was revealed what Khan was up to? But confronting Khan could also be a dangerous task for anyone but the most senior of military officers. "His status and that of his organization is so sacrosanct that if I point out anything, my own credibility and patriotism will be in doubt," explained Feroz Khan, who was one of those who tried to rein in Khan. "Everybody knows Khan is walking in to see the army chief and he doesn't meet anybody below that. Who dares question these things? He won't operate below that level. He meets the prime minister, the president, or the army chief."[35]

In 2000 the ISI took the outwardly dramatic step of raiding a C-130 plane chartered by Khan that was heading for North Korea from a military base at Rawalpindi. However, they found nothing incriminating. According to President Musharraf, the ISI only found SA-16 missiles that KRL was developing in conjunction with the North Koreans.[36] But President Musharraf claimed that Khan may have been tipped off. "We got some suspicious reports through the security agencies that there is some suspicions of some items to be loaded and taken somewhere in the plane. So, unfortunately, either you know, he was tipped off or whatever, we didn't find anything. But we were very sure that there was some activity likely . . . but we didn't catch them red-handed."

The autumn of that same year, Pakistani intelligence agents would follow Khan to Dubai on his travels.[37] There were meetings with what President Musharraf called "suspicious contacts." His trip was in clear violation of the NCA rules that Musharraf had imposed. When Khan returned he was confronted by Musharraf and warned to stick to the rules and not travel without permission. He said he was merely involved in the sale of some rockets in the Middle East. Despite numerous warnings from Musharraf himself, Khan clearly felt that he was simply too powerful to be sacked. Soon after, President Musharraf discovered Khan making arrangements to fly to the Iranian city of Zahedan. Khan refused to discuss the flight with Musharraf saying it was secret. "I said, what the hell do you mean?" Musharraf later recounted in an interview with the *New York Times*. "You want to keep a secret from me? So these are the things which led me to very concrete suspicions."[38]

Patience was now at breaking point. The warnings from the United States were also building the pressure. Secretary of State Colin Powell called up Musharraf soon after he took office in January 2001 to make the point.

When Musharraf finally decided to dislodge Khan, it was not easy because of Khan's popularity and Musharraf's relative unpopularity. The weak position first of Nawaz Sharif and then Musharraf in his early years in office meant that, at precisely the moment that evidence was emerging of Khan's activity, Pakistan's leaders did not feel able to take on a national hero who had many allies in the media, in parliament, in the public, and even in the military. It was not clear who would win such a fight. "We had to deliberate for hours how to handle the situation," explained Musharraf. "But we appointed him as an adviser to give him some comfort. I mean this had to be done as a gradual process. As I said, it was extremely sensitive. One couldn't outright start investigating as if he's any common criminal."[39] Some senior figures in the army resisted the idea of taking any action against Khan.

Khan was to be moved sideways but the path was not smooth. Khan was offered the position of "adviser to the chief executive" (the latter being Musharraf's formal title)—but he prevaricated, turning it down, then accepting it again. The main priority was to separate Khan from his KRL power base but not push him entirely out of the system—after all he was a man who knew all of the country's nuclear secrets and it would be dangerous to have him angry and at large. He also was an iconic figure for many in Pakistan. As "the father of the bomb," he had been idolized as a hero, as a man who could show that Pakistan was not a poor, dysfunctional, divided state but one that could stand tall as a nuclear power. He became a personal representation of the bomb and all its symbolic value and therefore his humiliation would be a national humiliation. Thanks to Khan's own propaganda, but aided by the Pakistani government placing him on a pedestal, it would prove hard to explain why the hero was in fact a villain who'd put the country at risk. It would also raise embarrassing questions over how exactly he had been able to get up to no good and who knew about it or helped him.

To make even a limited move against him, some work had to be done on public opinion and so anonymous briefings began against Khan in the press but in a controlled manner, focusing on his personal corruption. One story said that there was insufficient financial "discipline" at KRL because of lax auditing procedures of the more bureaucratic type that PAEC had. "Sources claim that 104 cars of KRL have been taken back from persons who were not working for KRL," wrote one newspaper. "They were using the cars for personal use. Fuel for these cars was also provided from the account of KRL."[40] Word spread that Khan had retired because of the probes into his financial corruption and that he had used KRL funds to finance the propaganda campaign to bolster his image as the father of the bomb. Khan fought back. He had never liked Musharraf, and now he started briefing journalists that Pakistan's leader was selling out the country's security. "Family sources" even leaked threats to the papers that Khan had offers from various Muslim countries to work for them in the field of nuclear technology.

It was clear to everyone that the displacing of Khan was not a voluntary move. Rumors swirled around Islamabad. There were different versions of Khan's semi-retirement for different audiences. [41] The semiofficial version put around to cover up the proliferation issue was that the infighting between KRL and PAEC had simply become too much and that Musharraf had decided to impose his authority on the two feuding groups, especially after the bitter rowing over who was responsible for the 1998 tests. Ishfaq Ahmed was also removed from being chair of PAEC at exactly the same time. Pakistan newspapers reported that the turf war between the two men was preventing the government from restructuring the nuclear and defense establishment and that Khan had resisted KRL losing its independence. Khan's stature and personality was said to have made it too difficult to impose the command and control that was now required. There were whisperings of U.S. pressure, "The hush-hush atmosphere has been forced by the military government because it has bowed completely to the demands of the United States" said a spokesman for a religious party.[42] Other right-wing parties worried that it might be a move towards stopping enrichment and signing the Comprehensive Test Ban Treaty and that Khan was the obstacle to this happening.

To soften the blow of his departure and alleviate suspicion, General Musharraf threw a lavish dinner for Khan on March 27, 2001. The two men were on their best behavior and made it look as if all was well between them. In an almost comically over-the-top eulogy, Pakistan's leader played to every aspect of Khan's ego and mythmaking about his own role. Harkening back to the bleak days in the wake of India's 1974 test, Musharraf said, "Allah Almighty answered the nation's prayers, had mercy on our situation and made a miracle happen. In walked a giant of a man, none other than Dr. Abdul Qaedeer Khan, the man who would give Pakistan a nuclear capability single-handedly. . . . Never before, in my judgement, has any nation owed so much to one single man's achievement . . . you are our national hero and an inspiration to our future generations. Nobody can ever take that away from you and your place in history is assured. You will always be at the very top."[43] Musharraf went on to explain to the elite of Pakistan gathered before him that he'd decided to appoint Khan an adviser so that he would be able to benefit from his "rich experience." While new leaders should be brought forward, "life must go beyond personalities and institutions must be strengthened," said Musharraf, the closest he came in the speech to a criticism or acknowledgement of the problem that was emerging. To those new leaders, Musharraf made a promise: "my government will provide you with every possible political and financial support. We will take whatever pressures come. We will do whatever it takes to ward off such pressures." Musharraf was hoping that Khan's removal would help shield Pakistan from Washington's growing pressure. But in his speech he also helped perpetuate those myths built up around the nuclear program that had given Khan so much power. "In a general sea of disappointments, the development of Pakistan's nuclear capability is a unique national success story. It is a story of selfless devotion, unbridled dedication, scientific brilliance, technological mastery and above all, supreme patriotism and religious fervour of thousands of silent workers. These men of science, these Mujahids, have put Pakistan in the exclusive nuclear club, they have made Islamic nations proud. They represent the best qualities of Pakistanis and have shown that when we want, we can move mountains."[44]

Khan's "promotion" should have been a major blow. Khan was told that he could not enter his lair, Kahuta, anymore. Yet for all the fuss made of it, Khan's "retirement" in March 2001 made almost no difference to his work. Having shunted Khan aside, Pakistan felt that they had dealt with the problem, or at least they hoped to have assuaged American complaints. By this stage, Khan had shifted from a Pakistani procurer to an international proliferator, operating in the private sector, making him much harder to stop. He was not prevented from traveling and his real base of operations had already been moved to Dubai which he was visiting increasingly regularly to run his operations. There was no attempt to trace back through KRL's books what had happened in the past or to inform the outside world of any deeper suspicions. And KRL was still Khan's domain, even if he was no longer resident. His people were still in senior positions and they owed their loyalty to him, not to the new chief, who very soon found himself in an uncomfortable position. Khan himself and senior KRL staff would still head off on their Africa trip in 2002. After Khan's activities were revealed publicly, Musharraf would initially say that Khan's shuffling of position had nipped his activities "in the bud."[45] That was far from the case. Stopping Khan would take much more than a promotion and a dinner.

WASHINGTON, D.C.

September 2001

THE HEAD OF PAKISTAN'S POWERFUL INTER-SERVICES INTELLIGENCE AGENCY (ISI), Lieutenant General Mahmood Ahmed, had arrived in Washington a few days earlier. He and his wife had flown over on a CIA plane for the standard tour given to visiting heads of foreign intelligence agencies. But with the attack on the twin towers and the Pentagon, suddenly the visit took on a much more serious purpose. It was immediately clear that Pakistan's help would be required in dealing with Osama bin Laden in neighboring Afghanistan. Mahmood was summoned early the next morning along with the Pakistani ambassador to Washington, Maleeha Lodhi, to see Richard Armitage, the pugilistic, barrel-chested deputy secretary of state. A plain-speaking former soldier, Armitage long had been seen by Islamabad as a friendly voice ever since his time as a Pentagon official in the 1980s when he travelled to the country to keep tabs on the Afghan campaign. But Armitage and his boss Colin Powell had decided to deal with Pakistan head on. Armitage delivered a tough message, so tough that Mahmood would complain that he'd been positively rude. Armitage pointed to a decoration sitting in his office that he had received from the government of Pakistan and said that if Islamabad did not help now, he would send it back and no American would ever want another decoration from the country. The United States wanted the Taliban gone in order to get to Osama bin Laden. He offered Pakistan a simple choice: side with the United States or the Taliban. "You are either 100% with us or 100% against us," he told them. "There's no grey area."[1] Mahmood was taken aback by the brusqueness of someone supposed to be a friend. He protested and said that Washington had to understand the history of Pakistan's involvement with the Taliban, which Pakistan and particularly the ISI had sponsored since the mid-1990s. Mahmood himself had been one of the strongest proponents of the ISI's relationship with the Taliban. History was one thing, but the future begins today, Armitage replied, telling him to come back the following day. Armitage and Secretary of State Powell spent that afternoon working on a list of seven demands that were delivered to Mahmood on his return. Mahmood was told it was a list, not an a la carte menu, and that a swift reply from Musharraf was expected. It was all or nothing.

Dealing with A. Q. Khan was not on the State Department list. Terrorism was now the overriding priority.

Mahmood called President Musharraf who made his decision immediately. By 3 P.M. that same day, at a second meeting, Armitage was given his answer and he followed up with detailed requests for logistical and intelligence support in dealing with Al Qaeda and ousting the Taliban. There had been debate within Pakistan's leadership for a number of years over the costs of supporting the Taliban, but the military, including Musharraf, had been among the most ardent supporters of ensuring that Pakistan had a client regime in Afghanistan to provide "strategic depth" against India. But now everything changed. Musharraf conducted a sudden reversal of years of policy. "Nine eleven came as a thunder bolt," according to Musharraf. "I confronted acute challenges on one side but also saw great opportunities on the other. I decided on the route of opportunities. I had to absorb external pressure and mould domestic opinion towards my decision."[2] Musharraf saw a chance to bring his government out of the cold, after the 1999 coup that had brought him to power and left relations with the United States strained. The September 11 attacks and a campaign against Al Qaeda offered the chance to recreate the conditions of the 1980s under Zia, where a partnership with the United States in Afghanistan led to the lifting of sanctions, a vast inflow of money and weapons, as well as the diplomatic cover for continuing other strategic activities. Musharraf had the decisiveness of a soldier; he took a cold, hard strategic look at the possibilities and decided that allying with the United States, even if it meant sacrificing the Taliban, was the best means of protecting the two other key national interests, Pakistan's nuclear weapons and Kashmir. In the end, events would conspire to make that trickier than expected.

On September 14 Musharraf met with his senior military commanders. He told them of his decision. In a heated six-hour meeting, Musharraf eventually prevailed despite the dissent of at least four generals including his deputy Chief of Army Staff Lieutenant General Usmani and General Mahmood. Mahmood's support had been vital in the coup that brought Musharraf to power, but he had become increasingly religious and anti-American. Soon after, Musharraf purged those opposed to cooperation with the United States, removing Usmani and Mahmood and making sweeping changes to the senior leadership of ISI. After this, the organization was under his control, whatever it might be up to. Within weeks, the remaining sanctions over both the nuclear issue and Musharraf's coup would be lifted. Over the next three years, Pakistan would receive $2.64 billion from the United States.[3] Once again, Pakistan's relationship with the United States would be transformed.

September 11 had a significant impact on the debate over what to do about A. Q. Khan. It increased the urgency of dealing with proliferation amid very real concerns that Al Qaeda might get its hands on nuclear weapons, but it also made dealing with Pakistan a far more complex task. The level of seriousness with which Khan's activity was treated grew after the attacks on the United States, but so did the problems in working out how to stop him.

CHAPTER 7

Watching

FROM THE EARLIEST DAYS OF KAHUTA, Khan was always conscious of the attention of foreign intelligence agencies. As someone who had been a spy and a stealer of secrets himself, he was more than aware of having become a target. He had a particular gripe about the British and joked that Britain's intelligence service, MI6, never paid enough to tempt his staff to betray their employer. Khan was under electronic surveillance by Britain's eavesdropping agency, GCHQ, and its American counterpart the National Security Agency (NSA) for a long period but it revealed little. Khan was too careful. Intelligence officers tried to get close to Khan and his senior staff but found it impossible. Kahuta was out of bounds and when individuals left KRL for events like conferences they were always escorted by security and never left alone and vulnerable to a quiet approach by foreign intelligence officers seeking to recruit them. But, for Khan and those around him, success bred confidence and eventually sloppiness. Having gotten away with things for so many decades, the key members of his network were also beginning to get cocky, thinking they would never get caught. They would often have security scares in which they thought they might be watched. When this happened, they flatlined and went quiet, but never for long. There would be so many of these scares that when the real thing happened, the network failed to tighten up its act.

In the latter half of the 1990s, the idea was growing in the CIA and Britain's MI6 that A. Q. Khan was up to something more than just his usual no good. The nature and scale of his activities was unclear. But the CIA and MI6 decided to aggressively target the Khan network and see what could be discovered. This was to be a joint Anglo-American enterprise. It was agreed early on for the plan to work there would have to be real information sharing between the United States and UK; all information, however sensitive, would be shared but only within the small team from both countries working on the case.[1] On both sides of the Atlantic, the intelligence was highly compartmentalized, few people were let in on the operations, and to the special code words associated with it. The same strict secrecy also applied internationally. Even Israel, America's usual partner on Middle Eastern nuclear proliferation issues, was kept out of the loop regarding CIA operations dealing with both Khan and Libya.[2]

The small trans-Atlantic team working on Khan centered its strategy on firstly identifying the key members of his business network and then gaining as much intelligence on their activities as possible. The United States and UK divided up the targeting based who had best leads on a particular part of the network, although some were targeted jointly. The U.S. intelligence community dwarfs Britain's in terms of resources and technical capacity but London often has an edge when it comes to traditional human intelligence partly because it has to provide a sharper focus for its more limited resources. And the old-fashioned recruitment of spies was at the heart of the breaking of the A. Q. Khan network. According to a former head of the CIA's clandestine service, it took a "patient, decade-long operation involving million-dollar recruitment pitches, covert entries, ballet-like sophistication and a level of patience we are often accused of not possessing" to first track and then break Khan.[3] Britain's GCHQ and America's NSA both systematically monitored the communication lines of suspect businesses involved in the nuclear technology trade, looking for suspicious orders and movements. New, innovative (and still classified) intelligence collection techniques were also employed. Conversations between Khan and his Libyan customers were listened into and recorded. There were many setbacks and the task was trying to put together a jigsaw from tiny pieces where the end picture was not clear. Although an element of luck would be important in providing a crucial breakthrough, there were no easy "walk-in" sources who provided the full story. Early leads in turn provided further collateral to exploit against other members of the network and slowly build the picture, trying to persuade one individual or another to betray their partners.

Eventually, a number of spies would be recruited within the Khan network in different sites. Multiple sources were vital as they allowed investigators to compare stories and look for gaps in information and then confront their sources to ask for more in those areas. But the sensitivity of some of these sources made confronting Pakistan more difficult for fear of exposing them.

George Tenet, who was CIA Director from 1997 to 2004, has been reported as telling audiences that "working with British colleagues, we pieced together [Khan's] subsidiaries, his clients, his front companies, his finances and manufacturing plants. We were inside his residence, inside his facilities, inside his rooms. We were everywhere these people were."[4] But that statement reflects the end state of knowledge in 2004 rather than anything in 2000 when the intelligence was beginning to flow in. It was only in the last six months of the operation that a deeper, broader picture was being built up as the growing body of intelligence was leveraged to confront more and more members of the network and persuade them to talk (although many may not have told the truth). Even at this point there were many mysteries. In many ways, the growing body of intelligence did not necessarily answer all the questions (such as the role of the Pakistani government). What it did finally provide were more solutions and options to dealing with a thorny problem.

Khan's overconfidence ended up being an advantage. Even after an Iranian opposition group revealed Iran's nuclear enrichment program in 2002, Khan did not stop work. Although, the network did begin to destroy documents in its offices in Dubai when it became concerned that it might have been penetrated. But by this point the United States and UK knew of the destruction because of a particularly audacious "covert entry" into the Khan network, a piece of "operational daring" according to George Tenet that involved considerable risk on the part of a spy.[5] By 2000 this entry had already provided access to some of the business records of the Khan network and a picture was just beginning to emerge of the range of Khan's activities.

Policymakers and intelligence officials agree that 2000 was the year when things began to become clearer as the new sources of intelligence began to flow in. The picture was fragmentary and evolving, but the fog was starting to lift on what Khan was up to. In April of that year the UK intelligence

community had fragmentary evidence that the Khan network was supplying enrichment equipment to at least one customer in the Middle East,
which was thought to be Libya. By September 2000 the intelligence community believed that the network was expanding to mass-produce components for large-scale centrifuge cascades.

In Washington the intelligence was coming in during the last year of the
Clinton administration. "We were then aware of the Khan-Libya cooperation in the area of centrifuge technology," remembers Robert Einhorn who
was assistant secretary of state for non-proliferation under President Clinton
and into the early period of the Bush administration. "We were aware of
some of its elements—especially in Europe and Dubai. At that early time
we didn't understand that network in its full dimension."[6] The administration looked at the options. The one recommended by the CIA was to watch
longer, understand the network better, and by doing so make it possible to
comprehensively shut it down. Previous attempts to deal with individuals
involved in the Khan network, like Henk Slebos in the 1980s, had led to
short jail sentences or no action, allowing the businessmen to quickly return to work. This time the aim was not to just do some weeding but pull
up the problem by its roots. But at this time no one had enough information to be sure the network could be shut down. They needed a lever to
prise open the network and make a shutdown possible. The international
nature of the Khan network also necessitated the involvement of other
countries in any shutdown. But at this early stage the intelligence was too
sensitive to share and not yet comprehensive enough to be convincing.

It did not take long for the dangerous scale of Khan's assistance to become apparent and begin affecting intelligence assessments regarding
nuclear proliferation. In 1999 a U.S. National Intelligence Estimate, un-
aware of the Khan deal, reckoned Libya could not have a nuclear weapon
until 2015. U.S. intelligence analysts viewed Libya as an "inept bungler,
the court jester among the band of nations seeking biological or nuclear
capabilities."[7] But as the intelligence on Khan filtered in, suddenly the
analysts did an about-turn and the estimate fell fast. By December 2001
when the full contours of the Libya deal were still only beginning to emerge,
a new estimate put the arrival time at 2007. Even at that early stage when
not much was known, Khan was estimated to have shaved a full eight years
off Libya's target date for getting the bomb.

In January 2001 the Bush administration took office and CIA Director George Tenet and his staff briefed a small group of the most senior officials on the Khan network. Reflecting the importance attached to the subject, the group was made up of top officials and their deputies, those who were going to be most involved in the actual decisions. The key players were Deputy Secretary of State Richard Armitage, the Deputy National Security Adviser Stephen Hadley, Deputy Director of the CIA John McLaughlin, Secretary of State Colin Powell, Director of the CIA's Clandestine Service James Pavitt and Robert Joseph, the senior director for non-proliferation on the National Security Council and the point man for day-to-day decisions. Knowledge was tightly held. In addition to the usual clearances process, everyone briefed on Khan had to be personally approved by the CIA Director George Tenet. The initial briefing provided a broad outline of the general parameters of Khan's activities but it was a clear that substantiating detail was lacking, as was the kind of actionable intelligence that would facilitate operations to shut down the network. Throughout the coming years, the U.S. president and British prime minister would both take a personal interest in the Khan network, receiving extensive briefings.

In the early months of the Bush administration, the group discussed whether or not to move against the network. There were no formal decision papers on the subject, but the initial meetings as with those that followed over the next few years had a familiar feel to them. The team would meet at the White House and the CIA would provide an update on its operations, the latest revelations and the emerging picture. Discussion would then turn to what to do. State Department officials would argue, "Why don't we just put a stop to this. We don't know how much damage Khan is doing, we don't know who else might be getting this technology, states or other groups." The CIA would then argue that this was precisely why operations should continue. If action was taken now, when maybe only half the network was known about, only half the job would be accomplished. The other half of the network could continue to operate. It had to be put out of business completely. And the scale of the business that Khan was engaged in was truly shocking. "As we learned more and more about the network's operations, we discovered that in fact it was similar to a multinational corporation in the sense that the network established field offices across three continents," Robert Joseph later explained.[8] It was also important to find out exactly who else was trying to buy from the Khan network—by doing this, it might be possible to hook a bigger fish than Khan himself. If others would hold off action just a little longer, the CIA would say, there was the chance of a real breakthrough with a new penetration of the network, perhaps a bogus buyer. The early decision to keep watching was close to—but not entirely—unanimous. Over the coming years, the debates would occasionally spill over into fierce argument. A few officials believed the intelligence agencies were "addicted" to collecting intelligence rather than using it to act and wanted to move faster. Senior members of the intelligence community countered that they were the only ones who really understood the breadth and depth of the problem and also the relative reliability of different sources and therefore only they could know when and how to act. Within a few months of the first discussion, the debate would be engulfed by far more imminent problems as Al Qaeda launched its attacks on the United States on September 11, 2001.

From September 11, 2001, the growing intelligence picture on A. Q. Khan and his proliferation activities was flowing into a highly charged and complex environment in which fears over a nexus between rogue states, terrorists, and weapons of mass destruction was thrust to the top of the agenda. America had been struck and would strike back. On top of that, U.S.-Pakistan relations had taken on an entirely new dimension, transformed in a way strikingly similar to that of December 1979 when the Soviet Union had invaded Afghanistan. Once again, Pakistan was a vital partner in America's defining struggle. As happened in the 1980s, there was now an issue—counter-terrorist cooperation and Afghanistan—that would be the overriding priority. This, according to senior U.S. intelligence officials, did delay taking action against Khan. But it did not stop it entirely. This time, unlike the 1980s, Pakistan's nuclear program was not shunted aside as a distraction but instead jostled for space in the inboxes of policymakers, although Khan was only one of a number of worries now within the nuclear context. There was also concern over domestic unrest in Pakistan and the danger of Musharraf being overthrown, perhaps by members of the military with sympathies for the Taliban and Al Qaeda. This was a particularly terrifying possibility when the new rulers would have the keys to Pakistan's nuclear arsenal. However, Pakistan was extremely sensitive to calls for increased controls on its nuclear weapons since it feared that growing U.S. intelligence on the location or nature of the arsenal could leave it vulnerable to rollback or covert action to seize the weapons (the United States did develop contingency plans for the latter but endeavored to keep them as quiet as possible).

There was also fear that Al Qaeda might get its hands on nuclear weapons. From the early 1990s, Osama bin Laden has been seeking nuclear material. Around 1993–94, an Al Qaeda operative tried to purchase uranium from a Sudanese individual for $1.5 million but the cylinder he received proved to be useless. Another individual in Sudan tried to get material for Al Qaeda but was probably scammed into buying low-grade reactor fuel or other useless material. In 1998 bin Laden said that getting hold of unconventional weapons was a "religious duty." Terrorists are unlikely to be able to develop their own infrastructure to produce fissile material. The Japanese terrorist cult Aum Shinrikyo tried to develop nuclear weapons but lacked the scientific expertise or access to do this despite huge financial resources. So if terrorists get hold of a weapon it will likely be from a state. Their best option is to buy or steal an actual device or obtain fissile material that could be used to make a simple bomb. Buying or stealing has always been a fear when it comes to the nuclear stockpiles of the former Soviet Union and Pakistan. In late 2001 this possibility was beginning to look very real. One CIA source called "Dragonfire" warned that Al Qaeda had already gotten its hands on a weapon that was to be detonated in New York.

Events on the ground in South Asia compounded the growing anxiety. As American troops and intelligence operatives swept through Kabul in October 2001, they found startling new details of Al Qaeda's ambitions regarding nuclear weapons—and the role of Pakistan. The speed of the Taliban's fall meant that safe houses were abandoned still filled with documents that offered up a huge intelligence haul. It revealed Al Qaeda's capabilities and intentions had been underestimated. It was further along with its biological weapons program than had been previously thought with several sites containing commercial production equipment and isolated cultures of a biological warfare agent—a development that had been missed by the CIA.[9]

What really set off alarm bells was that the documents found in Kabul made clear that Pakistani nuclear scientists had actually met with the Taliban and Al Qaeda to discuss the development of nuclear devices. One of the men who had met with them was Sultan Bashiruddin Mahmood, the same scientist who had caught Zulfikar Ali Bhutto's eye in Multan in 1972 with his zeal. After being shoved aside by Khan, he moved over to PAEC, rising to become the director for nuclear power, but he also became increasingly radical and religious, dabbling in occult ideas of science and religion with a belief in the power of genies. He wrote a book entitled *Doomsday and Life after Death* with flames on the cover. In 1999 he was forced out of the nuclear establishment amid increasing concern over his views (including advocating the transfer of nuclear technology and materials to other countries) after he protested at the Pakistani signing of the Comprehensive Test Ban Treaty.[10] Another scientist who went with Mahmood to Afghanistan, Chaudiri Abdul Majeed, had retired from Pakistan's nuclear program in 2000.

After the two men left Pakistan's program, they founded a charity called Umma Tameer-e-Nau (UTN) involved in relief work in Afghanistan. Mahmood's sympathies for the Taliban were well known and when he was visiting Kabul in 2000, bin Laden is reported to have heard of his presence and sent an Al Qaeda operative to his hotel to arrange a meeting. A second meeting with bin Laden occurred over several days in August 2001 in a Kabul compound.[11] Mahmood's son told reporters, "Basically Osama asked my father, 'How can a nuclear bomb be made, and can you help us make one?'"[12] Mahmood is said to have told bin Laden that it would be very difficult to build a bomb. According to the White House, during a follow up meeting, an associate of bin Laden indicated that he had nuclear material and wanted to know how to build nuclear weapons. No one is sure of the exact nature of the conversations and how much advice Mahmood may have given, although his son says he declined to help. If the Taliban had not been overthrown, the relationship could have moved further forward. When it emerged Mahmood had met with bin Laden as well as Mullah Omar and discussed nuclear weapons, there was panic in Washington. CIA Director George Tenet raced to Islamabad to personally investigate the subject. Pakistani officials stressed that nothing sensitive had been passed on by anyone but there were suspicions in Washington that other scientists had been over to Afghanistan. There was no evidence that Al Qaeda had actually gotten hold of fissile material for a weapon and there seemed to be a realization that a "dirty bomb" might be more feasible than an actual nuclear bomb. Mahmood and Abdul Majeed were arrested by Pakistani intelligence officers on October 23 along with the entire UTN board, which had ties to the Pakistani military—former ISI Chief General Hamid Gul was reported to have been UTN's "honorary patron."[13] Gul met with Mahmood in Kabul the same month Mahmood met with bin Laden, although Gul said he knew nothing of contacts with bin Laden, according to reporting by Wall Street Journal correspondent Daniel Pearl just before he was killed. Mahmood was interrogated jointly by the CIA and ISI and failed a half-dozen lie detector tests.[14] But for all the fears over nuclear leakage from Pakistan, Islamabad was not confronted in a detailed fashion about Khan. There were too many other priorities and too much still to learn about the network.

The tremendous danger posed by the nexus between the development of weapons of mass destruction by states and the desire for those weapons by non-state terrorist groups was fast becoming the new orthodoxy in Washington. Proliferation had always been high on the agenda for the key figures in the Bush administration, but after the surprise attack of 9/11 and fear that the next attack might involve unconventional weapons, a new forward leaning policy was acquired. This policy put the greatest emphasis on stopping states, and particularly, rogue states, from developing weapons of mass destruction rather than closing down the networks that might be supplying them—hence the identification of Iraq, Iran, and North Korea in President Bush's Axis of Evil speech in January 2002. The Bush White House never had much faith in traditional arms control regimes and treaties with their universalistic principles, perceiving them as ineffective and too focused on process rather than results, in turn constraining U.S. action. This was evident well before 9/11 with the rejection of the Comprehensive Test Ban Treaty and the Anti-Ballistic Missile Treaty. After 9/11, the Bush administration focused much more on the nature of the regimes that were seeking weapons and the importance of denying the capability to those it considered "rogue states." Rather than pursuing global disarmament, it wanted to change the regime of certain states seeking to acquire weapons of mass destruction (WMD). The problem was dangerous regimes not dangerous weapons. From universalistic ideals and treaties, the Bush administration would shift towards developing "coalitions of the willing" to act against those countries who were deemed a threat. Each country would be dealt with differently. Additionally, there was a new focus on pre-emption, partly because of the fear of nuclear material getting into hands of terrorists who would not be affected by traditional ideas of deterrence. By the end of 2001, with the military phase of Afghanistan appearing complete, Iraq was already becoming the next focus for U.S. officials. And from early 2002, Iraq became an important backdrop to the Khan story—occasionally intruding to the foreground of events.

The decision to go after Iraq reflected a focus within the Bush administration on the notion of rogue states as the primary problem. It was also driven by officials for whom the issue of weapons of mass destruction proved the most useful rallying cry when the real motives ranged far more widely, from deep-seated antipathies to Saddam to a desire to redraw the political map of the Middle East and project American power.

In London Tony Blair decided it was important to remain close to the United States and influence it rather than criticize it. But a long-running concern over proliferation meant that Blair had a much higher propensity for signing up to a confrontation centered around weapons of mass destruction. Blair had been concerned over proliferation and rogue states prior to the September 2001 attacks and had long pushed for more proactive policies, including with President Bush during a meeting in February 2001. British intelligence officials in the 1990s had been concerned that they were collecting plenty of information but that the policy framework hadn't been in place to actually do anything with the information. Blair set up a high-level policy group to coordinate more vigorous action.

Senior British officials later described the sense of a "creeping tide" of proliferation in the nuclear, biological, chemical, and ballistic missile capabilities amongst countries of concern over this period. After 9/11 Blair wanted to act against the range of threats. "After the attack on America, it was vital we took a completely different attitude to the proliferation of nuclear, chemical and biological weapons because of my fear that if terrorists managed to get [their] hands on these types of weapons, then terrorists that killed 3,000 people would kill 300,000 people," Blair later explained. "So the reason why we then discussed the issue of Iraq as a live issue for the first time after September 2001 was because [9/11] had changed the paradigm within which I thought these things through. My thought then was look: Iraq is the place to start on WMD, it's not that you don't have Iran, North Korea, and Libya and the network of A. Q. Khan and others who were a big WMD problem. But the place to start was Iraq because of the history of UN resolutions. I may be wrong in that but I thought you had to send such a clear signal across the world that regimes from then on would know that they had to comply with international obligations and terrorists would have a reduced chance of getting hold of those weapons."[15] Blair's desire was to take a stand on weapons of mass destruction but the problem was that, of all the intelligence available through 2002 over proliferation activities, the United States was pressing to act first and most aggressively against the place where the evidence was actually weakest: Iraq.

Downing Street's decision to follow Bush in going after Iraq first was not one with which everyone unanimous within the British government was happy. Other government departments and intelligence agencies saw other proliferation activities as more serious in terms of being a direct challenge to British interests.[16] However, the United States was in the driving seat and Tony Blair had decided to stick close to President Bush. The growing concern over Khan and Libya in intelligence assessments formed only "part of the background" for Tony Blair's discussion on Iraq with President Bush at Crawford on April 6–7, 2002. At a meeting between Tony Blair and Britain's top national security, military, and intelligence officials on July 23, 2002, Jack Straw, the foreign secretary, noted that the evidence when it came to stopping proliferation did not point to Iraq as the logical first target. "Bush had made up his mind to take military action, even if the timing was not yet decided," said Straw according to an official memo. "But the case was thin. Saddam was not threatening his neighbours, and his WMD capability was less than that of Libya, North Korea or Iran."[17] These were of course the three primary customers of Khan.

Iraq distracted from other proliferation challenges, including those linked to A. Q. Khan. Although perhaps not appreciated publicly at the time due to the relentless focus on Iraq, 2002 was an enormously important, even frenzied, year when it came to nuclear proliferation. Just weeks after the Downing Street meeting, a group opposed to the Iranian regime held a press conference and revealed Iran's secret enrichment facility at Natanz (almost certainly having been passed the information on the site by another country, perhaps Israel). The intelligence agencies were aware of the site but this was the first much of the world had heard of an Iranian program. Information was also beginning to flow into London and Washington from a crucial penetration of the A. Q. Khan network which was providing access to past transaction records of the network. This led to a realization that Khan had provided much more assistance to Iran than had previously been understood. Details were emerging that Khan had done much more than give some small-scale assistance in the late 1980s but had gone on to provide much more know-how and actual material in the following decade. However, the political reaction was muted because energy was focused on building up the threat from Iraq.

The Bush administration had probably planned to move on the Iran issue after the invasion of Iraq was complete on the basis that the U.S. military presence in Iraq would intimidate the Iranians into cooperating. A chance to dialogue with Iran may also have been lost in May 2003, when Iran, worried about facing the same fate as Iraq, made a secret approach to the United States through channels in Geneva that had been open since 9/11. This was one of a number of attempts to open up back channels to allow secret communication. But on this occasion orders for a series of car bombings in Saudi Arabia the same month were traced back through phone intercepts to senior Al Qaeda members in Iran, leading to a belief in some parts of Washington that there was no point talking since President Khatami and his moderate government weren't really in control. Iran could wait. The International Atomic Energy Agency (IAEA) had an eye-opening visit to Natanz, which revealed the scale of Iran's ambitions, in February 2003, just weeks before the war with Iraq was to begin. The Iraq war (and its aftermath) dragged away valuable resources in areas like satellite technology and imagery collection that would otherwise have been available to spy on nuclear programs in countries like Iran.[18] As the Iraq insurgency later spread, it would reduce the amount of leverage on Tehran and embolden Iranian ambitions. Iraq's nonexistent program had totally overshadowed the much more substantive reality of Iran's nuclear ambitions.

In October 2002 another substantial proliferation issue intruded as U.S. negotiator James Kelly went to meet the North Koreans. Relations with North Korea had been in free fall. The 1994 Framework Agreement was unravelling fast. There had been little enthusiasm on the U.S. side for delivering the assistance the North Koreans wanted as part of the deal, and September 11, 2001, transformed the new Bush administration's attitudes, leading to North Korea being placed in the "axis of evil." By the time of

Kelly's October 2002 meeting, the United States had collected strong intelligence that Pyongyang had a clandestine enrichment program. Kelly expected a flat denial when he confronted his opposite numbers. At first the North Koreans were shocked but they came back the next day and, according to the United States, confessed—a fact that U.S. officials initially kept quiet while they tried to work out how to respond over the following ten days. "We do not need another crisis now," a Bush administration official told the *Washington Post*.[19] The news was finally made public on October 16. One reason for waiting was that in the intervening period, the U.S. Congress was voting on whether or not to authorize the use of force in Iraq. The Agreed Framework deal offered fuel as well as help in building light-water nuclear reactors in return for a freeze of Pyongyang's nuclear weapons program. While hardliners in Washington were keen to see the deal collapse they were not keen for the issue to get in the way of the build up over Iraq.

In November the North Korean leader tried to pass a personal written message to President Bush to open up a dialogue through two American visitors to Pyongyang, but the two men who passed the message on believed that the U.S. administration was too deeply embroiled in the build up to Iraq and so ignored the offer.[20] The United States was also focused on regime change as the answer to North Korea rather than negotiations. Within weeks North Korea accelerated the crisis. In December 2002 the North Koreans upped the stakes by restarting work at the Yongbyon plant and ejecting IAEA officials and monitoring equipment. It also said it would begin reprocessing the eight thousand spent fuel rods that it had left from 1994. U.S. intelligence believed that this could provide enough material for up to half-a-dozen bombs. In January 2003 North Korea exercised its right to withdraw from the Non-Proliferation Treaty (NPT). When the United States had begun to complain about Khan's links with North Korea in 1998, there was only suspicion. But once it became clear that Khan was providing a full service to the Libyans, including weapons designs, the level of concern over his links with North Korea also began to grow rapidly.

To all intents and purposes, there was policy paralysis over what to do regarding Iranian and North Korean nuclear ambitions. Almost all energies in Washington were devoted to Iraq.[21] Iraq was clearly to be first, but perhaps not last, in the U.S. drive against proliferation. In a reported telephone conversation with Tony Blair on January 30, 2003, Bush told Blair he "wanted to go beyond Iraq in dealing with WMD proliferation, mentioning in particular Saudi Arabia, Iran, North Korea and Pakistan."[22] Exactly what was meant by the list is not clear from the memo, although it was from this point that evidence pointing to contacts between Khan and Saudi Arabia was emerging. One piece of intelligence from the watching of the Khan network that caused particularly alarm amongst officials was evidence that Saudi Arabia appeared to have recently begun directly financing Khan Research Laboratories (KRL). Could this be in return for help with a bomb? It was known that post-9/11 tensions had led some in Saudi Arabia to believe that the United States would not always be the reliable guarantor of Saudi security like it had been in the past. The realization from August 2002 that Iran—a major regional rival—was further down the nuclear road than previously thought also may have led to a re-evaluation in Riyadh of whether the nuclear route should be pursued, particularly when Saudi conventional forces are well equipped but largely unproven. In September 2003 a British newspaper reported that a Saudi Arabian strategy paper was proposing the acquisition of nuclear weapons for their deterrent value as one of a number of options. The Saudi government vehemently denied the report.[23] Israel's head of military intelligence claimed that an October 2003 visit of Crown Prince Abdullah to Pakistan saw the concluding of a secret nuclear agreement, providing weapons for cheap oil, a view allegedly confirmed by the Iranians.[24] The contacts between Saudi Arabia and Khan and his frequent travels to the kingdom were the source of considerable interest in Washington but evidence was circumstantial.

From 2000 when the intelligence picture was building, Khan was still operating, still selling, and still passing on material and knowledge to Libya and North Korea. It would later become clear that between late 2001 and early 2002 a nuclear weapons design was passed onto Libya. Khan's planes were still arriving in Pyongyang and were suspected by the CIA to have been transferring more and more material. There was no guarantee any of the material could ever be recovered. Could Khan have been stopped earlier? Although the intelligence had begun to trickle in from 2000, it wasn't until 2002 that a clear picture of Khan's activity had emerged. Alarm bells were now ringing in London. Every Wednesday afternoon, the heads of Britain's intelligence agencies and senior policymakers gather in a room inside the Cabinet Office building on Whitehall. Papers are requested by the Joint Intelligence Committee (JIC) on matters of strategic importance and then produced for discussion around the table. Unusually, the intelligence on Khan was so sensitive that an "inner JIC" was formed to look at the subject in detail with a smaller number of officials. A JIC report is the measured view of the entire British intelligence community and is based on consensus, every word argued over in a tradition of detailed drafting. In March 2002, the issue on the table for the JIC was Khan. Staff had produced a detailed assessment pulling together all the available information from the different services. The picture was an alarming one. It showed just how widespread Khan's activities had become, with Dubai having now become the new base of operations and a production hub established in Malaysia.[25] In July 2002 the committee was looking at Khan again. It now concluded that the A. Q. Khan network was "central to all aspects of the Libyan nuclear weapons program."[26] Since Khan had access to nuclear weapons designs and had been involved in the development of Pakistani missiles, the government feared that he might not only pass on the technology for enriching uranium but that he might also enable his customers to build nuclear warheads for missiles. The JIC assessed that this was the first case of a private enterprise offering a complete range of services to enable a customer to acquire highly enriched uranium for nuclear weapons. Intelligence also identified further individuals involved and the finance and transportation methods, including details of the banks across the world and the shipping companies. There was also more detail on other overseas facilities.

The JIC came back to Khan again six months later in January 2003. Then it expressed particular concern over Libyan progress due to the network's assistance. Something needed to be done. As well as the concern over what was going to Libya, the CIA and MI6 also had another major worry as they penetrated deeper into the Khan network. They picked up talk amongst the members of the network that Khan had already lined up another customer, along with the existing Libya deal. It was not clear who that customer was but word was going around the network that Khan had landed them another catch. Discussions between and within the U.S. and UK governments were intensifying over how long to watch the network and when and how to act against it. Both governments agreed that it was becoming too dangerous to let it continue.

There were a number of brakes on speedier action. The first was the need to protect sources. Some voices from the CIA's Directorate of Operations argued that nothing should be done to compromise the flow of information, partly because of the value of the intelligence and partly because of the personal danger for some of those sources. "There was tension because we had several very sensitive sources," remembers a senior intelligence official. Public disclosure could put lives at risk. There had been considerable operational daring by members of the clandestine services, which had been crucial in penetrating the network but in turn that complicated moving against Khan for fear of revealing the identity of spies and sources. "Some day it will make a great movie," explained another of those involved. "But it wasn't a movie. If people got hurt, they wouldn't just get up off the ground and go home to dinner." The second brake was the desire to learn more. Contrary to some statements, the intelligence was never comprehensive enough for those watching to be sure they knew absolutely every part of the network. This was vital since the plan was to attack the tentacles—the businessmen and middlemen—and not just the head, Khan himself. This was partly out of knowledge that it would be hard to get to Khan because of Pakistan's protection. As a result, it was vital to be sure that all the tentacles were under surveillance. Otherwise they could simply go underground and emerge soon after in a new—and unknown—form. Because the full customer list was still unclear the fear was that an undetected part of the network could keep supplying. Preventing this meant continuing to gather as much intelligence as possible to be sure that when action was taken it would be effective. It was also hoped that the question of who in Pakistan was supporting Khan might be answered in order to increase leverage to do something about him.

Another related issue was that the penetration of the Khan network was providing a unique window on not just his activities but also on a much wider world of rogue state activity. By watching his connections it was becoming possible to understand the interlocking webs of proliferation that centered on—but extended far beyond—Khan. North Korea was a black hole for U.S. intelligence and Khan offered one of the few potential vantage points on its activities. It was revealing activity and relationships that had not been known previously, and Washington was particularly keen to keep watching. The United States was trying to develop missile defence options and anything it could get on the North Korean missile program and what it was supplying to other states of concern was perceived as highly valuable.

And as more intelligence trickled in it often raised more questions than it answered. Much of the most intriguing information only came in during the later stages of the intelligence operation as it penetrated deeper into the network late in the day. As each stone was overturned, there would be something new. Trails of intelligence were leading into China. Were some of the people Khan was meeting in Beijing linked to Chinese intelligence or the People's Liberation Army or were they independent players? What of his close relationship with Saudi Arabia? How many countries were involved? How big was Khan's web? As signs began emerging of a potential new customer for the network, there were questions over whether it would be worth finding out who it was. "Our fear was that he was on the verge of proliferating again. And he was setting up his network to do just that," explained Richard Armitage.[27] Was it Syria? Egypt? Sudan? Saudi Arabia? Would it be worth waiting longer to find out? But what if waiting meant crucial material was transferred?

London was becoming jittery by the start of 2003 about Khan's continued activity and wanted it stopped. The growing intelligence on what was going to Libya was a concern—there were suspicions that Libya might be receiving nuclear material in the form of UF6 and also even a weapons design. Khan risked undermining the entire non-proliferation regime. Soon the signs of material continuing to flow to Pyongynag and Tripoli made even the United States believe it had to do something. The hardest question was not whether to act against Khan, but how? If it had been a simple question of either roll up the entire network or watch it, the choice would have been much easier. But how could you roll it all up?

Debates in Washington were becoming fractious. When intelligence indicated the transfer of materials through friendly countries, some officials pushed for telling those governments to allow an interception but the intelligence professionals blocked it, arguing that a limited interception would simply stop one shipment of goods but do nothing to shut down the whole enterprise and simply alert the network that it was being watched. Telling other countries was also problematic, not least because material was often being produced or flowing through "friendly" countries—including NATO allies like Turkey. "There was lots of diplomatic activity," said one former

State Department official, "but we were not always telling governments anything specific. We would say things like, 'we have indications that missile parts are moving through your ports or we have indications of production in your country.'" "The CIA would complain about the fecklessness of diplomatic demarches but the extent to which their effectiveness was limited was because the information supplied (by the intelligence community) was so non-specific," remembers one State Department official. "Countries allied to the U.S. would say they need more information and then the CIA would say no. In other cases governments would say that they did not know what their companies were up to." This approach did not look like really halting the network.

There were other, more dramatic options. One that was discussed by the senior players was covert action. The CIA's clandestine service proposed what one official described as "dirty tricks, putting sand in the gears" of the Khan network by attacking it using the CIA's covert capability. This would involve discreet, specific activity, such as sabotaging production or manufacturing at one of the plants associated with the Khan network—the SCOMI plant in Malaysia was one site considered at the very highest level. This would be made to look like an accident. Another option was to interfere with transport such as shipping, perhaps by debilitating or even sinking a vessel. The Israelis were the acknowledged masters of this kind of activity and were suspected of using it in Europe in the early 1980s against the nascent Iraqi program to intimidate scientists and businesses, as well as in the early 1960s against Egyptian missile development.[28] But with Khan, the U.S. policymakers decided against the CIA proposal, arguing that any covert operation risked discovery, which would then have an impact on diplomacy, especially since some of the activities might have to take place in friendly or at least neutral countries where manufacturing or transport was located, such as Malaysia. And maybe it was possible to take down the SCOMI operation with no one knowing who had done it, but would that really wrap up the entire network?

By 2003 the small trans-Atlantic team was in intense discussion looking at ways of exposing the Khan network. The discussions were intense and lively, according to those who took part. "It was a real marriage, we argued a lot," commented one official. By this point there was a general agreement on the need for action. The debate largely focused on tactics. None of the options looked easy. Proposals went back and forth. The discussions were difficult. "There were endless meetings," one participant remembers. The objective was to eradicate the Khan network in a way that wouldn't just push it underground and allow it to regenerate itself. The head (Khan) and the body (the network) had to be put out of business. Senior intelligence officials argued with those who wanted speedy action against Khan alone, warning that there was no guarantee that the body would die even if the head was cut off.

The problem was finding a way of bringing the issue into the public domain that would be convincing. The hope was to draw international attention to the network to a sufficient extent to force President Musharraf to shut it down, something which years of carefully worded warnings had so far failed to do. But this also had to be done while balancing other demands—not least the need to maintain cooperation with Pakistan over fighting Al Qaeda and avoiding destabilizing Musharraf.

One option was simply to go public with what was known. But some were sceptical about what would happen if Khan's activities were suddenly sprung on the world. Most of the public had no idea who A. Q. Khan was. What if everyone just shrugged their shoulders? And given the fact that the build up of the Iraq War was underway, there may have been deep scepticism about this being manufactured to fit in somehow. It would take other countries like Turkey, Malaysia, South Africa, and, of course, Pakistan to shut down Khan's operations, but would they really be so quick to trust U.S. intelligence that was presented to them? The whole process could go off half-cocked with Khan and his network left in place, knowing that the United States and UK were on to them. What was really needed was some trigger that could allow the issue to be brought into the international spotlight and that could generate independent evidence and validation of the secret intelligence. This could in turn spark domestic inquiries and also an investigation by the IAEA. Washington and London needed to find a way to show their hand to the world but without revealing their sources. They needed to shift from a clandestine intelligence gathering operation to a public roll up of the network. But how could this shift take place? No one was sure. And then in March 2003 came a surprise intervention. Without realizing that the Khan network had already been penetrated, one of its customers decided, for its own reasons, that the game was up. An intricate, tense endgame was about to begin.

LONDON

March 2003

THE CALL CAME OUT OF THE BLUE, just as the bombs were about to fall on Baghdad. It was from a Palestinian intermediary well known to Britain's Secret Intelligence Service, MI6. The message from Colonel Gadaffi of Libya was short and simple: the issue of weapons of mass destruction was on the table. And the leader's son, Saif al-Islam Gaddafi, wanted a meeting.

Two officers from MI6 went to meet Saif al-Islam in the private room of a hotel in London's exclusive Mayfair district. For the young Gadaffi, it was a strange and nerve-wracking experience. "It was quite unique at the time for me because I was face to face with the British secret service for the first time in my life—the people who I had regarded for a long time as devils, enemies."[1] Would they double cross him, he wondered? Did they and the Americans have an agenda for regime change in Tripoli in the same way they had embarked upon in Baghdad?

Saif started by telling them he had a message from his father: Colonel Gadaffi wanted to work with the UK and United States to launch a new initiative to reform the Middle East. A British officer cut to the chase. We would be happy to work together but first there is an important issue to resolve, he explained. What about the weapons of mass destruction? Saif replied that "the leader" was ready to deal with the subject. There were no more details about what this would involve and whether everything—including the nuclear issue and Khan's deals—were on the table.

From the hotel, a call was put in to Sir David Manning, Tony Blair's foreign affairs adviser, at Downing Street to discuss how to proceed. Ten minutes later, Manning called back. Downing Street was skeptical but intrigued. Keep going was the message. Saif was told that this was a fascinating offer and good news. But there was a need to hear it from the mouth of the father, not just the son. Three days later, on the day the war with Iraq commenced, a plane took off from an airport near London carrying a small team to Libya for a meeting.

The team working on Khan realized that the Libyan offer was potentially the break they needed. It could offer a chance to expose the network's activities to the light of day in a way that no one could deny. But this would mean carefully synchronizing the breaking of Khan with dealing with Libya. And, given the suspicions on all sides regarding the Libya negotiations, who knew how long that would take? The next few months would prove to be far from easy as the breaking of the Khan network and the disarming of Libya became closely intertwined and entangled. At times, it looked as if both might fail.

CHAPTER 8

Dealing with Gadaffi

COLONEL GADAFFI HAS A HABIT OF KEEPING HIS VISITORS WAITING before they are ushered into one of his vast Bedouin tents to talk, and more often than not, to listen. His favorite location to meet guests is his birthplace, Sirte, which has also become his desert headquarters. Visitors fly to a tiny airstrip in the middle of the desert. From there, it's a short drive before arriving at Gadaffi's remarkable hideaway. Camels wander to and fro amongst campfires and bushes that litter the dusty landscape. The center of activity is a vast tent—the size of three tennis courts—decked out in drapes and coverings. The tent is largely empty with only a solitary television and a few chairs and cushions set in one corner. Many of the key meetings over the coming months would take place here, others in a similar tent in an army barracks in the Libyan capital, Tripoli.

Gadaffi, one of the great survivors of international politics, can be at once charismatic and inscrutable. His craggy, weathered face is instantly recognizable but hard to read. But when the two British intelligence officers arrived to meet him in March 2003, he gave his visitors a simple message— yes, he would disarm. There would be many bumps along the road but one of the things that kept the negotiations on the road was that every time anyone went back to the source of the initial decision—Gadaffi himself— he made clear that he was sticking with it.

Gadaffi's decision to gingerly step out of the cold was not sudden but the product of a long period of reflection. Tripoli had been gently probing for openings with the West for some time. The revolutionary ardor that had once fired Gadaffi had cooled over the years and the Libyan leader had been seeking a way out of his isolation—on his terms. But doing so would not be easy. Over the preceding decades, Libya had come to be characterized by its opponents in London and Washington as an almost archetypal rogue state and its leader as a picture book dictator who had supported international terrorism and had tried to develop weapons of mass destruction. By 1979 Libya was designated a state sponsor of terrorism. In 1984 Britain broke off relations after a police officer, Yvonne Fletcher, was killed by shots believed to have come from inside the Libyan Embassy in London. In 1986 a Berlin disco was bombed and intercepted communications revealed that Libya was behind the attack. That same year, U.S. planes, flying from British airbases, bombed Tripoli, including Gadaffi's home, killing his eighteen-month-old adopted daughter.

Then in December 1988, Pan Am 103 was blown up over Lockerbie in Scotland. Two hundred seventy people were killed, including 189 Americans. Until September 11, it was the largest single terrorist attack against the United States in terms of the loss of civilian life. The intelligence was murky but pieces of clothing found in the suitcase that carried the bomb were traced to a shop in Malta whose owner identified a Libyan intelligence officer as the purchaser of a number of items. The evidence seemed to point to Gadaffi as having carried out the attack, possibly in retaliation for the U.S. air strike in 1986 (although a number of people still believe that Iran and Syria may have been behind it). New sanctions were imposed, including by the United Nations. Libya found itself more isolated than ever. Dealing with Lockerbie would be the central issue in relations with Tripoli for more than a decade to come.

There had also been a long-standing concern over Libyan interest in unconventional weapons, primarily mustard gas and other lethal chemicals. By the 1980s Libya had succeeded in developing a limited chemical weapons capability and may even have used it against Chad in 1986–87. From 1988 the United States openly accused Libya of building a plant at Rabta, seventy-five miles southwest of Tripoli. Gadaffi attempted to divert attention with an unusual ruse. He claimed the plant had been destroyed by fire, a fact seemingly confirmed by satellite imagery. But intelligence analysts soon realized the fire had been faked with burning tires. On the nuclear front though, the general perception in the U.S. and British intelligence communities was that the Libyan program was going nowhere fast. That is, until Khan revealed a different story.

The Libyans had sought nuclear weapons for different reasons at different times. Gadaffi first tried to buy the bomb, including from Pakistan, in the early 1970s. In these early days of his reign Gadaffi believed that nuclear capabilities would provide him with the leading role to which he aspired in world politics. Then in the mid-1980s there was a renewed purchasing campaign. This time, the effort was driven less by a quest for status than by a desire to ensure Libya's survival as its relationship with the West had begun to deteriorate rapidly. The bomb was the best means of deterrence, especially after the 1986 air strike by the United States and then the reaction to Lockerbie. "We thought of obtaining WMD's at the beginning when problems with the West started," explains Libya's Ambassador to London Mohamed Azwai. "They refused to have dialogue with us and we considered this was a sign that they were planning something bad for us. We came to the conclusion that—in the end—a military confrontation will be imposed on us. So from then, we started looking to obtain weaponry that could protect us from that attack. When Lockerbie came it made us convinced that this decision was right. . . . At the same time, we tried to convince the other side to sit with us and negotiate. Regrettably, the West's response took ten years."

From the early 1990s on, Libyan thinking shifted again and it began to pursue a dual-track strategy to obtain the bomb and also cut a deal with the United States. The Libyans would follow this approach right until the end. For a long time, and largely secretly, Libya had been trying to open up relations with the United States. The first attempt came as far back as 1992 when Libyan officials approached former Senator and presidential candidate Gary Hart. The Libyans signaled to Hart a possible willingness to hand over the Lockerbie suspects and discuss nonconventional weapons in return for the lifting of sanctions. There was no interest from the White House.[1]

Clinton administration officials have also said that Gadaffi was trying to open back channels with them. Martin Indyk, assistant secretary of state for Near East affairs, and Bruce Riedel, from the National Security Council, met secretly in Geneva with the head of Libya's intelligence service in early 1999, beginning a series of contacts that would persist into the Bush administration.[2] Libya offered to give up its chemical weapons program in return for sanctions being lifted. How genuine the Libyans were is an open question because at exactly the moment they were trying to talk to the United States, they were also pushing ahead with the deal with the A. Q. Khan network to buy a nuclear bomb. By 2000 the Libyans had placed the order for the full enrichment program offered by Khan. At this point, the United States did not know of the Khan deal and did not see the chemical weapons program as sufficiently advanced to constitute a major threat whose termination would justify bringing Libya in from the cold. U.S. officials made clear that at these meetings in Geneva that Libya would have to pay compensation and admit responsibility for Lockerbie first before any dialogue could begin on broader diplomatic reengagement.

The Bush administration followed the same script when it continued the process of meeting secretly with officials from Tripoli. U.S. officials told the Libyans directly that resolving Lockerbie would only remove UN sanctions. Lifting U.S. sanctions, by contrast, would require opening the WMD file. However the administration would not even begin the latter conversation until after they had dealt with Lockerbie.[3] This approach slowly began to pay dividends, especially after an October 2001 meeting in the United Kingdom. "When we returned to Libya to report on what had come up in London, it started a debate with all of those responsible in Libya on the benefits of keeping nuclear weapons versus giving them up," remembers Mohamed Azwai, one of those involved in the negotiations. Within Libya, the handful of individuals at the top of the regime who made the decisions about the costs of maintaining a nuclear program had begun to question its benefits.

Slowly, the Lockerbie issue also began to move off the agenda. In April 1999 Libya agreed to hand over two suspects to be tried under Scottish law in the Netherlands. The handover led to the suspension of European sanctions, but the comprehensive deal that the Libyans sought was still remote. By 2003 the appeals process was largely over and Libya agreed to pay $2.7 billion to the families of the victims. The Libyans turned to Britain to negotiate a broader deal, partly because they perceived a greater willingness on Britain's part to listen but also because it was hoped that Britain could bring the United States on board because of the close relationship between London and Washington.

The UK had restored diplomatic relations with Libya in July 1999, but 9/11 provided another opening to transform the relationship. Initially, Gadaffi's reaction was panic. A diplomatic cable, recently declassified, reveals that Gadaffi feared being a target of the U.S. and was calling "every Arab leader on his Rolodex" to try and dissuade the U.S. from action.[4] But soon Gadaffi also saw an opportunity. He had long been an opponent of Al Qaeda since his regime had been the target of Islamic militants allied to Osama bin Laden. Gadaffi had actually issued the first Interpol arrest warrant for bin Laden in March 1998. Gadaffi's intelligence chief arrived in London with a list of more than a dozen Libyan residents in the UK whom the Libyan government accused of being linked to bin Laden and whom they hoped the UK would arrest as well as of other militants in Europe.[5] Libya clearly hoped that by providing this intelligence it could make use of the post-9/11 shift in Washington's priorities and buy itself out of isolation. But the U.S. and UK remained adamant that Lockerbie had to be resolved first and that the WMD program was next on the list. The Americans and British had just recently begun to learn of Libya's nuclear ambitions through Khan, and they had their suspicions over Gadaffi's intentions and reliability.

There was more progress on the diplomatic side in August 2002 when UK Foreign Office Minister Mike O'Brien visited the Libyan leader—the first time a British minister had done so since Gadaffi came to power. O'Brien was kept waiting for hours before being escorted into Gadaffi's tent by the Libyan leader's female bodyguards. When O'Brien brought up the issue of nonconventional weapons, Gadaffi did not utter his usual denial. Instead, Gadaffi surprised O'Brien by acknowledging that weapons of mass destruction were a serious issue, and said he was keen to improve relations in order to get foreign investment for his oil and gas industries. Gadaffi asked if the West was serious about disarming Saddam and O'Brien said they were.[6] O'Brien reported back to Foreign Secretary Jack Straw that he believed Gadaffi was genuine in his desire to move on the issue.

On O'Brien's return to the UK, Tony Blair wrote to Gadaffi. There was a sense that after having denied the existence of any chemical, biological, or nuclear weapons programs for so long, Libya might at last be willing to move on the issue. British officials felt that they would not be able to persuade Libya to come clean without holding out the offer of improved relations with the United States, so when Blair met with President Bush at Camp David in September 2002 he raised the issue and received agreement from the U.S. president to move ahead. Blair kept exploring the subject through letters and envoys sent out to Libya. Then in March 2003 came the phone call and the Libyan approach. But was it genuine? Many in Washington and even at 10 Downing Street were dubious. So what was driving Gadaffi?

Through the 1990s Gadaffi was keen to move in from the cold for a number of reasons, primary amongst them was simple economics. He had come to recognize that he needed investment in Libya's economy, particularly to exploit its oil revenues that make up a quarter of the economy, but this was impossible under the crippling sanctions regime. The timing of the phone call to MI6, coming just as the invasion of Iraq was about to begin, has inevitably raised questions. Was Gadaffi afraid that the road from Baghdad led to Tripoli? Could it be that Gadaffi feared that, like Saddam, he could be singled out as a sponsor of terrorism seeking WMD and be next on the list for regime change? Did he fear that any future WMD attack on the United States might be blamed on the Libyans as a pretext for war? Some in the United States have claimed Iraq was a major factor. "It became more urgent for him to get off the bad list when he saw the fate of the Taliban regime and the Saddam Hussein regime," said one senior Pentagon official.[7] The most explicit statement came from Vice-President Cheney in August 2004 when he said: "A year ago, Libya had a secret nuclear weapons program. But after our forces ousted Saddam, and captured him in his hiding spot north of Baghdad, Libya's leader, Muammar Ghaddafi, had a change of heart."[8]

Gadaffi's son has been adamant that Iraq was not a factor. "There is no foundation for that statement. First of all, we started negotiating before the beginning of the war, and it is not because we are afraid or under the American pressure or blackmail."[9] It is true that the desire to improve relations had been long-standing on the Libyan side, based primarily on economics and a realization that confrontation with the West was a dead-end. But Iraq accelerated a process that was already under way, increasing Libya's sense of urgency. Secret messages were also passed from the United States to Libya in the run-up to the Iraq war. These intimated to the Libyans that if they continued to act in a way similar to Saddam then the international community would not stand idly by. No detail was given but it was communicated to the Libyans that it was known that they were flouting both

UN resolutions and their commitments under the nuclear Non-Proliferation Treaty. There was no precise threat, as it was judged to be more effective to leave the exact consequences of Libyan activity hanging in the air unspoken. But alongside the stick, a carrot of being brought into the international community was also dangled in front of the Libyans, including the lifting of sanctions and even security assistance. It was deemed advantageous to be clear about what the carrot was but leave the stick somewhat ambiguous.

Iraq may also have played a role in confirming in Colonel Gadaffi's mind a long-developing sense regarding the actual utility and value of nuclear weapons. "We made this step," Gadaffi later stated, "because this programme is not useful to Libya, but it actually represents a danger and threat to Libya's very integrity."[10] Gadaffi's thought process, according to those who discussed the subject with him, was that the United States had possessed nuclear weapons since 1945 but still found itself embroiled in conflicts like Vietnam and Iraq and was never able to use its weapons. Libya's program had cost a huge amount of money and yet he still didn't have the bomb. And even if he did have it, would it actually be that useful? All it promised was further sanctions and isolation. "We realized if we obtained weapons then [we would be] in more danger than if we don't have them," says Mohammed Azwai, Libyan ambassador to London. The revelations over Iran's facility in Natanz and the visit of IAEA inspectors in February 2003 added further impetus. The Libyans realized that Khan's help to Tehran might be exposed and in turn that might lead investigators to realize that Khan had also been supplying Libya.

But getting to the point where Libya would actually come clean and disarm fully and transparently would not be an easy process. Gadaffi may have tried to draw closer to the United States and UK from the 1990s onward, but he also seemed to believe that he could hedge his bets and do so while retaining his weapons of mass destruction programs. Even in March 2003 when the new approach to British intelligence took place, it would emerge that the Libyans were still not really owning up to developing nuclear weapons, perhaps out of fear of the consequences, perhaps to retain a capability. Making the Libyans understand that they really were going to have to strip themselves of all their illicit activity was going to take some work. And in this task, the penetration of A. Q. Khan's network would prove pivotal.

In the first meeting with British officials in March, Gadaffi made clear he wanted the United States involved in the deal. The Libyans suggested that they had already tried to make a similar pitch to the United States but had been ignored. For the Libyan leader, used to exercising absolute power, his initial promise to disarm was all that needed to be said on the matter and he moved the conversation onto other areas. The British officers were conscious that disarmament would still take some difficult negotiating and asked with whom they should deal on the matter. Musa Kusa, Gadaffi answered. Kusa, the head of Libya's foreign intelligence service, was a shadowy and deeply controversial figure. Few photographs of him exist but those who have met him describe him as surprisingly charismatic (for a spy chief at least), clearly intelligent, and clearly ruthless. On later occasions when he met with British officials, Kusa would sometimes turn up wearing jeans and a leather jacket. But he is widely understood to be the mastermind of the darker side of the Libyan regime. In 1980 he had openly talked of the assassination of Libyan exiles in Britain, leading to his expulsion as head of the Libyan mission in London. He was also wanted in France in connection with blowing up a French airliner in 1989. He was educated at Michigan State University and had risen to become one of Gadaffi's closest advisers.

When they sat down with Kusa for the first time, British officials made clear that Britain knew more than Libya thought about its nuclear program (due to Khan, but this could not be revealed). The whole process, it was explained, would only work if Libya itself came clean about what it had. The United States and UK believed that they would have to keep the Libyans guessing as to how much they really knew in order to test their sincerity.

The officials returned from Libya and reported back to the Foreign Office and Downing Street. The view from 10 Downing Street remained one of interest matched by scepticism and caution over Gadaffi's true intentions. There was no doubt in the minds of the prime minister's closest national security advisers that Gadaffi wanted to rejoin the international community but that was not the same as being willing to give up all his weapons. They told MI6 to proceed—but with care. Tony Blair brought up the subject with President Bush during his March 26–27 visit to Washington and encouraged the President to support exploring the Libyan contact. The view in the United States was at least as skeptical but it was agreed that the UK should take the lead and at least see where the process could end up. The White House was conscious of the powerful Lockerbie lobby that would have to be handled very carefully if a deal was to be struck with the Libyan leader. In April a senior British officer who had met with Gadaffi flew to Washington. Sir Richard Dearlove, the head of MI6, was over anyway for a scheduled visit and together with CIA Director George Tenet went to the Oval Office to brief President Bush. The President told them he supported a move forward.

With agreement on all sides to go ahead, the question was how? The first thing to do was to introduce senior Americans to the Libyans. The two sides had rarely met and lacked even the limited familiarity with each other that existed on the British side. MI6 arranged for a senior CIA official, Steven Kappes, who had considerable experience in the Middle East to meet with Musa Kusa in Geneva.[11] It was now time to flesh out what an actual agreement would look like. Kusa had been asked to bring details of Libya's WMD activities to Geneva but he said he hadn't been able to do so because of a lack of time. It was the first of many signals that the process was not going to be easy.

Over the coming months, the Libyans kept fishing for what the British and Americans already knew about their program. They were told that they had to come completely clean to prove their bona fides. When asked about nuclear weapons, the Libyans replied that, perhaps, they had one or two things on the nuclear side that they were not supposed to have, but nothing serious. It would almost have been comical if the stakes were not so high. There was no sign that the Libyans were ready to own up to what they were receiving from Khan. The Libyans asked for non-aggression pacts and other security guarantees but the United States and UK stuck to the position that Libya had an illegal program and needed to give it up before anything would be guaranteed. Once the Libyans gave up what they had, then, and only then, relations would improve.

By the start of September, the Libyans began to worry that the whole courtship could fall apart. They pointed out that everything that had happened so far had been done in secret and could be denied by the British and American governments. The British emphasized that the negotiations had to remain secret or else the publicity could complicate the already tricky process to the point of collapsing the deal. The Libyans insisted that they meet with someone who was not an undercover intelligence officer and of sufficient authority to show that the UK government as a whole was committed. It was agreed that a prominent British individual would pay a visit to Libya along with senior CIA and MI6 officers and that this individual would personally meet Gadaffi. He brought a letter from Tony Blair reassuring the Libyan leader that he would be re-admitted into the international community if all went well. The official was a sufficiently distinguished figure to show the Libyans that this was a serious negotiation. The individual asked Gadaffi directly—was he really prepared to give up his entire WMD capability and everything associated with it? The answer was yes.

It was made clear throughout the initial negotiations that Libya would have to allow the U.S. and UK to visit facilities. U.S. and British officials wanted to visit all the sites and wanted to know that the Libyans were going to take them everywhere rather than just the places they asked to see. Even with the excellent intelligence coming in, it would require full and open access to really be sure that the country was serious about disarmament. In a country the size of Libya, it would not be hard to hide a small installation somewhere and retain a program. Gadaffi consented to the visit but nothing happened. There were a few false alarms on getting the green light to go to Libya but each time nothing materialized. This was proving to be the major stumbling block. Frustrations grew. The Libyans were not being open about what they had and were not letting the CIA and MI6 come in to check. What's more, there was intelligence showing that the Khan network was still producing and supplying components for its Libya deal. Were the UK and United States being double-crossed? Was Gadaffi after a deal while he still went for the bomb? Was he, as most now believe, hedging his bets and keeping an eye on events in Iraq?

On the Libyan side there were concerns over whether the UK would deliver. They feared that London and Washington might simply gain all the knowledge they could through the secret negotiations in terms of Libya's activities and then turn round, stop the negotiations, and accuse Tripoli of being part of the axis of evil for having pursued nuclear weapons. Nervousness over such an outcome meant that the Libyans were reluctant to come clean about what they really had, fearing it would lead to shock and condemnation rather than a successful conclusion. But of course, on the other side, British and American intelligence already had a clear idea of what the Libyans possessed because they had penetrated the Khan network. So the

Libyans' failure to be open about their program raised serious concerns in London and Washington. Perhaps the Libyans were not actually committed? Were they hoping to cut a deal that would bring them out of the cold without giving up their secret nuclear program? The result was gridlock.

By summer's end, the mood was becoming gloomy. The Libyan deal looked stuck. Maybe Gadaffi had only made the offer when the war with Iraq was imminent and had now backed off? Meanwhile, Khan was still going about his business. Action on breaking his network had been stalled because Libya had seemed to be the perfect hinge to prize it open. And now the two thorny issues had become entangled. If the end of a Libyan nuclear program that no one had known about was revealed, there would be immediate questions over where the capability came from and the finger would soon point at Khan. If the intelligence agencies weren't truly ready to shut down Khan's network, the Libyan revelations would tip off all the tentacles of the Khan network and they would go further underground, making them much harder to stop. Equally, if the Khan network was shut down in full public view before the Libyan negotiations were complete, it risked upsetting the Libyans and doing in the entire deal. The whole of 2003 would see some delicate, at times high-wire, intelligence and diplomatic efforts to close both deals. At the top of the Bush administration there was more interest in Libya than breaking A. Q. Khan, not least because the public was aware of Gadaffi but few had heard of the Pakistani scientist. Closing the Libya deal would provide a bigger political payback and would demonstrate that the administration's tough policy on proliferation was paying dividends. But by the summer, what had once been seen as a promising chance to both bring a rogue state in from the cold and break the Khan network was looking like a swamp in which London and Washington had become mired.

And then in mid-September came the tip-off. The *BBC China* had stopped in Dubai and was heading to Tripoli with key parts for the Libyan program. It was agreed that it had to be stopped whatever the impact on the Libyan negotiations. It was too large a consignment and represented too much latent capability to allow it to go through. A process was set in motion by the small CIA/MI6 team to track the key containers on board and the ship's location. The interception of the *BBC China* would have to be carefully orchestrated in order to avoid derailing the Libyan process, while still applying the right sort of pressure on the Libyans.

The difficult question was where to intercept it since the whole incident had to be kept secret. Italy seemed a good choice based on the route. This meant the Italians would have to be brought on board. The Germans would also have to be told since legally either the country that operated and owned the boat (Germany) or the country whose flag it sailed under (Antigua) had to be notified. At a meeting in Rome in late September, the UK asked Italy and Germany for assistance. The meeting was not without its difficulties since the European officials could be informed of Khan supplying Libya but could not be told of the ongoing Libyan negotiations—there were strict orders from Bush and Blair to keep it under wraps. There was surprise in some quarters at the idea that Libya could really be developing a nuclear program. It was explained to the European officials that a number of balls were in the air and sensitive intelligence assets were at risk so nothing could come out publicly. They would keep their promise.

The packages on board the *BBC China* were opened up in the early hours of Saturday morning. Once the contents were confirmed, MI6 contacted Musa Kusa and sought an urgent meeting. Why, when the outlines of a deal to renounce WMD were already in place, was Libya still buying more material? Was the material going to be buried in the desert to use after the inspectors had left? The Libyans explained that the *BBC China* was part of a series of regular deliveries and that the intention was always to give up the material as part of the long-planned final deal. It was conveyed that any hints of evasiveness could undermine the deal and provide ammunition to those who might be sceptical. For months, negotiators had been emphasizing that they knew a lot and expected full cooperation. The interception of the *BBC China* forced the Libyans' hand. It was now all too clear that British and American intelligence knew exactly what the Libyans were up to and what kind of capability they were assembling.

The dramatic operation paid off. Within two weeks, the first team would be allowed in to Libya to visit the key sites. The Anglo-American team met beforehand to decide tactics and pool their knowledge of what would need examining once there. Drawn from the CIA and MI6, there would be one expert in each discipline—nuclear, missile, and chemical/biological—from each country, plus a technical team leader and senior CIA and MI6 officers running the negotiations. According to flight logs, a CIA plane operated by a front company left Britain's Northolt airfield at lunchtime on October

19. The plane carrying the joint team arrived in Libya later in the afternoon. When details of the flight later became public it was wrongly thought to be involved in the CIA's practice of "extraordinary rendition" involving the transfer of terrorist suspects.[12]

The circle of people with knowledge of the approach to Libya and the ongoing negotiations was even tighter than that that had been around the Khan intelligence. In London, those involved remember it as the most tightly held diplomatic exercises in which they had ever been involved. In Washington, beyond the president and vice president, only half-a-dozen senior CIA officials and Secretary of State Powell, his Deputy Richard Armitage, and Assistant Secretary of State William Burns were aware. The rest of the State Department was not informed, including John Bolton, the undersecretary of state for arms control. The dovetailing of the Khan and Libya operations would also be extremely tricky. Some of the key people who knew about A. Q. Khan and the material being transferred to Libya did not know that at the same time Libya was in negotiations with the UK and United States over disarming. When John Bolton became aware of the interception of the *BBC China* and wanted to make it public at a conference, he had to be told in no uncertain terms that this was not an option. Bolton had been an advocate of regime change in Libya. As a result, there were people on both sides of the Atlantic who did not want him involved in the negotiations and the decision was taken at the highest levels to leave him out of the loop. Everyone on both sides of the Atlantic was relying on the visit by the team of experts to determine whether the deal could be made to work.

On their arrival in Libya, the teams were introduced to their guides, individuals who had run each of the secret programs. These guides were profoundly nervous and appeared unsure how to act. Most likely they had been told simply to make the visitors happy. But what if they revealed more than they were supposed to? It is also possible that their nervousness stemmed from having profited personally from the procurement activity and so they had something to hide even from their own government. The guides immediately asked the visitors what they knew already. They were told that this was not the way things were going to work and that they would have to open up first.

The progress on the missile and chemical and biological side was relatively quick and the teams were soon out visiting sites. But it was a different story when it came to the nuclear program. The Libyans initially claimed there had been no work on the fuel cycle and no work on enrichment. When challenged and asked if they were aware of the seizure of the *BBC China*, the guides looked blank and said no. Building trust proved difficult. The Libyans, unsure where the negotiations might lead, were cautious about allowing the teams to meet those working at facilities and refused to allow photos to be taken. After an exhausting day of up to twelve hours of inspections, the team would return to their accommodation and be up until the early hours writing up reports and sending them to their headquarters.

The mutual suspicion between the nuclear team and its Libyan interlocutors grew as the days went on. The Libyans adamantly refused to admit that they had any plans for nuclear weapons (as opposed to just working on a fuel cycle). This made no sense in terms of the way the program was structured, but they stuck to their line. The visitors also had suspicions that the Libyans were hiding the degree of outside help they were receiving and maybe even a number of foreigners working on the program, possibly from North Korea or Iraq.

After the teams departed on their unmarked plane from Tripoli airport on the afternoon of October 29, they returned to London and Langley to sift through and assess the information they had collected. On missile and chemical/biological weapons progress was good, but on the nuclear program it was patchy. There had been some progress—they'd seen centrifuges that had come from the Khan network but the Libyans had not admitted that any uranium hexafluoride (UF6) had come from the network, nor were they mentioning the weapons design, both of which the CIA and MI6 suspected had been transferred. If anything, the team was more disappointed than the political leadership who was briefed on the progress. When then-U.S. National Security Adviser Condoleeza Rice heard the report, she commented that if she were negotiating she wouldn't give everything away on the first visit.

After the problems over the nuclear program in the October trip, it was decided another visit was needed if the deal was going to work. In November, the senior MI6 and CIA officers handling the negotiations met with Kusa in the UK, at a location away from London. It was decided to reveal to Kusa more of what the intelligence agencies really knew. At a tense meeting, a number of very specific examples were laid out before him on the table, highlighting the difference between what the Libyans were claiming and what M16 and the CIA knew to be true. Among the evidence was the recording of a long conversation between A. Q. Khan and Libyan nuclear chief Matuq from February 28, 2002.[13] The message got through, and the Libyans agreed to another trip.

On December 1 the team set off for round two. The CIA plane flew overnight from Washington, D.C., arriving at Northolt airfield in the UK just before nine in the morning, providing a couple of hours for the British team to board before taking off again. When they arrived in Tripoli, the team received much more cooperation than they had on their previous visit. The Libyans finally revealed the UF6 cylinders that they had received from Khan. They also took the visitors to sites they hadn't previously seen. The only remaining problem was that the Libyans were still not admitting that the nuclear program was geared towards weapons. By now the personal relationships were good enough with the Libyan guides to warn them that, despite everything else, this obstacle would force the intelligence officers to qualify their assessment to political leaders.

The last full day of the trip, December 11, was a rainy day in Tripoli. The fate of the negotiations hung in the balance with the possibility that the team would have to report back that the Libyans were continuing to hide aspects of their work. But at 3 P.M. there was a sudden flurry of activity. The Libyans finally admitted that the purpose of their program was to develop a nuclear weapon. It was still dark when the exhausted team arrived at the airport to depart the following morning. They were met with a surprise. The un-marked thirty-two-seat Boeing 737 was waiting on the tarmac, having arrived a few days earlier from its waiting position in Malta.[14] As the team approached the foot of the plane on the runway, the Libyans said they had something for the team to take back with them. They handed over a stack of six or seven brown envelopes about a foot high. Once on board the aircraft, the team opened them. Inside was a nuclear weapons design. All along the United States and UK had suspected that the Libyans had received a design from Khan but here was the final proof. Enclosed were nearly all the instructions required to manufacture and assemble the components for a bomb. The last-minute admission by the Libyans transformed the report that the intelligence officers would send to their political masters. A deal now seemed close. Closing it would go down to the wire.

The final agreement was to be hammered out on a memorable day in London. The day of December 16 began with a meeting around 11 A.M. in offices on Whitehall. Looking back, British officials express amusement at the optimism of their initial plan that the final details could be completed in an hour before all sides headed off for a pleasant lunch to celebrate. In practice, the talks got nowhere in the first hour and the group headed off together at 12:30 P.M. A private room for lunch had been booked at the Traveller's Club—one of London's most exclusive clubs sited in an elegant building on Pall Mall. Founded in 1819 for members who had traveled or resided abroad, it was a favorite haunt of members of MI6. Gentleman were expected to wear ties but some of the Libyans hadn't come dressed for the occasion and so they were hustled through the door by British officials keen that the doorman didn't spot them and unwittingly stymie the negotiations.

The small group gathered in a grand chandeliered private room whose walls were adorned with paintings of past British explorers and diplomats, At the negotiating table, the British team included William Ehrman, director general for Defence and Intelligence at the foreign office, David Landsman, the head of the Counter Proliferation Department, and two officers from MI6. Representing the United States were Robert Joseph from the National Security Council and two CIA officials, one of whom was Stephen Kappes who was the point man on the Libyan negotiations.[15] On the Libyan side were Musa Kusa, Abdul Ati Al-Obeidi, the ambassador to Rome, and Mohamed Azwai, ambassador to London.[16] It would turn into a long, long lunch with discussions dragging on through the entire afternoon and not finishing until around 6 P.M. "It was very much a nothing is agreed until everything is agreed negotiation," explained one of those at the meeting. Both sides profoundly lacked confidence in the other side. "We lacked confidence the Libyans would really go ahead with this—Gadaffi was the kind of mercurial character you could never be sure was going to do it."

The exact choreography and sequencing of the public announcement that Libya was going to disarm its nuclear program was a major sticking point. They argued over every word of the final text of the Libyan announcement. British and American negotiators wanted to ensure that there was absolutely no doubt about what was being announced and its significance. It had to be perfectly clear that the Libyans were going to explicitly admit that they had weapons of mass destruction programs and were going to give everything up. Originally the Libyans wanted to say they were giving up "any" WMD that they had—as though they might not have any at all but if they did have any, they would relinquish them. This proved to be a key sticking point. There could be no room for hedging, British and American officials insisted. Robert Joseph made clear that Libya would have to surrender its entire enrichment capability, even though this could be used for a civilian nuclear energy program, not just the weaponization aspects of the nuclear program. The long-range missile and chemical programs also had to go.[17] The White House was firm in its desire not to be seen to be offering anything that looked too much like a deal—after all, the stance they had taken with "rogue states" was that the United States would take a tough line and as a result those states would have to decide how to behave. The United States had been resistant to the idea of one-on-one negotiations with countries like Iran and North Korea. The Americans did not want to be seen as either having been drawn into a long process or "rewarding" illegal behavior, and so they resisted any explicit deal with the Libyans in which sanctions would be lifted.

The Libyans meanwhile had reservations about the idea that Gadaffi himself should make the announcement. This was partly because he bizarrely has an unusually informal position within the Libyan "revolutionary" state as a "guide of the revolution" (even though in practice he is an authoritarian leader). But the Libyans also perhaps felt it would simply be too embarrassing for the "leader" to make the announcement. At first the Anglo-American team rejected any alternative. Eventually, a compromise was reached that the foreign minister would make the detailed announcement and then Gadaffi would personally endorse it. Suspicions remained right to the end. The Libyans feared that they could be double-crossed. What if they went public with an admission of a nuclear weapons program and the White House and Downing Street failed to congratulate the Libyan leader or even worse condemned him? There were high stakes for the Libyans and to the end trust was not overflowing on either side. Both sides wanted to know exactly what the other would say to have confidence that they would not be left high and dry at the last minute but neither side wanted to be too explicit. The capture of Saddam Hussein three days earlier increased Libyan jitters. The pictures of Saddam raised fears that the U.S. and UK were planning a similar humiliation for Gadaffi. The British-American team reassured the Libyans that Bush and Blair would respond and gave a rough idea of what they would say but refused to present precise texts, indicating only that they would issue a warm welcome to Gadaffi and initiate a process to bring Libya back into the international community.

Finally, the exhausted teams came to a conclusion. The UK team reported back to Downing Street that they believed they had a deal. Tony Blair made the first of a number of calls to the White House over the following days and spoke to Condoleeza Rice about the text upon which they had all agreed. However, the Libyans then announced the text wasn't necessarily final as Gadaffi himself would have to approve it. A number of changes were proposed. Frantic phone calls ensued right down to the wire to go through every word all over again.

On December 18 Tony Blair's new Foreign Affairs Adviser Nigel Sheinwald summoned the negotiating team to 10 Downing Street for a meeting and a telephone call was arranged between Blair and Gadaffi—the first time the two men had spoken. In a half-hour conversation, Blair emphasized the need for clarity and sticking to the text that they had been provided. If that happened there would be an immediate response from Blair.[18]

The plan was set and December 19 was to be the day. But even just a few hours before the announcement, it was uncertain whether or not the deal was still on. Officials in London and Washington were worried and knew that Gadaffi could be unpredictable. The deal was that the Libyan foreign minister would read the announcement on Libyan television on Friday, and then Gadaffi would endorse his statement, beginning a sequence of public announcements from London and Washington. The final draft of the statement was faxed from Tripoli to London to confirm the contents—three drafts had gone back and forth over the previous twenty-four hours. Condoleeza Rice and Tony Blair both suggested some minor changes, which were then sent onto the British embassy in Tripoli to be forwarded onto the Libyan government.[19] Blair and Bush then conferred privately on the phone as they waited for the broadcast.

In an element of farce that only added to the tension, Libyan TV was showing a football match that night which ran over schedule. At 9 P.M., the moment that the Libyan announcement was supposed to be broadcast, there was nothing. Sitting up late in their offices, British officials were finding the evening excruciating. They wondered if the whole deal was going to fall apart.

Calls were made to the British ambassador in Libya to ask what was going on. Eventually around 9:30 P.M. the match ended and the Libyan foreign minister appeared to make the statement. Then Colonel Gadaffi released his crucial statement confirming the deal—the final confirmation that had been such a concern. At 9:55 P.M. the go-ahead was given. Blair was out of London and had to race to make it in time to be in front of the cameras for the evening news at 10:15 P.M., broadcasting from Durham near his constituency home, fifteen minutes before President Bush's appearance.

A few days later a messenger flew from Tripoli to London. He brought with him boxes of dates and oranges for the prime minister and a senior MI6 officer who had been involved from the start. There was also a message, expressing Gadaffi's pleasure at the outcome. The tone implied a certain degree of surprise that London had carried through on its part of the bargain. Few in London could also believe that it had all worked out as planned. In Libya the relief would later turn to disappointment as in months following the announcement Tripoli felt it had not gained as much as it hoped, particularly from the United States. But for Tony Blair and George Bush, battered by criticism of their policy over Iraq, that December night of the Libyan announcement appeared to be a triumph. The White House used the public disclosure to emphasize the way in which Iraq had forced Gadaffi to make a choice. However, there were still some doubts; after the deal, the CIA asked its "red cell," which is tasked with looking at alternative viewpoints, to look into whether Gadaffi's abandonment of nuclear programs had been merely temporary.[20]

Halfway across the world in Pakistan, the news of the Libyan announcement was a disaster for A. Q. Khan. In Islamabad President Musharraf was livid. Libya's declaration had come at a very awkward moment. It would now be impossible for Musharraf to deny A. Q. Khan's activities any longer. Around the world Khan's network also began to panic, realizing that the game was nearly up. The combination of the interception of the *BBC China* and Libya's announcement provided ample publicly usable and independently verifiable information with which to go after the network. Time was running out for Khan.

NEW YORK

September 24, 2003

THE CITY WAS SUFFERING from its annual bout of gridlock as the world's presidents, prime ministers, and dictators descended on the United Nations for the annual General Assembly meeting. Amid the hustle and bustle and the overlapping security details, the most interesting meetings often took place on the sidelines of the main conference as world leaders engaged in some unobtrusive diplomacy. These so called "bilaterals" offered the chance for leaders to meet privately without the public spotlight of a formal visit to each other's country. There were endless arguments within Washington over to whom the President should give his precious time. That morning he would be breakfasting with Caribbean leaders and then talking to leaders of Ghana, Mozambique, and India. But there was one meeting that day that was of particular importance. After years of often hazy and circumspect warnings, the time had come to lay out the case before President Musharraf; there would now be no room to hide when it came to A. Q. Khan. The president and the director of the Central Intelligence Agency (CIA) would together see to that. Khan's time was running out. But it was not quite up. Even now, Musharraf would not put a final end to Khan. It would still take more nudges, more pushes, more pressure to bring him down.

CHAPTER 9

Confronting Musharraf—
Dealing with Khan

THE NOOSE AROUND KHAN'S NECK had been tightening for some time but almost imperceptibly slowly. One by one, his clients' secret nuclear programs were being revealed and the trail was leading back upstream towards its source. But for a long time, the evidence was too weak, and the shield of his reputation too strong, to strike a telling blow. Khan remained confident that he would not be stopped. Complicating everything was the intricate, multi-layered relationship between the United States and Pakistan. Fighting the war on terror was the number one priority for the United States and, for this, Pakistan's support was essential. President Musharraf was seen as the only guarantor of cooperation but he was a leader whose position was vulnerable. Losing him would be a disaster. Any move against Khan would have to work within these constraints.

Perhaps in the early days after September 11 it had been hoped that Pakistan's pivotal position would only delay action against Khan for a short while. But as time went on, Pakistan and its leader became more, not less, important to the war on terror. As Osama bin Laden and the Al Qaeda leadership fled over the border into the tribal areas of Pakistan, President Musharraf's cooperation in hunting them down became essential. Dealing with Khan was hugely important. But not so important that it was worth causing the kind of domestic turmoil that might lead to Musharraf's downfall in the process. The scientist remained extremely popular within elements of the military as well as with Islamists. Imperfect an ally as Musharraf might be, the alternative for the United States would likely be worse. Musharraf is not only aware of his perceived value; he understands how to exploit this. This meant getting Musharraf to confront Khan would take some hard choices—and compromises.

For many Pakistani policymakers, memories of 1990 were still uppermost in their minds when it came to dealing with Washington. If Osama bin Laden was caught and Al Qaeda crushed, what use would Pakistan be to the United States anymore? Would it be just like the end of the Afghan campaign? Would Pakistan again be abandoned? This is a possibility even President Musharraf acknowledges: "after the Soviets left we were left in the lurch and then there was a sense of betrayal and abandonment. It will take some time to overcome this feeling. The fear exists in Pakistan that after the War on Terror is over the U.S. will abandon us again. However, promises I have received from the U.S. make me certain that the U.S. has learnt from the follies of the past and this will not occur again. It will not be in U.S. interests."[1]

The complaints over Khan and his dealings with North Korea had been coming in from Washington since 1998 but they had lacked detail. An American official who transmitted some of those concerns describes them more as "awareness sessions" so that Musharraf knew the issue was on their mind rather than confrontations. The problem was finding evidence that was sufficiently convincing but that could be used without compromising its source. Musharraf had taken some action in 2001 by trying to sideline Khan, but this had little effect. Given Khan's reputation and support in the country, far more than Musharraf himself enjoyed, getting the Pakistani leader to act was not going to be easy.

The failure of the warnings about Khan to have any impact was made all too clear in the summer of 2002. There had been growing evidence of air traffic between North Korea and Pakistan and planes linked to the Pakistan military traveling to Pyongyang. In July U.S. spy satellites spotted a C-130 Pakistan Air Force cargo aircraft at a North Korean airfield. What looked like missile parts were seen being loaded onto the cargo plane. But even more worrisome were the items being unloaded for delivery to North Korea. The activity was blatant with little attempt to hide what was going on. Secretary of State Colin Powell called President Musharraf soon after and made his displeasure clear. Powell told Musharraf that the United States didn't know what was on the plane but it would have to assume the worst. Musharraf replied that the planes were simply returning defective equipment and picking up shoulder-fired SA-16 missiles. Powell warned Pakistan's leader that Islamabad did not need to be looking for trouble at a time like this, adding it would make it harder to cooperate in other areas. Musharraf gave an assurance that nothing would happen again.

After the North Korean enrichment program was exposed publicly, following James Kelly's October 2002 meeting, word began to leak out (often from U.S. officials) that Pakistan might have helped Pyongyang by supplying technology. The accusation met with the most furious denials that Islamabad could muster. There was an extensive debate within the U.S. administration on how to act. "There was a lot of pressure not to embarrass Musharraf," one senior administration official told the New York Times.[2] Powell told reporters that he had talked to Musharraf about the subject and that Pakistan's leader had given him a "four hundred percent assurance that there is no such interchange taking place now." But then added with a smile, "We didn't talk about the past."[3]

Powell pressed for action but did not publicly express frustration as he felt Musharraf was dealing with the issue as fast as he could. Before 9/11 Powell had barely talked to the Pakistani leadership but would go on to have an intensely close working relationship with Musharraf, unusual between a head of state and a foreign minister. They would speak more than eighty times while Powell was in office. Both were former generals who had moved into politics but retained a preference for straight talking. U.S. officials believed Musharraf was a man of his word. But they also knew that he chose his words very carefully, a lesson they had learned from dealing with him over a range of issues, not just A. Q. Khan.

In March 2003 Khan Research Laboratories (KRL) as well as North Korean organizations were placed under sanctions by the United States. This was ostensibly for missile cooperation but word began to leak about suspected nuclear cooperation. The move was a public shot across the bows that patience was running out. It was hoped that the relatively light sanctions on the organizations (and not their host nations) would at least send a public signal to the Pakistani government that it had to act against Khan without undermining Musharraf and exposing his position. With the Iraq War beginning as the sanctions were announced, most of the world was looking elsewhere, which would also limit the public fallout and allow the squeeze on Musharraf to be gentler. The sanctions were carefully targeted against KRL and not the state of Pakistan itself. Musharraf protested against the move and demanded more evidence, continuing to deny that Pakistan had transferred any nuclear or missile technology. But Musharraf still cited a lack of evidence for the charges. "If they knew it earlier, they should have told us," he told the *New York Times*. "Maybe a lot of things would not have happened."[4] It was a line he would continually use with U.S. officials as they pressed him on Khan.

As well as the exposure of North Korean links, pressure began to build from the exposure of Iran's plant in Natanz in August 2002. Questions started to be asked about where the outside help that Iran had clearly received might have come from. By May 2003 the International Atomic Energy Agency (IAEA) was sure it was from Pakistan—the similarities in the centrifuge design allowed few other possibilities. In July the senior IAEA official investigating Iran, Olli Heinonen, wrote to the Pakistanis and asked a Pakistani diplomat to meet with him. At first the diplomat refused but eventually agreed to come as long as he didn't have to answer any questions. In early October Iran began to provide the IAEA with documents about overseas procurement networks including the names of five middlemen from Europe and the Middle East who Iran claimed had helped provide the components.[5] They were all well-known members of the Khan network. Although the Iranians did not spill the beans for a while, claiming Iran only dealt with intermediaries, the finger was clearly pointing through them at Pakistan and Khan. What's more the Iranians were in a bind. When IAEA inspectors analyzed their samples from Iran they found traces of highly enriched uranium particles that were between 36 percent and 70 percent U-235, well above the 1.2 percent U-235 level that Iran had admitted to enriching. These minute particles were to prove another vital clue in the detective work of unravelling the A. Q. Khan network. The question immediately asked was whether these were evidence that Iran had indeed been secretly enriching uranium to weapons-grade levels— potentially the definitive proof the U.S. was after in terms of proving Iran had a weapons program. Faced with a potentially catastrophic problem, the Iranians had no choice but to reveal where the centrifuges had come from and try and shift the blame elsewhere. The centrifuges, they admitted, came from Pakistan and the particles must have been left over from previous use of the machines. Slowly, and far from openly, the Iranians began to talk. By the summer of 2003 the IAEA was writing to Pakistan asking for clarification and comment.

In late June 2003 there was a stalled attempt to confront Musharraf. There was no doubt that persuading the Pakistani leader to act had to be done in person and at the very highest level. The Pakistani president was traveling first to London and then to the United States, where he would first see his son in Boston and then to go to Washington to meet the president, vice president, secretary of state, and other officials. It was agreed that the issue would not be raised in London but that the United States would lay out the case during Musharraf's visit to Camp David. But as the Pakistani leader's plane took off from London on June 20, a call came through from U.S. officials to their British counterparts. There had been a change of plan. The issue of A. Q. Khan would have to be taken off the agenda for the Camp David meeting and would have to wait. It was not explained why. It was a worrying moment for officials working on Khan in Britain, coming at the same time as the Libyan negotiations appeared to be gridlocked. The complicated crosscurrents in dealing with Pakistan after 9/11 seemed to be slowing an already difficult voyage.

By September the CIA and MI6 were tracking the *BBC China* and made the decision to intercept it. Events were moving apace. Musharraf had to be dealt with even if the Libyans didn't come clean. The face-to-face discussion had to take place in person and the General Assembly in New York was the best opportunity when Presidents Bush and Musharraf would be in the same town and when the whole incident could be kept secret. The location of the meeting was the Waldorf-Astoria hotel in New York at a seven-thousand-dollar-a-night suite on the thirty-fifth floor. It was where President Bush stayed during UN meetings and the suite was commonly used for his bilateral meetings with foreign heads of state during the two days of the UN meetings. Late in the morning on September 24 President Bush met with Musharraf. The two men were both soberly dressed in dark suits. Afterwards the press would be told by State Department and White House spokespeople that the men discussed cooperation in the war on terror, providing troops for Iraq, Kashmir, and dialogue with India. "It was an excellent meeting," a senior administration official said immediately afterwards.[6] But at the end of the nearly one-hour session, the president had told the Pakistani leader to be prepared for another visitor and that Musharraf should pay great care to what he said. President Musharraf's visitor was George Tenet, director of the CIA. Tenet made the first detailed presentation of the evidence that his agency along with the British had collected against Khan. It represented indisputable proof that A. Q. Khan was selling nuclear technology and personally profiting from it. The multimedia presentation included an array of detail on Khan's travels around the world, his finances and bank accounts, the scope of his network, his offers to other countries, and the facilities some of those countries had developed based on Khan's assistance—including Iran. Some of the intelligence had to be carefully vetted and presented to hide its real source. The aim was to make sure Musharraf could not claim this time that the evidence was lacking and he didn't have enough to act on. The scale of detail made Khan's activities undeniable. Musharraf was in a tight corner, with little room for maneuver. He later described discovering A. Q. Khan's role as the "most embarrassing" moment of his life and perhaps his "biggest challenge." "I found myself between the devil and the deep sea."[7] The day got worse for Pakistan's President. He would miss a scheduled appointment to meet with President Putin. It was blamed on the traffic.

The meeting was kept secret. Nearly two weeks later a high-powered U.S. delegation came to Islamabad. On October 6, Richard Armitage and the Assistant Secretary of State for South Asia Christina Rocca made their way past the well-manicured lawns as they entered Army House in Rawalpindi, the plush but low-key residence and main office of President Musharraf. The bulk of the meeting was about the War on Terror and Kashmir. But Tenet's message was reinforced. There was a need to act on Khan or else there would be consequences in Pakistan's relations with the United States. The close ties built up post September 11, 2001, should not be taken for granted. Armitage was particularly influential in Islamabad because of his long history in the region and military background. His trip in June 2002 had played a pivotal role in talking down India and Pakistan from what many believed was an imminent nuclear war between the two countries. At this point and for much of the period, the main worry in terms of Pakistan and nuclear weapons wasn't Khan selling them but the Pakistani government using them against India (and vice versa). Armitage,

Powell, and British Foreign Secretary Jack Straw managed to prevent a very close shave following an attack on the Indian Parliament in December 2001. Just before he left for one key trip, Armitage asked a collection of intelligence analysts which of them thought that a war would start. They all raised their hands. Many people in South Asia believed it was only the threat of nuclear annihilation that prevented a conventional war from beginning. In turn, this actually strengthened the reputation of Khan within Pakistan for having brought "security" to Pakistan through its nuclear arsenal.

In October 2003 Armitage could not discuss the ongoing Libyan negotiations to which he, but not the other U.S. officials, was privy. His job was to show that it was not just the intelligence community, but also the diplomats who were saying that it was time to act. Armitage's close relationship with Musharraf and Pakistan would ensure the message was not lost. That same day the head of the Pentagon's Central Command General Abizaid also arrived in Islamabad on a separate visit to meet Musharraf at Army House. The two American delegations did not go in at the same time but virtually passed each other in the corridor. Abizaid also emphasized the need for action in meetings with General Muhammad Yusuf Khan, the number two in the army. Military-to-military contacts often carried as much, if not more weight than those at the highest levels. In addition, British ministers followed up the New York meeting saying they shared the same concerns as the United States. The belief was that it would be more productive to be cooperative than confrontational; better to offer support to Musharraf than be seen as bullying.

Keeping the George Tenet meeting secret, officials within Pakistan later pointed to the Armitage meeting as the key point at which evidence had been presented. "That initiated the process," claims President Musharraf. "That is the time when we first came to know the extent of an involvement, the depth of involvement. And then we certainly started moving and investigating."[8] Pakistani newspaper reports later claimed the U.S. officials presented "mind boggling" evidence against Khan when they arrived.[9] "It seemed that Americans had a tracker planted on Dr. Khan's body," a Pakistani official later told a journalist.[10] But still Khan was not stopped.

Soon after the visit, the IAEA sent further letters to Islamabad requesting comment on the source of the Iranian program. Iran began to reveal more for fear of being implicated in an upcoming report from the IAEA, admitting it bought items from the Khan network but claiming that none of them were related to weapons purchases. By December 2003 Pakistan retracted its denials that anything could have happened with Iran. Just before Christmas a Pakistani team came from Islamabad to Vienna. In a strange meeting, they told IAEA investigators that there was no government involvement whatsoever in whatever had happened. The delegation proceeded to leave the room but then the head of the group returned by himself and handed over a piece of paper with a list of fifteen names, all of them European, who had been part of the Khan network. The combination of Iran, North Korea, and the *BBC China* meant that Khan's days were numbered, and the strategy of continued denial was crumbling fast. But Khan's days numbered more than many expected. It would still take four months for Musharraf to bring him down.

Musharraf was adamant in his conversations with foreign diplomats that he would deal with Khan in his own way and that he knew best how to act. Representations might be made by others over what to do with the scientist but it would be Pakistan that would make the decisions and then inform the United States and UK what these decisions were. The latest U.S. evidence may have been detailed in a way never previously witnessed, but Pakistan was not going to take on trust that it was all true. Musharraf ordered the Inter-Services Intelligence Agency (ISI) and Strategic Planning and Development (SPD) cell of the National Command Authority (NCA) to independently check every single piece of evidence that had been presented. Teams went abroad, including to Dubai, but they found nothing with which to discredit the evidence and avoid the unpalatable conclusions. Of course, since at least 2000 the Pakistani government had already known much of the truth from previous investigations, including intelligence on Khan's full bank accounts and foreign travel. But the government now needed to slowly leak these secrets to the public, to prepare the way for Khan's final, belated dismissal.

It was clear to Khan by December that the net was closing in around him. From late November, one by one his senior aides from KRL were being detained. Pakistani intelligence agents first picked up Mohammed Farooq and Yassin Chauhan, two of KRL's directors.[11] Rumors swept Islamabad that English-speaking individuals were also present, meaning the CIA and FBI must have been involved. Farooq had worked in KRL since the 1980s and was in charge of liaison with foreign customers and suppliers. He had been demoted after A. Q. Khan left in 2001, but still remained at Kahuta and was reported to have been a key figure in dealing with Iran and Libya.[12] More than a dozen individuals from KRL were held and interviewed. Their homes were put under surveillance and their passports seized by the ISI—in part to prevent escape, but also to follow their travels. The government ordered The State Bank of Pakistan to investigate their bank accounts. Publicly, these arrests were attributed to information coming out of the IAEA and the Iranian deal since nothing was yet known to the outside world of Libya and the *BBC China*. "It is too early to make a final judgement, but it seems that some senior people were involved in an activity that was not compatible to their status," a senior official told a Pakistani newspaper.[13]

Other arrests would follow in a second wave in January. Those detained included Major Islam Ul-Haq, a former staff officer to Khan who was arrested while dining at Khan's home, Brigadier Tajwar, former head of security, and Dr. Nazir Ahmed, KRL director of science and technology who was involved with the missile program and North Korea. Security officials came to the men's houses late on a Saturday night and early on Sunday morning in mid-January. The men were detained and held in solitary confinement at a "secret location" in small, hot rooms.[14] The temperature often exceeded 110 degrees, according to family members. Many of these men had been part of the "Timbuktu" group of travelers. Eventually, security officials would detain at least twenty-six individuals, all of whom were later released. At least three KRL director-generals, two retired brigadiers, and one retired major were being debriefed by intelligence officers and many of them began to talk and implicate Khan. The list gives some idea of the degree of support that KRL provided to Khan's activities. Generals Beg and Karamat would be "subjected to debriefing" because of accusations linking Beg to Iran and Karamat to North Korea. They were found innocent.

But moving against Khan himself was a difficult matter. After all, he was someone used to dealing directly with only the highest officials in the country. Two top officials, Lieutenant General Khalid Kidwai, the man in charge of nuclear oversight within the National Command Authority and leader of the investigation, and Lieutenant General Ehsan ul-Haq, head of the ISI, went to Khan's house in December with the evidence.[15] The meeting was tense. The visitors began deferentially talking of the respect in which Khan was held but then moved onto the allegations. Khan, usually a soft-spoken man, was used to being treated with the utmost of deference and did not take well to being confronted. As they began to ask him questions, he reacted with disbelief and started to shout, asking why they were abusing him. They told him to confess or it would all be made public—he denied everything. They began to use veiled threats. Some reports claimed that they warned that they could not protect his daughter, although it was not clear what this meant.[16] The phrase Guantanamo came up according to some of Khan's friends. The two interrogators left empty-handed.

At this point, Khan himself began to panic. Previously, he had considered himself impervious. Now, he began to realize that even his reputation might not be enough to save him. He hastily tried to cover up as much as he could. He sent an emissary to Dubai three times in November and December to remove as much evidence as possible and told Iranian contacts to destroy everything and claim the Pakistani interlocutors were now dead. The emissary was later arrested.[17] Khan also began to organize his rearguard defense. Close aides called up friendly journalists in Pakistan and abroad to say that it was all a lie and Musharraf was giving into the Americans. Khan in at least one case followed this up himself with coded conversations to assert his innocence. At the same time, there were also heavy hints from those around him that Khan would not easily allow all the blame to fall on himself. He told friends that all the army chiefs since Zia had known of his activities and that he would "expose everyone and everything if he was made a scapegoat."[18] His daughter Dina appeared on the BBC on December 24 saying, "there is a definite feeling in this household that my father is being made a scapegoat for the use of other people, and we're also waiting to see what's going to happen."[19]

Khan was no fool and knew how to survive in the internecine, winner-take-all world of Pakistani politics. He needed an insurance policy. In December word went out that information had been smuggled out of the country including videotapes, audiotapes, and documents that directly implicated the military in his activities, allegedly proving that successive chiefs of army staff knew of his deals (particularly deals with North Korea)—this would, of course, include Musharraf himself. There may have also been evidence that some officers had benefited from the deals to the tune of millions.[20] It was reported that Khan's daughter Dina, who could travel easily with her British and Dutch passports, was possibly in London, the Netherlands, Paris, Dubai, and Timbuktu where she spent Christmas Eve at the hotel named after her mother. There would have been plenty of evidence in Khan's hands. Since he returned to Pakistan from the Netherlands in 1976, Khan kept a diary written in English.[21] "That was presumably his insurance policy," believes Peter Griffin who occasionally helped Khan with English words for the diary when he was staying over at the guesthouse. Khan kept the volumes upon volumes of diaries in a large metal trunk in the hallway of his house (Khan once joked that he locked it and lost the key). The current whereabouts of the diaries are unclear, although they are believed to be out of the country.[22]

Meanwhile, pressure from Washington for action was growing. There was deepening frustration at the slow pace of events. Well-sourced articles in the U.S. media were pointing the finger directly at Pakistan for helping the Iranian nuclear program. External events would again complicate matters. On December 14 and 25 President Musharraf narrowly survived two assassination attempts. After 9/11 Musharraf had initially hoped to simply rein in the jihadist groups that the ISI had once created, but the organizations had developed their own momentum and their own agenda, independent of the government. They had nearly brought India and Pakistan to nuclear war after an attack on the Indian parliament in December 2001. In January 2003 Musharraf banned two of the biggest militant groups and now the militants were gunning for him personally. Getting Khan was important to the United States, but not losing a key ally in the War on Terror was an even more important priority. The United States had invested so much in Musharraf personally rather than building broader democratic institutions that it found itself with little leverage to influence Pakistani policy. The failed assassination attempts strengthened the idea in Washington that Musharraf had to be given space to work out a solution that stopped Khan but left Pakistan's president in as strong a position as possible.

Bringing down Khan was proving slow. Despite all the reports of Iranian and North Korean transfers, Khan was looking suspiciously difficult to dislodge. That made Libya vital. When Colonel Gadaffi made his dramatic announcement in December 2003, it was a shock to the Pakistani leader who had no idea it was coming. There was no doubt who had given Libya its program. What's more Khan had supplied a weapons design. There could be no more pretense that any illicit transfers were only of civilian technology. It was the final blow to Musharraf's hopes of withstanding the pressure and avoiding a direct confrontation with Khan.

Though, even then, Musharraf hesitated before moving against the nation's hero. The United States kept ratcheting up the pressure but the Pakistanis kept saying that they were still looking at it and needed more information. Frustration grew in Washington. There was a sense of drift. With patience finally at end, Colin Powell called Musharraf at the end of January. "We are now going to talk general to general," Powell told Musharraf. It was a phrase he used when serious matters were to be discussed between the two men who otherwise had a friendly relationship. It was clear from his tone of voice that this was not going to be a friendly conversation. The secretary of state said Washington had had enough. Powell explained that the information about Khan's provision of nuclear technology to Libya was about to come out. President Bush himself was going to make a speech on it in the coming days and it risked putting Pakistan in a very harsh light with no room for deniability. "You may want to—and I strongly recommend that you do—act," Powell told Pakistan's leader. Behind the advice was a warning. Musharraf got the message.

And so the end finally came a few days later on Saturday, January 31, when the National Command Authority met and formally removed Khan from his position as special adviser to the prime minister. The same day a military guard appeared at Khan's house and he was formally placed under house arrest. Officially, the military would only say that his security had been "enhanced."

From the outside, there is no sign that the complex of buildings on the outskirts of Islamabad is home to the notorious Pakistan intelligence services. It is only after you enter through the ten-foot-tall black gate and go past the green courtyard that the glass doors reveal the insignia of the ISI inside. It was here that Khan was taken for interrogation. The head of the ISI and others told him that he needed to be clean about everything. In the final move of the game, Musharraf ordered Khan to be personally brought to him on February 1. Musharraf told Khan to be straight with him. Khan continued to deny everything. There was no evidence, he said. The United States was making it up. Musharraf then threw the evidence before him.

Musharraf later told aides that he only became angry once when Khan claimed that two (now dead) aides to Bhutto had persuaded him to trade with Iran. Musharraf showed evidence to contradict this and much else, including confessions from others at KRL, details of bank accounts in Dubai opened in false names containing millions of dollars, and a letter he had written to Iranian officials telling them to dismantle the equipment they had received from him.[23] Khan had no way out. His defenses were suddenly breached and then buckled entirely. Khan literally collapsed before the president begging for mercy.

The question remained: What to do about Khan? There were incessant meetings on the subject between top officials. It was not a simple matter. The United States and UK had been promised that if anyone had broken any laws they would be prosecuted. But prosecution was not a pleasant thought for the Pakistani government. A public trial could be a disaster and because of Pakistan's weak export control laws it wasn't immediately obvious what Khan could even be charged with apart from perhaps violating the Official Secrets Act. Khan had so many supporters that it could destabilize the government. There was also the crucial question of what information Khan had on senior military figures. Khan could not be put on trial, nor could he be handed over to the Americans without fear of everything being revealed. The remaining option was for Khan to confess publicly, admit guilt, and take full and sole responsibility for his actions, saving the state and military from any embarrassment. In return he would be pardoned and saved from a worse fate. A deal had to be struck.

An old friend of Khan's, former law minister Senator S. M. Zafar, was brought in to negotiate the final deal over the last two days. Zafar, whose advancing years and receding hairline hide a razor sharp mind, had defended Khan in his court case in the Netherlands in the 1980s; he visited Khan at his house in Islamabad. Khan appeared depressed, tense, and nervous, clearly unsure of his fate. Khan said he was being accused but those accusing him were in part responsible for the misdeeds. But the deal was clear. Confess, say nothing more, and there will be a pardon. He was told that he should reveal everything because if new information later emerged he would be held responsible.

Khan agreed to sign a twelve-page confession, known officially as the First Information Report, which has never been made public. The United

States was never explicitly involved in the detail of the negotiations but made clear its minimum conditions within the context of what it felt Musharraf could achieve. Khan had to be put out of business—including no travel. The United States made it clear that the surveillance and intelligence techniques that had allowed Khan to be monitored so far would be used to make sure these conditions were met.

On February 4 the National Command Authority held a special session to rubber-stamp the final details of what to do with Khan's confession. Khan met Musharraf again for forty-five minutes—pictures show Musharraf in his combat fatigues leaning back and looking sternly at the grey-haired scientist in a dapper suit. In the meeting with Musharraf, Khan accepted full responsibility for activities and submitted a mercy petition to the president, asking for clemency. The president said that the nation had been traumatized by the events of the previous two months and he would consult with the National Command Authority about the mercy position. Khan said that Musharraf "appreciated the frankness with which I gave him the details and Inshallah he will discuss with the cabinet, with the prime minister and with other colleagues and then he will take a decision how to proceed and close the matter."[24]

That afternoon Khan was driven to the squat, yellowing building that housed the studios of Pakistan TV in Islamabad so that he could speak to the nation that had idolized him. His friends had vigorously opposed the idea of a televised confession, arguing it was simply too humiliating but the government had insisted, believing it was the only way of breaking the spell Khan had cast over the populace. Importantly, Khan spoke in English, not Urdu. The real audience was the rest of the world as much as it was the Pakistani people. They were being told that the problem was now being dealt with. Khan declined to use the teleprompter and frequently looked down at his notes, but he spoke firmly and clearly. "It is with the deepest sense of sorrow, anguish and regret that I have chosen to appear before you in order to atone for some of the anguish and pain that has been suffered by the people of Pakistan on account of the extremely unfortunate events of the last two months. . . . My dearest brothers and sisters, I have chosen to appear before you to offer my deepest regrets and unqualified apologies to a traumatized nation. . . . It pains me to realize in retrospect that my entire lifetime achievement of providing foolproof national security to my nation could have been placed in serious jeopardy on account of my activities which were based in good faith but on errors of judgment related to unauthorized proliferation activities." Khan admitted "much of" the evidence he was confronted with was "true and accurate."

The original statement given to Khan to read out talked of an "error of judgment" but Khan himself is believed to have added the phrase "in good faith," which was not in the original agreed text, an attempt to obviate the idea—spread by the government—that he had acted out of greed but instead give the impression he had his own patriotic motives that he simply wasn't being allowed to elaborate upon. His supporters continue to point to these three words as evidence that Khan had really only ever acted in the national interest, and with national approval, but was now being forced to take the fall. For the government, emphasizing Khan's greed was a useful way of de-legitimizing him in the eyes of the people and trying to reduce his image as a self-sacrificing national hero. He ended by taking full responsibility for his actions. "I also appeal to all citizens of Pakistan, in the supreme national interest, to refrain from any further speculations and not to politicize this extremely sensitive issue of national security. May Allah keep Pakistan safe and secure." With those words, the broadcast—and Khan's long career—was over.

Khan's confession was the talk of Pakistan that night. The tension had been building up with the public arrests of Khan's aides and news of investigations. Both Khan's supporters from the conservative wing and opponents of the army on the more liberal side all believed that Khan was taking the rap in a stage-managed process. Initially, many refused to believe what he was up to, still seeing him as a hero rather than someone who might have threatened Pakistan's security through his activities. To have the nuclear program—something that for years had been the source of so much national pride and sense of achievement—suddenly turned into something embarrassing was a shock. It was much easier to blame the whole affair on one man alone and his greed, not the system as a whole. Others, taking their lead from the Pakistani government line, said that in reality it was greedy Western companies who were to blame for selling the technology and Pakistan had once again been made the scapegoat. "His seeking of pardon from the nation should now close this painful chapter and the much revered scientist be allowed to retire in peace with dignity . . . It is sad that our top scientist who is also known as the 'Father of the Islamic bomb' should have been pushed to such a point where he had made an admission in humiliating language. But in spite of this painful development he has in no way lost any of the esteem he enjoyed," wrote one newspaper in an editorial.[25]

Banners appeared saying, "We want Qadeer Khan as President not Prisoner." Demonstrations and rallies cropped up around Pakistan's cities, often orchestrated by the religious parties and the friends and families of the scientists. On the day of Khan's confession, the leader of the Islamic opposition party Jamaat-e-Islami, Qazi Hussain Ahmad, demanded that Musharraf step down because of the humiliation of Khan, accusing the president of "character assassination." "The nation will never forgive this humiliation of national heroes and one person is responsible for it," he said in a statement. Ahmad even went on the Arabic TV station Al-Jazeera by phone and said that Khan had only confessed due to "pressures that were brought to bear on him . . . in fact they reach the point of torture, if you like." Khan's supporters began an effective domestic political campaign to prevent him from being handed over to the United States.

The religious parties used Khan as a chance to attack Musharraf. At a stormy session of parliament on February 16 opposition parties said that Musharraf was selling out to the United States. "The public believes that [Khan] has been forced to do this and that he was shamed. Musharraf went on sinking deeper in the quicksand," said Senator Sami Ul-Haq. "So to save himself, instead of sacrificing himself, he let the disaster fall on the poor scientists. And to help their generals escape from their doom in their quicksand they're trapped in, these scientists took the blame on themselves. . . . [Dr. Qadeer Khan] must have been intimidated. They must have told him to say what they want him to say, otherwise he too shall be sent to Guantanamo."[26] Many darkly warned that the whole episode had been concocted by the United States to weaken Pakistan and particularly to make its nuclear weapons vulnerable. Former ISI Chief Hamid Gul claimed that the United States would use Khan to get "joint custody" of Pakistan's nuclear weapons. Khan had succeeded in identifying himself so strongly in the public's mind with the bomb itself that an attack on Khan was an attack on the nuclear program, an attempt to strip Pakistan of what it had and leave it defenseless. Owning up to Khan's activities, let alone allowing in UN or American investigators, was perceived as virtually handing over the keys to the Pakistan nuclear arsenal to those who wanted to deprive Pakistan of its defense against India.

But some in Pakistan, including in the military, did recognize that it was Khan who had jeopardized the country's security and national interest. Through his activities he had opened up the country's nuclear program and arsenal to sustained international scrutiny, raising question marks over its safety and security and over the credibility and honesty of those officials who guarded it. Pakistan's reputation as any kind of responsible nuclear power had been severely undermined if not permanently shattered. Khan had compromised the security of the technology on which Pakistan's deterrence was based and also sold, partly for his own profit, the work accumulated over decades of thousands of scientists and engineers—work that belonged to the nation as a whole. He'd given Pakistan's many enemies the perfect excuse that Pakistan was a country that could not be trusted with the bomb. "What hurts me is that he betrayed our trust," explains one former Pakistani diplomat. "The trust we had behind the program where we decided to eat grass to get the bomb."

Even with his confession of having been a lone actor, events threatened Pakistan's international image, not least because the possibility of any proliferation had been so adamantly denied for so long. After years of denial, Pakistan was now slowly being forced to take back almost every statement it had made. The Pakistani government needed a careful but aggressive public relations offensive. Even before the confession was made public, select Pakistani journalists were summoned to be briefed by the President's office on Sunday night of February 1. In a detailed two-and-a-half-hour briefing, officials said that the government had known nothing of Khan's activities but that he had indeed passed on technical information to other countries for personal profit. But all proliferation had stopped under the new NCA brought in by President Musharraf. Khan, it was said, had only acted for a short period—with Iran between 1989 and 1991, with Libya in the 1990s, and North Korea until 2000. In the end, all of these dates would prove to be wrong.[27]

In its early stages, the carefully constructed deal, in which Khan confessed, was pardoned, and not handed over to the United States, nearly collapsed. Officials became nervous over Khan's cooperation and his possible insurance policy, partly because the incriminating documents and tapes had not been returned as agreed. As a result, senior Pakistani officials made clear that the pardon given to Khan was only "conditional" and that if more evidence of his activities arose he could still be in danger of being prosecuted.[28] The message got across and the deal held.

On February 5 General Musharraf held a dramatic press briefing to answer the avalanche of questions from both Pakistani and international media. During it, he gave a very detailed explanation of how he believed Khan was able to get away with his actions. In a session that went on for hours, Musharraf began by saying he had just returned from Europe where everyone had repeatedly hurled accusations against him and Pakistan for supporting terrorism and supporting proliferation.[29] The "sad thing" in the president's eyes was the way in which even the Pakistani media were jumping on the bandwagon and saying that the government and military were involved in proliferation. Some were perhaps acting on "foreign instructions," implying that they were being disloyal. He warned that the result of the whole affair could be UN sanctions. "There should be only one thing in our minds. Pakistan—it has to be defended," said Musharraf.

Would the United States now force Pakistan to give up control over its prized nuclear assets, as was being speculated? "Rollback is not being done. No one is telling me. Stop saying this," Musharraf told the journalists. "I have seen death very closely, not once but six times. We are not one of the cowards. We will put our lives at stake for these strategic assets . . . The foremost concern for Pakistan, for all of us, for me is rollback . . . Ladies and gentlemen, this country will never roll back its nuclear assets, its missile assets. I will be the last man doing it. . . . I repeat once again that there is no compromise on vital national interest. We have two national vital interests, our nuclear program—being a nuclear state and the Kashmir cause is our national vital interests. No leader can go back on these two."

Musharraf played down the scale of Khan's activity. There were sixty-five hundred scientists and forty-five thousand people working in nuclear organizations and only eleven individuals had been detained. Musharraf gave a detailed explanation of KRL's autonomy and lack of oversight as a justification for the lack of government knowledge. "This is absolutely true that neither the government is involved, nor are government officials involved. Nor is the army involved. Because there was maximum autonomy for clandestine cover operation, financial autonomy, administrative self control. . . . Security was under the organization itself. . . . And this was the correct approach I tell you. Otherwise, we'd have been unable to move ahead."

The proliferation ended "roughly around 2001" when Khan retired and proper controls were established, Musharraf said. Even now though, he was still wary of Khan's status, saying, "He is my hero. He always was and still is, because he made Pakistan a nuclear power." He added that he had decided to pardon him on the basis of cabinet and NCA discussions. Musharraf was pressed on why he had allowed Khan to be humiliated by having to appear on TV and why a face-saving solution had not been found. "I thought I provided him this face saving," said Musharraf. "Really, whatever I have done I've tried to shield him actually . . . [but] you cannot shield a hero and damage the nation. . . . The only question that arises here is that—is Pakistan important or the hero important? Pakistan is important."

There was careful choreography in the response by Musharraf and the United States as well as in Khan's statement; they were all designed to give the impression Pakistan had dealt with the rogue scientist Khan. Pakistan had been "very forthright in the last several years with us about proliferation. We do not have any information they are involved," Richard Armitage told those who pressed him on the role of the government just as the story was breaking.[30]

But both sides knew that this could not have been the case even if they were loath to acknowledge it publicly. At a private meeting with a senior American official soon after Khan's confession, Musharraf claimed that he had known nothing about Khan's activities because everything Khan did had been run through different channels of authority to which he did not have access. Even when he was army chief, Khan's work had been run through the former president's office in the 1990s, he explained. Musharraf may have been trying to shift the blame but in doing so he was also acknowledging that Khan had not been acting alone and did indeed have the backing from some parts of the state. But the Pakistani and U.S. officials kept even this admission, however partial, secret. Admitting any form of state responsibility would undermine the notion, propagated extensively by both sides, that Khan was a lone "rogue" actor. The man who was once lauded for bringing his nation the ultimate means of security was being cut loose and hung out to dry for the sake of the strategic relationship between the two countries. It was a final reversal of the situation in which that relationship had been his protector and shield.

U.S. officials quickly said that they were content with Pakistan's explanation and actions and were careful not to push for Khan to be handed over. They refused to be drawn into judging Khan or even on whether they wanted access to him. U.S. officials were conscious that the first peace talks between India and Pakistan were about to start in mid-February 2004. Speaking in Islamabad on March 18, Colin Powell referred to the whole A. Q. Khan affair as an "internal matter," and said he was confident that the Pakistani government would fully disclose whatever it learned.[31] It was remarkable that the United States should be so happy to accept Pakistan's investigation of itself. Of course, a finding of state-led proliferation would have threatened the three-billion-dollar U.S. aid package that the United States had promised to Pakistan in 2003 and the U.S.-Pakistani alliance on which the United States was relying to deal with Al Qaeda.

President Bush and all U.S. officials have always been lavish in their praise for President Musharraf's cooperation. In turn, they have also been distinctly muted in their public pronouncements over Pakistan's nuclear proliferation activities. Officials consistently said that they had no evidence that President Musharraf or the government as a whole had been complicit or knowledgeable of Khan's activities. As happened in the past, for instance with the sale of Chinese ring magnets to Pakistan in the mid-1990s, the United States found it easier to focus on the individual rather than the state in order to avoid sanctions at a difficult time.

Congress was a major concern for the Bush administration during the period when Khan's activities became public. Many congressmen believed that the leadership of Pakistan had to be complicit in Khan's activities. With its historic tilt against Pakistan and favor of tough action on proliferation, there was a danger that Congress could undermine Musharraf and counter-terrorist cooperation. Richard Armitage provided classified briefings on Capitol Hill in order to convince congressional members that Musharraf was worth supporting. Armitage argued that Musharraf was the best available option for both Pakistan and the United States and that President Musharraf had shown great courage in taking down Khan, a figure whom Armitage likened to a Pakistani version of George Washington and Thomas Edison combined.

Musharraf's final deal with Khan was clearly not to everyone's liking. Critics argued that Musharraf is a "marginal satisfier" of everybody with whom he deals, including Washington, doing just enough to satisfy demands but going no further. And though this might appear necessary for his survival, it led to incomplete and inconsistent policies and conclusions. Some argued that the United States could have been tougher on Pakistan and demanded Khan be handed over. But in Washington, it was simply viewed by key figures within the administration as the most that could be achieved without risking bringing down an important ally. In the midst of the Iraq War, Khan, the world's most dangerous proliferator, had been put out of business, Libya had been disarmed, and Musharraf was preserved to fight other battles. It might not be ideal but for many in Washington it was enough. But was it?

Access to Khan was important because even though the head of the network had been put out of business, his colleagues were still at large. And while Libya was out of the game, other customers like North Korea and Iran were still working hard off the information and material provided by Khan. But just how much had Khan given them? There was still much work to be done to ensure that the network really was dead and that its damage could be limited. But many of the questions still outstanding were ones only Khan could answer.

KUALA LUMPUR

November 10, 2003

IT WAS EVENING WHEN THE HEAD OF THE SPECIAL BRANCH of Malaysian Police, Bukit Aman, received two visitors, an American and a Briton. The CIA and MI6 officers had flown over to deal with a delicate issue. The officers laid out the information their agencies had collected on the activities of associates of A. Q. Khan within Malaysia. They explained they were tracking an international proliferation network and one in which a Malaysian resident, B. S. Tahir, was a key figure. They explained that a workshop in the town of Shah Alam in Malaysia had been used to manufacture components for centrifuges. They knew this because they'd stopped the *BBC China* a month earlier and had found the five containers full of wooden boxes packed with components. The boxes had the logo of the Malaysian company stamped on them. The officers asked for help, in view of the "intense interest in this matter at the highest levels of the U.S./UK governments." They also stressed the need for secrecy. The meeting occurred while the Libya negotiations were ongoing but it was perceived as important to bring Malaysia on board before the issue exploded into public view.

The Malaysian prime minister was briefed by his officials three days later on November 13 and he ordered a "detailed and transparent investigation" by the police. Tahir was picked up. By February the police had released a twelve-page statement, based largely on Tahir's interrogation. The statement had been designed to exonerate the Malaysian Company SCOMI from having had any knowledge of the Libya deal and what the parts being manufactured in its plant were intended for. The press release did not mention the links between Tahir and the company, SCOMI, in which the prime minister's son had been involved as an investor, although there is no evidence that the prime minister's son knew anything about the Libya deal.

Around the world, the network was unraveling, but the process would be far from simple, as the Malaysian experience would reveal. The *BBC China* was to be used to confront not just Libya and Pakistan but also other governments in an attempt to enlist their help in pulling up the network from its roots. Since the first disclosures about Khan, arrests have taken place all over the world from

Europe to Africa to Asia. Investigators have been consistently surprised by its scale and reach but also remain deeply worried that there may be more that they do not know. Getting access to Tahir and others was vital to find out the full story of the Khan network but proved far from easy. This was a particular problem when some major questions were either unanswered or beginning to emerge about how much damage had really been done, and what dangers might still be out there.

CHAPTER 10

Unraveling the Network

As THE NEWS ABOUT LIBYA BROKE, the Khan network went into a tail-spin. Urgent messages filtered out as Tahir began to panic. "He got a message to me at the beginning of 2004 in January to say destroy all your records," remembers Peter Griffin. "I said, 'What records?' He said, all the records of everything you've got that we've done business with. Just destroy it. I said, 'why?' He said because I'm telling you to. I said no, you give me a reason. Because if you are that desperate to destroy records of what you have been up to and if you can't answer that, I'm keeping those records." Griffin, like others, would keep the information, realizing it was his only evidence as everything unraveled.[1]

For the international team working against Khan, speed was of the essence in exploiting Libya's surprise move. There was now the chance to unite the wider international community in an attack on the global tentacles of the network. But there were also some ruffled feathers to smooth over. The morning after Libya made its announcement, two senior British officials who had been involved in the operations against Khan were on a flight to Vienna. The Director of the International Atomic Energy Agency (IAEA) Mohamed ElBaradei was supposed to be on holiday by now, but a few days earlier he had been persuaded not to go but without being told why. He was not in the best of moods. He had found out why he had been asked to stay in Vienna as he switched on the news on the evening of December 19 and saw Libya's surprise announcement that it had nuclear weapons and would be dismantling them. The Libyan deal was embarrassing for the IAEA. Another country had managed to evade its safeguards and develop a nuclear weapons program without the agency's knowledge. What's more, two of the organization's members—Britain and the United States—had known about it and engaged in negotiations over its future without telling the IAEA.

But for IAEA investigators like Olli Heinonen, the Libyan admission was one that promised to bear much fruit. There would be a whole new case opened on Libya, and the United States and UK offered all the visit reports and information that they had collected. The agency also now had a huge range of new leads on Khan and Iran that they could begin to utilize.

On December 20 El Baradei met in Vienna with Libya's nuclear chief Matuq Mohammed Matuq who promised that Libya would now disarm. But there followed the first of a number of messy rows between the IAEA and Washington over the actual process of disarmament. The IAEA felt that now that the program had been declared and the Libyans had invited them in, they, as the nuclear watchdog, should play more than the supporting role that some in Washington had in mind. John Bolton, then the top proliferation official at the State Department, was now involved in the process, which complicated matters. The U.S. relationship with the IAEA had dipped to a new low as Bolton had been leading a campaign to prevent El Baradei from being reappointed for a third term as director. El Baradei even reportedly believed the United States was bugging his phone. "It becomes unpleasant when you apparently cannot even have a private phone conversation with your wife or your daughter," he told journalists. (Although the bugging would have been performed to listen into conversations with Iranian diplomats).[2] Some in Washington also pointed out that the IAEA technically was not supposed to be involved in nuclear weapons. In fact, almost all of the organization's senior members (including El Baradei, an Egyptian, and Heinonen, from Finland) were not cleared to even look at a Libyan warhead design since they did not come from an existing nuclear weapon state. To try and work out who would do what, Libyan intelligence chief, Musa Kusa, came to London for talks and on January 19, British official, William Ehrman, and Bolton flew to Vienna to meet with El Baradei. The resultant careful compromise was one in which the IAEA was in charge of verifying the disarmament of Libya's weapons of mass destruction (WMD programs but the United States and UK would provide "logistical help," although in practice this meant that the United States and UK did the actual dismantling while the IAEA watched.

A small IAEA team had gone into Libya at the end of December to get some sense of the size of the existing program. The team included ElBaradei, Olli Heinonen, and Jacques Baute, the head of the Iraqi inspections team who, coming from France, was authorized and had the expertise to examine the weapons design. The real disarmament began on January 20. The priority was to get the most sensitive materials out fast, just in case the Libyans changed their mind. The plane that brought in the U.S. team, led by Don Mahley, waited at the airport for the most important item after its passengers had disembarked. The weapons design was "officially" handed over to Mahley and his British counterpart David Landsman by the supervisor of Libya's program, Matuq, in a slightly odd ceremony in a meeting room of the Libyan National Board of Scientific Research, which was the main front organization for the nuclear program. The designs were in a white plastic bag with the name of an Islamabad draper, "the Good Looks Fabrics and Tailor" emblazoned across the front. It wasn't the subtlest of signs of the real source of Libya's imported expertise. The Good Looks Fabrics and Tailors in Islamabad caters to Pakistan's elite, past and present. One of its regular customers for many years was Abdul Qadeer Khan, who, as well as purchasing his own suits there also referred many of colleagues and friends. After the story of the Libyan bag broke the proprietor reportedly removed the framed picture of Dr. Khan from the wall of the shop.

Jacques Baute and his team from the IAEA examined the papers inside the bag and said that they looked like the real thing. The papers were placed in a locked briefcase with seals from the IAEA and taken out to the waiting plane to be flown to the U.S. A mechanical problem that delayed the plane gave the IAEA more time to inspect the papers after arguments with U.S. officials, one of whom slept with the designs to keep them safe. The whole process had to be carried out secretly. The British and American officials were conscious of Libyan spies watching every movement and also of the sensitivity for the Libyan leadership in handing over material for which they had paid so much. At the other end, armed couriers were sent to Dulles airport to take the weapons design straight to the high-security vault in the

Department of Energy building to which the IAEA was offered access if they required it as part of their investigation.

The designs were important not just for their forensic value in the investigation but as a very public sign that A. Q. Khan was in the nuclear weapons business, not just nuclear energy as he and others in Pakistan claimed. The designs were for a bomb that would weigh around five hundred kilograms, not the latest, most advanced Pakistani design.[3] The papers were a compilation of many different elements and included drawings, instructions, and notes. Many of the notes were in Chinese. Others were handwritten in English. The latter apparently came from Pakistanis who had attended seminars given by weapons experts in China in the early 1980s. Some of the lecture notes were in English and include the date and location of the lecture as well as drawings. One note said, "Munir's bomb would be bigger"—possibly a boast since the smaller a design , the easier it was to fit it on a missile.[4] The weapon was crude by modern standards. The package handed over by the Libyans included around 95 percent of the blueprints needed to make a bomb, including manufacturing and assembly instructions. But some crucial designs required for implosion were missing for reasons unclear. Was Khan scamming the Libyans or holding something back for a final payment? The Libyans claimed that the network had, unasked, given them the designs as the "cherry on the cake" of the deal. But this didn't make sense since the designs were far too valuable to have been given away for nothing. There were no obvious indications that Libya had done any work using the documents or yet purchased any parts for a weapon. It was impossible to know if any further copies had been made.

A few days later more of the most sensitive nuclear material was sent out on a chartered flight, again in a hurry. This included the cylinders of UF6, the largest of which was the size of a small car. Before they were taken, the IAEA team took swipes of the inside and outside, which could later be tested in laboratories to determine the origin of any nuclear material. Also removed were key components like power converters, control panels, and components for the centrifuges, which meant that whatever was left behind would be useless. In March a chartered ship would take away the rest of the centrifuge material and also the North Korean missile equipment. Some of the material was still in cargo boxes marked KRL for Khan Research Laboratories and clearly had come straight from Kahuta in Pakistan.

Politics—and Iraq—complicated the aftermath of the Libya deal. Soon after American journalists were taken to the U.S. government facility at Oak
Ridge in Tennessee to be shown these spoils of the Libyan deal. Because
many of the centrifuge parts were still in their original packing crates, there
would be some debate over whether the United States was over-hyping the
progress of the Libyan program in its briefings to the press. "The program
was much more advanced than we assessed. It was much larger than we
assessed," Robert Joseph, head of non-proliferation at the White House,
told reporters. The administration skirted over the fact that what was on
display were casings—not working centrifuges—the actual rotors were
missing and Libya had not actually managed to enrich any uranium yet.
There remains a debate over the quality of the material Khan supplied to
Libya and whether the Libyans really had the capability to put it together.
Much of it remained in boxes. However, the Libyans had run UF6 in the
test stands and were being provided equipment to make their own rotors.
The politicized nature of proliferation in the wake of Iraq meant that every
claim was treated with scepticism and examined for spin. The reality was
that Khan had taken Libya far further than they could ever have gone alone,
but the Libyans were not yet close to the bomb.

For Libya, the road out of the cold was bumpier than it had hoped.
Through 2004 the U.S. began to lift its sanctions and restore diplomatic
ties. In March Tony Blair visited Gadaffi in his tent for two hours of talks.
But the high expectations on the Libyan side have not always been met.
Gadaffi's son talked of expecting help "economically, politically and even
militarily."[5] But his father would later claim he had received no "concrete
rewards" for his decision.[6] One problem was that in the summer of 2004,
details emerged of a Libyan plot to kill Crown Prince Abdullah of Saudi
Arabia, a plan that had emerged out of a clash between the Saudi leader
and Gadaffi at an Arab summit. This slowed down the process of normaliz-
ing relations with Libya and removing it from the list of state sponsors of
terrorism. Finally in May 2006 U.S.-Libyan relations were normalized.

The playing out of Libya's disarmament was intended to have wider
significance since some, including the Libyans themselves, hoped it could
act as a model for other "rogue" states like Iran, Syria, or North Korea. But
Gadaffi himself has said Libya did not receive enough in terms of security

guarantees and civilian technology to make that possible. The Bush administration was keen—some felt too keen—to make the point that it had succeeded with Libya simply by taking a tough stance and forcing the Libyans to act. There was a desire on the part of the United States to downplay that there had been any direct negotiations. This was partly because of the Iraq policy in which it was argued that Saddam had been offered a simple choice of full cooperation or regime change and had failed to take it while Libya had been offered a similar, simple choice and accepted it. But critics argued that with Libya, negotiations with the United States and UK had occurred that included the implicit, but perhaps not explicit, offer of incentives and cooperation in return for disarmament.[7] Because U.S. policy was based around making countries believe that pursuing weapons of mass destruction made them less rather than more secure, the fear was that some countries might believe that the lesson of the Libyan experience was that by developing a weapons program, a country could acquire a bargaining chip that could then be negotiated away in return for other incentives.

One key advantage of breaking the Khan network through Libya was that it provided a wealth of documentation and hard evidence that would be difficult to dispute, unlike the secret intelligence that had previously been collected. There was no need to protect any intelligence source or method since the Libyans had voluntarily handed over so much information about who had supplied them. What's more the IAEA was now involved. This was critical as it meant that those countries that were sceptical of the U.S. intelligence on weapons of mass destruction in the wake of Iraq had a completely separate, independent organization validating all the information. The IAEA also had a record of standing up to the United States and not supporting its policy on Iraq. This made the evidence hard to resist, even for those states that might have been keen not to confront the reality of proliferation within their borders. Once the BBC China had been intercepted in October 2003, the work began with the United States and U.K in going after the network with a division of labor based on who had the best contacts and information on each country. There were at least a dozen countries in which Khan and his associates were known to have operated—and the real figure could have been higher.

John Wolf, the U.S. assistant secretary of state for non-proliferation, was tasked with the diplomatic legwork of dealing with countries like South

Africa, Malaysia, Turkey, and Dubai. For the first few months of 2004, exploiting the documents and preparing the case was the priority. "We were then able to go to individual countries and demonstrate the way in which this organization operated clandestinely within countries to do things that violated some combination of their international obligations under the treaty for the non-proliferation of nuclear weapons, their own export controls, their own tax laws, their own customs and export licensing regulations, their company registration procedures—whatever. A lot like [dealing with] Al Capone we didn't care what countries used to wrap up the network. What we wanted to demonstrate is that a very dangerous network had operated in their countries—so we showed clear evidence of what that contribution was. We provided them with ideas but they made decisions about which aspects of their national law they were going to invoke and how they were going to deal with people and assets within their borders. We did that in all the countries. The result was a kind of snowballing investigation in which new information came up that helped to add to what we already had." [8]

Kuala Lumpur, the Malaysian capital, was one of Wolf's first stops. Being a former ambassador to the country made the potentially tricky task somewhat easier. "We had a picture that showed a centrifuge. The picture had black and red and all the pieces that were red were things made at SCOMI. We were able to describe to the Malaysians that these pieces were unique. They had no application outside of the centrifuge. They certainly weren't rotors for oil equipment or whatever the invoices said they were. And they weren't going to Dubai. They were going to Libya. We provided them with a pretty full description of what appeared to us to be to attempts to deceive Malaysian authorities as to the truth of what was going on at SCOMI. This was politically sensitive for a number of reasons. We made clear that B. S. Tahir was our target—that he was knowledgeable and at the heart of it. We also provided some information on the larger network beyond just SCOMI, [on Tahir's] role as the chief operating officer of A. Q. Khan Worldwide Inc." The relationship with Malaysia was not the easiest, partly because of Tahir's connection and partly because it was the most public wing of the network and therefore attracted considerable amounts of publicity. The Malaysians were unhappy with a statement by CIA Director George Tenet that one of the Khan network's largest plants had been shut down because they believed that it made it sound as if all of those at the SCOPE factory were complicit (SCOPE being the plant set up by the Malaysian parent company SCOMI to manufacture the components). Staff provided tours to journalists to show that the factory was still operating. They denied any relation to Khan and emphasized that the deal had just been a one off order over a period that wasn't repeated and that the parts made in Malaysia were not sophisticated. They said that not only had the staff at SCOPE not known what was being manufactured but also that SCOPE had not broken any Malaysian laws. Nor had Tahir technically broken any laws either but eventually, he was placed under arrest in May 2004 under Malaysia's Internal Security Act, which allows individuals to be held without trial or specific charge. The Malaysian prime minister has made clear on a number of occasions that Tahir will not be handed over to anyone else. The IAEA has been given some limited access to Tahir but not as much as it wanted. The CIA was able to talk to him only twice in the first twenty months of his detention and on the second occasion he claimed to have remembered previously forgotten details of sales to Iran.[9]

The U.S. State Department team also traveled to Turkey in the spring of 2004 and gave an exhaustive presentation of what it knew about Turkish firms who had been involved in the Libya deal. This led to an aggressive move by the Turkish government to clean up their end of the Khan network. The Turkish customs service developed enough evidence to indict several corporations and proved highly effective in trying to root out the problems. A key individual involved in the Libya deal, Gunas Cire, died of a heart attack. Spanish and British investigators also began investigations regarding citizens and businesses in their countries. Some of these countries were tipped off by British and American officials after the *BBC China* was raided in October but before the Libya deal was announced in December. Their aim was to have the countries prepared to move against key individuals once the Libya deal became public and for them not to be caught by surprise. They were asked to keep their knowledge secret until then.

On the evening of September 1, 2004, the South African division of the Khan network was attacked. Nine months earlier, in December 2003, the United States had asked South African authorities to look into the company Tradefin, which had been tasked with building the piping and feed systems for the Libyan centrifuge plant. Armed police surrounded and searched the Tradefin factory and offices and arrested Johan Meyer. They also took away truckloads of equipment. The investigators were in for a surprise when they raided the factory. Behind a corrugated wall, they found eleven containers holding 200 tons of piping for the centrifuge plant still intact. Investigators also found a video from KRL, documents with Khan's signature, and a business card from Tahir, in a steel trunk.[10]

The panic engendered by Gadaffi revealing his nuclear program in December 2003 had spread to South Africa as well as to Tahir in Dubai. According to a South African indictment, Gerhard Wisser is alleged to have sent this message to Meyer: "the bird must be destroyed, feathers and all." Another text message said, "They have fed us to the dogs," but Meyer didn't destroy the centrifuge equipment as the message requested.[11] Wisser's lawyer says he was innocent and that he told Meyer to destroy the components when he realized that they might be heading to Libya illegally.

The South African authorities charged Meyer with importing and exporting a Spanish-made lathe without permits and possessing components of a centrifuge plant without necessary authorization. On September 8 the charges were dropped as Meyer agreed to turn state's witness. On the same day, Gerhard Wisser and Daniel Geiges were arrested in South Africa. The men deny the charges and say they did not know the destination of the material they had put together.

Gotthard Lerch, the long-time German supplier of Khan, was arrested in November 2004 in Switzerland on an arrest warrant from the German authorities. He went on trial in early 2006 and German prosecutors alleged he received up to $34 million for helping Libya from 1999.[12] Urs Tinner, son of Friedrich Tinner (another long-time supplier of Khan) was arrested in Germany and was handed over to the Swiss authorities at the border near Basel in May 2005, following an extradition request. Rumors swirled around the German press that the CIA might have recruited Tinner as a spy in Malaysia where he was overseeing the SCOPE plant in 2003.[13] According to some reports, Tinner claimed that he sabotaged some of the equipment coming out of SCOPE to make it unusable. Swiss authorities have complained that the U.S. has failed to offer legal assistance in its case against Tinner despite repeated requests.

In December 2005 Henk Slebos, Khan's longtime friend and associate, was sentenced by a Dutch court for shipments between 1999 and 2000 of dual-use technology to the Institute of Industrial Automation in Pakistan—an organization that acted as a front for Khan. For decades, a major source of frustration for those trying to halt proliferation has been that proliferators are not punished severely enough, even when they have been caught red-handed, especially when contrasted with the damage they have done. The weak sentence handed out to Slebos of only one year does little to assuage those concerns over the failure to put individuals out of business.

The aim of the roll up was always to expose as much of the network as possible in order to make it impossible for its members to continue to go about their business or for states to tolerate their activities. "We probably have achieved our objective of putting so much sunlight and bleach on this network that we killed it off," argues Wolf. "But did the perpetrators pay a price commensurate with the damage they have done to international security? The answer is probably no. Are governments sufficiently chastened and knowledgeable about what happened literally under their noses that they have taken the kinds of action necessary to prevent this ever happening again? Not yet. They are doing some of it. But . . . when I hear about countries that have or haven't upgraded their export controls and still aren't aggressively enforcing them then I worry that the situation hasn't been fixed and I think the perpetrators should have paid a serious price as a message to the market place that the international community won't tolerate this and will act aggressively."[14] A few U.S. hawks have suggested that the only way of stopping proliferation is to make the consequences more like those for being involved in terrorism—a life-risking venture for those involved, whether businessmen or scientists, with the hope of making them rethink the cost-benefit calculations of helping a program.

Unraveling Khan's operations has given investigators much new material to use against Iran in trying to understand its nuclear program and determine whether or not it is aimed at acquiring weapons rather than just energy, as the Iranians assert. The IAEA has mounted its own wide-reaching investigation, led by Olli Heinonen. As well as being passed information on Libya's dealings from Libya itself and from the U.S. and UK, the IAEA searched through warehouses in Dubai where the network had housed centrifuges and parts destined for customers. Iran named some business-men who formed part of the Khan network in October. When they were contacted by the IAEA they initially refused to talk and said it was all some kind of mistake. It was harder for them to do so when the Libyans also disclosed their names in December.

Intelligence from the Khan network would become a key lever to pry information out of Tehran. Information that Tahir and other members of the network have provided in interviews has forced Iran to slowly admit to things it had previously concealed. That the network had passed P-2 centrifuge information to Libya made the IAEA go back to Iran and demand to know whether it too had received designs for this more advanced machine. Thus far, the Iranians had only admitted a P-1 program, but under questioning, the Iranians for the first time, in early 2004, admitted that they also had received P-2 data. Members of the Khan network told the IAEA that there was more paperwork behind the 1987 deal than the one-page offer that the Iranians produced in January 2005, forcing the Iranians eventually to reveal more as the IAEA began investigating. As happened with Libya, diplomatic tensions began to appear between Pakistan and Iran. In May 2005 Iran demanded an explanation after President Musharraf gave an interview to a German magazine in which he said that Iran was "very anxious" to develop nuclear weapons.[15]

The Iranians took a number of steps to conceal the origin and extent of its enrichment program as the IAEA began to increase pressure for access. The Kalaye Electric Company was a large warehouse facility on the Ab-Ali Highway in Tehran where Iran had been secretly testing and developing centrifuges since 1995. An Iranian opposition group had revealed its location, but the Iranian authorities delayed access to inspectors, saying it was simply a private clock factory. As the wrangling continued, satellite imagery revealed trucks moving a large amount of material out of the site. Eventually the Iranians allowed IAEA inspectors in to investigate. They found that the entire site had been sanitized. Even the flooring and ceiling tiles had been removed. "It was even smelling of paint," remembered one inspector. "It was obvious they wanted to hide something."[16] The Iranians' aim was to stymie the ability of the IAEA to collect environmental samples that contained traces of uranium. Unfortunately for the Iranians, they had underestimated the technical capability of the latest sampling equipment. Inspectors began taking samples from places that the Iranians hadn't thought to cleanse, including doorframes and even the rubber seals in toilets. When the samples were analyzed, inspectors still found particles of uranium, forcing the Iranians to concede that they had carried out enrichment activities at the facility. What's more, some of the particles were enriched to more than 30 percent, far higher than needed in a nuclear fuel program. Did this come from a still secret enrichment program or, as the Iranians claimed, from Pakistan? The only way of knowing would be to compare the particles with those in Pakistan's program, since each facility in the world has its own "signature," which labs have learned to trace.[17] At first Pakistan refused to hand over any of its centrifuges. Mohammed El-Baradei tried to convince the Pakistani envoy at the UN. "We just take a swipe sample, that would help us a lot frankly and get you off the hook," he told him. "We also need some people to talk about what happened to validate the Iranian story again in a very confidential ways because the Iranians now tell us who came and who did what." "There have been a lot of sensitivities and suspicions," replied the Pakistani diplomat. "We have to be very careful how we do this."[18]

In Pakistan, prickliness over accusations of Pakistan's support for the Iranian program grew with the demand for Pakistan to hand over equipment that would verify Iran's claims. In March 2005 there was a stormy debate in Parliament with dozens of lawmakers walking out. "This will serve as an excuse for the U.S. to attack Iran first and then Pakistan," said one member of parliament.[19] But eventually parts from the same set sold by Khan to Iran were flown to Vienna for testing. Scientists spent months forensically examining the data—both in the IAEA's own labs and in those operated by other countries—looking at the unique oxygen signature of the particles. Nuclear forensics has close similarities with criminal forensics in searching for tiny clues and scientific fingerprints or signatures that can identify the source of a nuclear material. This is done by analyzing the age of a material, the types of impurities, and the chemical forms associated with it. So far, the signs point to Pakistan, not a secret Iranian program, as the source of the contamination.[20]

The Iranians clearly learned lessons about the combination of commercial satellite imaging and environmental sampling from their experience at Kalaye. When inspectors next asked for access to another site at Lavisan-Shian, which was alleged by Iranian opposition groups to be the site of weapons related activities, the entire site was razed and all buildings removed. The Iranians claim that this was due to a dispute between the municipality of Tehran and the Ministry of Defence, but even the soil was removed, making it hard for the IAEA to carry out sampling activities when it was let in. But they still found traces of highly-enriched uranium, a significant discovery because the site is controlled by the military, which Iran has denied having been linked to the nuclear program.

The IAEA believes that the Khan deals in the 1980s and 1990s are the key to understanding the Iranian nuclear program and whether it is peaceful or military in intent. IAEA officials are adamant that they want to see all the documentation associated with the 1987 meeting and not just the short note that Iran provided in January 2005, which has no dates, names, signatures, or addresses. The IAEA believes that there was more to the offer and is sceptical that it is getting the full story. Agency officials have repeatedly requested more information, including shipping documents. An Iranian opposition group has claimed that between 1994 and 1996, Khan handed over the same weapons design that he sold to Libya. Both British and American intelligence officials also strongly suspect—but cannot prove—that Khan provided the design. "Why would that part of the deal be so different from Libya?" asks someone involved in the investigation. If so, then is another copy of the Pakistan-China weapons design being worked on somewhere in Iran?

In late 2005 the Iranians slipped up. In an office in Tehran, they handed over two boxes crammed full of papers to IAEA inspectors and told them they could examine the documents, but could not take them away or photograph or copy them. While the inspectors leafed through the papers, the Iranians videotaped them.[21] One set of ten to fifteen pages caught the inspectors attention—documents on how to cast uranium into metallic spheres, something which would only be useful if you were building a bomb. The Iranians maintain that they never asked for this document and it was simply handed over by the Khan network and was never used in any way.

What makes these documents even more intriguing is that, according to reports, those who have seen both sets say they also contained similarities to weapons design and manufacturing plans found in the Good Looks Fabrics and Tailor bag handed over by the Libyans.[22] This could be evidence that the Iranians had indeed received weapons help from Khan and were not just interested in civilian energy.

The Iranian missile program also fuels suspicions. Iran has received help on ballistic missiles from Russia, North Korea, and China to the point of being self-sufficient in the production of the long-range Shahab 3. North Korea was a particularly important supplier from around 1993, roughly the same time Pyongyang began assisting Pakistan and Khan and in 2006 Pyongyang was reported to have supplied more long-range missiles. Given the expense and difficulties of developing long-range missiles, it makes little sense to go to all the cost and effort without also developing some-thing to actually deliver, such as a nuclear warhead. More evidence came in late 2004, when an Iranian walk-in intelligence source provided the United States and Germany with thousands of pages of laptop computer files that had been allegedly stolen from another Iranian.[23] Included were drawings, diagrams, and test data that seemed to relate to a number of Iranian attempts to place a device on top of a Shahab-3 missile between 2001 and 2003, which looked suspiciously like a nuclear warhead (slightly smaller than the design A. Q. Khan had provided to Libya).[24] The informa-tion was quickly shared with European allies who were negotiating with the Iranians to try and organize a suspension of Iran's nuclear activities, and in the summer of 2005 Robert Joseph, now the undersecretary of state for arms control, took it to Vienna. Other information from the same source included designs for a small, previously undeclared uranium conversion facility, which could form part of a parallel clandestine program run by the military or be a backup in case of military strikes against existing sites. Many suspect that the military research may have taken place at a site called Parchin where the Iranians have provided only limited access to the IAEA.

Another key question is whether the Iranians are being completely hon-est about the work they have done on the P-2 centrifuge design that they received from Khan in the mid-1990s. The degree of Iranian evasiveness on the P-2 has raised intense suspicions that it could be at the heart of a parallel clandestine program run by the Iranian military and which remains undetected. Initially, in October 2003, Iran neglected to mention that it even had possession of any of Khan's P-2 designs. Next it claimed that while it did receive the designs it did no work on them for seven years, a claim the IAEA finds surprising given their value. Iran claims there were staff shortages and problems making the more advanced rotors. However, having gone to such effort to procure the designs, not acting on them seems strange and has raised concerns over undeclared work or even secret facili-ties. It appears that from 2002 those working on the P-2 managed to make modifications to the cylinders suspiciously quickly given that it was claimed that the person doing the work had only just seen the drawings for the first time. In an April 2006 speech, Iran's president referred to the fact that the country was indeed working on the P-2 but provided no more details.

In another highly suspicious and unexplained transaction, an Iranian official under questioning from IAEA inspectors eventually conceded that a contractor had made enquiries with a European intermediary about getting thousands of magnets for use in P-2 centrifuges. The Iranian also mentioned that orders for many more might be on the way. The Iranians claim that none of the magnets were actually delivered by that supplier but magnets from other Asian suppliers did turn up in 2002.[25] Why would the Iranians want so many magnets for a P-2 when Natanz was based around the P-1 centrifuge and when Iran claimed it had done almost no research on the P-2? In early 2006 reports also emerged that Tahir may have revealed in one of his later interrogations that Iran was sent three actual P-2 machines; Iran has never admitted to receiving them and continues to deny it has them in its possession. But in April 2006, Iran's president did admit carrying out more research on the P-2.

The P-2 mysteries are significant because of the fear that Iran might have concealed a parallel enrichment program or another plant that could operate clandestinely and that, even though it might be smaller, might be able to operate more efficiently than Natanz thanks to the use of the advanced P-2s. Because Iran has a far more advanced technical and industrial base than Libya, it is far more likely to be able to develop its own indigenous production based on Khan's help. This local production would be far harder to detect or stop. If Iran did in fact have the ability to produce higher quality centrifuges than already known and had some of these assembled or ready to be quickly produced, then it could only take a year or two for Iran to develop a bomb even with just a few thousand centrifuges. All estimates of how far Iran is from the bomb are essentially guesswork because so little is known about how much the Iranians have been able to overcome technical hurdles in operating cascades. The existence of possible undeclared sites adds another variable. The most important question is how far is Iran from the so-called "point of no return," when it has the technological capability to manufacture, assemble, and run centrifuges without any need for outside input. At this point, any number of export controls, interception of deliveries, and diplomatic demarches are too late. Perhaps the second most important question is when does Israel believe this point is about to be reached, as it may replicate its 1981 operation against Iraq using air strikes in Iran. But because the Iranian program is far more dispersed and better defended, a similar outcome is far less likely.

Another unresolved issue is the identity of the fourth customer that members of the network said Khan had lined up just before it was broken. One of the biggest concerns—and mysteries—has been whether Khan could have sold technology to countries other than the three known customers. Some of the order books and invoices found in Dubai point to just this possibility and U.S. officials have talked of "several" more customers.[26] But while there are many signs of possible offers and negotiations and even a few whispers of deals and transfers, hard evidence about the identity of additional customers is difficult to come by. This remains one of the most urgent priorities for investigators, but it has involved piecing together limited amounts of often circumstantial evidence.

Saudi Arabia is one country whose links with Khan cause concern, not least because of the long relationship between the Kingdom and Pakistan's nuclear program. Some wonder whether it was a customer, and others whether it was a sponsor of Khan's work, especially given the fact it was providing direct funding to Khan Research Laboratories. Late in the day, reports came into the UK indicating that the trail of evidence led into the country. Phone records from front companies in Dubai also showed contact with the Kingdom, although it wasn't immediately clear what they were about.[27] Hard details of Saudi involvement with Pakistan's nuclear program are not easy to come by, although in 1994 a Saudi diplomat defected with fourteen thousand pages of official documents.[28] The documents allegedly show that Saudi Arabia provided something like five billion dollars of financing to Baghdad in the 1980s in exchange for any bombs that would be developed. Some reports claim that the CIA was aware of this deal.[29] The documents also allegedly detail the Saudi financing of Pakistan's program. The Saudi's have claimed that the diplomat who handed over the purportedly official papers was fired and the documents are not real, but ten years later he remains in hiding.

Khan himself also visited Saudi Arabia a number of times, including in November 1999 and September 2000. On the latter trip, he officially expressed his gratitude saying that it was "thanks to the Kingdom's assistance for various developments projects [that] we were able to divert our own resources to the nuclear program."[30] Khan received a standing ovation from a packed audience speaking on Saudi National Day. Some suspect that that Saudi Arabia did buy equipment from Khan and has stashed it away in a warehouse ready to be brought out and used to kick-start a program if the international security environment changes. Senior U.S. officials say they raised the subject in their discussions with their Saudi counterparts over the period. In what could be seen as a brilliant piece of salesmanship, by supplying Iran, the Khan network may have generated more business for itself by driving Iran's neighbors like Saudi Arabia, the UAE, and others to reassess whether they also needed to buy nuclear technology.

Another country that has raised suspicions is Syria. Khan certainly met Syrian officials on numerous occasions over an extended period and investigators believe that offers and negotiations occurred. Pakistani investigators in late January 2004 confirmed this was the case. However, they are unsure whether a final deal was struck or whether there had been any transfer of material. Khan traveled to Syria in the mid to late 1990s and also held meetings with Syrians in friendly countries like Lebanon and later in Iran (some see a possible joint deal between Syria and Iran).[31] From 2001 meetings intensified with KRL scientists accompanying Khan to Iran to meet Syrians. As the intelligence on Khan built up, there was also a parallel rise in the CIA's apprehension over Syrian nuclear intentions. A CIA report to Congress in the middle of 2003 warned: "Broader access to foreign expertise provides opportunities to expand its indigenous capabilities and we are looking at Syrian nuclear intentions with growing concern." John Bolton on September 16, 2004 stated, "We are aware of Syrian efforts to acquire dual-use technologies that could be applied to a nuclear weapons program." Some experts at the CIA felt he was exaggerating and pushing beyond the limits of available intelligence.[32] However, the CIA is investigating whether enriched uranium or any expertise or technology was sold to Syria.[33]

The list of states of concern over contacts with Khan does not end there. Khan traveled to Egypt although analysts believe Cairo may have spurned his advances.[34] The concern is that Egypt, like Saudi Arabia, Turkey, and Syria, might well be motivated to develop a program if it saw Iran moving forward. Egypt, like Syria, has been a member of the ring of countries involved in ballistic missile proliferation. In 1999 the United States imposed sanctions on Egyptian companies for transferring dual-use U.S. technology and missile components to North Korea.[35] The ability of relatively poor countries like Pakistan and North Korea to develop nuclear weapons programs has shown the dangers of underestimating who can get the bomb—if the political will is strong enough to drive the project forward. Additionally Turkey, Sudan, Nigeria, the UAE, Kuwait, and even Burma have been mentioned as potential customers. "Just look round the Middle East bit of a map and put your finger on it," explains one British official glumly. "The most exciting thing would be to find A. Q. Khan's receipt book but we haven't done that. He had contacts with a lot of countries. Whether they were significant in this respect or in some other, it is hard to know."[36]

The picture of Khan's network and activities is still evolving and becoming more complex as the investigation throws up new leads. "We've uncovered many new things," explained CIA Director Porter Goss a year after Khan's confession. "And we have found that in uncovering those things, we have not got to the end of the trail. Getting to the end of that trail is extremely important for us."[37]

One trail centers around the cylinders of uranium hexafluoride (UF6)—the actual nuclear material—found in Libya that it had received from the network. The network supplied the Libyans with two tons, but promised a total of 20 tons. It's known that Khan was charging one million dollars a ton, but where was it coming from? The Libyans swore to investigators that they had no idea where it came from and had merely paid money into a bank account. Good quality UF6 is a highly valuable commodity since the conversion of yellowcake into a gas pure enough to enrich is a difficult task. KRL would not normally have large stocks (PAEC had control of it) and even if there was a lax regime at KRL, it seems surprising that Pakistan would allow such a valuable item to go missing in such large quantities. Tests of the material and the container in which it was found in Libya have proved controversial. Early in 2005 U.S. officials visited a number of Asian capitals, making the startling claim that it actually came from North Korea, based on the "signature" of the samples. The retrieved UF6 did not come from any known Pakistani site, although it is possible that it came from an unknown site. The officials also produced evidence such as the tracking of suspect bank accounts. However, debate soon emerged over whether the test results really were conclusive.

Some members of the network have pointed to Pakistan, others to North Korea, as the source of the UF6, or some combination of both. For instance, could Pakistan have converted uranium from North Korea, and could the container have come from a different country than the contents? If it did come from North Korea, did Pyongyang intend it to end up in Libya or did Khan independently sell it on? Could it have come from a secret production facility hidden somewhere in North Korea traded as part of Khan's centrifuge-for-missile dealings? This might explain the strange route of the cylinders and the mysterious chemical signature associated with the UF6 and also why Khan was so relaxed about providing it. The trail is important because North Korea, unlike Khan, is still in business.

A major problem in bottoming out these investigations has been the inability to speak to Khan himself. For all the emphasis on breaking up the network, there are still real questions over knowing what damage it has done. Answering some of these key questions is impossible without direct access to Khan but this has not been forthcoming from Islamabad. The IAEA and CIA have been able to send written questions to Pakistan which are then supposed to be submitted to Khan before being sent back but few believe the answers are full and open. It is almost impossible to discover the full story of Khan's dealings with Iran for instance—and therefore how close Iran might be to a bomb—without interviewing Khan. President Musharraf told the *New York Times* that despite two years of questioning Khan, they had not been able to answer the question of whether bomb designs had been passed on to either North Korea or Iran. "I don't know. Whether he passed these bomb designs to others—there is no such evidence."[38] "Why is it that we are not being trusted for our capability in interrogating him? Why is it that we are not being trusted that we are sharing all the intelligence and information that we get out of him?" he asked other journalists.[39]

In an echo of the 1980s, the White House clearly believes that sanctions against Pakistan would be a mistake. Officials stress the lack of evidence of any complicity from the government when it comes to explaining how Khan could have acted for so long. "There are a variety of explanations," says

John Wolf. "The positive fact is that the U.S. government never had information that showed the complicity of certainly the Musharraf administration. We had some pretty strict legal obligations and the facts never added
up. It is just difficult to believe they weren't aware that something was
going on, but whether they ever investigated it, whether they wanted to
know, is a question you'd have to ask them."[40]

Critics still wondered whether America's three-billion-dollar aid package shouldn't be made dependent on the United States getting access to
Khan. But U.S. policy focused instead on rewarding Pakistan. In March
2005 the United States announced it would resume the long delayed sale
of the F-16s that had gotten Richard Barlow into such trouble over a decade and a half earlier. A year later President Bush visited both India and
Pakistan. This was part of a broader strategy of trying to engage India as a
strategic partner but ensure at the same time that Pakistan did not feel
sidelined. The aim was to get away from "hyphenated" U.S. foreign policy
towards India-Pakistan relations, which had created a zero-sum mentality,
and instead engage each country on its own terms. But there is also the fear
that in the wake of the Khan saga, the sale of the F-16s presents a mixed
message to Pakistan. Rather than a slap on the wrist for knowing about,
being involved in, or even just not stopping proliferation activities, the Pakistani military has been rewarded with the hardware it long coveted. President Bush continues to press for more access to Khan—and especially the
possibility of joint interrogations with Pakistan—including during his March
2006 visit to Islamabad. "We are going forward on that," was all that President Musharraf would say about discussions on the subject.[41]

And what of Khan himself? Since February 2004 he has been confined
to his house with his wife in the comfortable Margalla district of Islamabad.
Soldiers stand guard outside and he is forbidden to have contact with foreigners. The neighboring guesthouse where Khan hosted so many of his
suppliers and friends now serves as a security headquarters. He is not allowed to use the phone. Supporters of Khan paint a picture of a man suffering—they say he has high blood pressure and has lost thirty pounds. In
June 2005 Khan fell sick. Some even claimed he had a heart attack but
government ministers were quick to emphasize that he had merely had
some chest pains and that all was well. The developments were still major

news in Pakistan, some even whispering that he was being poisoned to prevent him from spilling his secrets.

His friend and biographer, Zahid Malik, claims he has depression, brought on by his humiliation. "Sometimes, he looks towards the sky as if he expects some help from Almighty Allah," Malik has said. Friends tell him that, despite having once been a national hero, he now needs to recognize that he has to submit himself to the wider needs of the state, which he once served and which once idolized him. "Dr. Khan must reconcile himself with the requirements of the time," says Malik. "This is what I have been telling him. I have been consoling him that 'Dr. Khan you have to reconcile, you have to submit with the interest of Pakistan.' But whether he has reconciled to that or not, I'm not sure. It's difficult to say." [42]

Slowly, one by one and with little fanfare or publicity, the fiber glass models of the Chagai hills that once proudly sat in every town center across Pakistan and celebrated the nation's most glorious achievement have been dismantled and with them the legend of A. Q. Khan. While one model can still be found by a busy road on the outskirts of Islamabad, not too far from the house where Khan spends his days, it attracts little attention anymore.

EPILOGUE

The Spread

Towards the end of October 2003 a strange coda to the tale of the *BBC China* occurred. Weeks after its unscheduled diversion in Taranto, the ship finally docked in the Libyan port of Tripoli. As the crates were unloaded, the Libyans were surprised to find an unexpected delivery—another pair of containers with centrifuge components. The material inside had been missed by the CIA and MI6 because it had come from Turkey rather than Malaysia. Because it was consolidated in Dubai, it was not tracked in the same way as the other boxes. The Libyans immediately told their British and American visitors who were in town at the time and the material was surrendered. But the incident raises wider concerns not just over whether there was more material destined for Libya which has remained at large but also whether, even now, enough is really known about just how much damage the A. Q. Khan network has done—and how far it spread nuclear technology. Two related phenomena call for pessimism about the future of proliferation—one is the growing supply of nuclear technology, in which Khan's legacy is vital. The other is the growing demand, which Khan has also fuelled.

One dangerous legacy of the A. Q. Khan network lies in the physical material to which he had access and for which remains unaccounted. Complete P-2 centrifuge machines have gone missing. They were last seen in Dubai and the network claims that they were destroyed but there is no evidence for this and it seems unlikely given their value. Are they still being held somewhere for a later sale? Were they sold or passed on to other clients, either known customers like Iran or those that remain unknown? Have any of the twenty tons of uranium hexafluoride promised to Libya been diverted elsewhere?

But even more than the physical material, the most worrying question is how much of the previously secret, tightly held knowledge on nuclear technology may now be circulating on the market. Khan would sometimes claim that he had passed on only old, used parts to countries like Iran. Even if that were true, which it isn't, the real damage Khan inflicted was the release of designs and technical information into the marketplace and into the hands of customers. It was this knowledge that allowed countries like Iran to go about building their own program with a high degree of confidence and eliminated the need for a huge swathe of difficult and time-consuming research. How much further the information may have spread is a concern that keeps those trying to prevent proliferation awake at night.

Technology has greatly facilitated the spread of highly sensitive information. From 2002 the Khan network in Dubai began transferring material from paper into electronic formats. The process began slowly but picked up pace towards the end of the network's life. Eventually, investigators found the entire plan for an enrichment program in electronic form on a set of discs in Libya. On one single disc was the complete set of drawings for the P-1 centrifuge, including how to manufacture, test, and assemble every component. Another disc held data for the P-2.[1] The material was in German, Dutch, and English and clearly originated in URENCO in the 1970s. In this form, the highly sensitive material that Khan stole so long ago and based his career around can be copied in a few seconds and passed around or even emailed. This makes it far easier for anyone who has hold of the plans to build their own network, without having to undergo the kind of atomic espionage with which Khan began his career. A number of copies were thought to have been made in Dubai but only the Libyan copy has emerged. "One of our jobs is to find who got this," explains Olli Heinonen of the IAEA. "We are talking to people who made copies and . . . trying to get from them a list of who got it."[2] There's no concrete evidence, but the suspicion is that the same could have happened to the nuclear weapons design and this could now be on the market. Khan certainly passed some material on different parts of the weapon design around the network in order to help with the procurement and development process, but no one is sure how much of the design is now readily available out on the open market. The combination of the availability of dual-use machines, the globalization of production capacity, and the availability of computerized designs means that any future network may find it far easier than Khan did to set up for business by piggybacking on his pioneering work.

Khan was at the center of a web but he may not have been the only supplier of material within it. The question of the source of the uranium hexafluoride (UF6) that came to Libya is an important unanswered question. There were some indications in 2002 that North Korea was planning on becoming a supplier of equipment and maybe of actual material. North Korean front companies also received a number of payments routed through the Khan network. This would make no sense if they were simply a customer of the network. Was North Korea instead more of a partner in Khan's work? Evidence pointing to North Korea as a supplier of nuclear material direct to countries like Libya would be a major worry, not least because North Korea could still be out on the market, exploiting the channels of contact opened up through Khan. And because Pyongyang already has so much missile traffic with countries like Syria, Iran, Libya, and Pakistan, this could easily provide cover for UF6 cylinders, which could be disguised as missile parts. A secret trade might mean that countries like Iran had received material without anyone knowing, which could dramatically shorten the time frame, and increase the potential secrecy, for developing weapons since uranium conversion was one of Iran's major technical problems. Given Pyongyang's record of selling missile technology to anyone who is looking to buy, the fear has always been that North Korea would do the same with nuclear material—and not just to states but also possibly to terrorists. "The export of arms equipment is currently reckoned to be North Korea's most important source of income," read a 2005 European intelligence report and there is a fear in many quarters that North Korea could step into the gap left by the Khan network, not least because it is perennially short of cash.[3]

The rings of proliferation among states—of which Khan was but one part—still continue to operate, spreading and perfecting illicit technology, trading on each other's comparative advantage. In 2003 the British Joint Intelligence Committee assessment found that the North Korean missile export program was continuing apace with Pyongyang, looking for new customers and offering upgrades to existing customers.[4] North Korea's expertise in digging tunnels has extended to advising Iran on how to protect its nuclear facilities in underground bunkers. There are reports that North Korea has been secretly helping the Iranian nuclear program since the 1990s.[5] It was also reported that in October 2005, during a visit to Pyongyang, Iran encouraged North Korea in its nuclear program by offering oil and natural gas.[6] Iran reportedly hoped to spread the pressure over nuclear development to other countries rather than see it all focused on Tehran alone—the same motive that may have driven Khan in his early years of spreading technology. Iran also has explicitly threatened to pass on its nuclear technology. The country's Supreme Leader, Ayatollah Khamenei, told Sudanese officials in April 2006 that his country was "prepared to transfer the experience, knowledge and technology of its scientists."[7]

Even Pakistan remains active. In May 2005 the United States indicted a Pakistani military supplier for running a clandestine nuclear technology procurement network in conjunction with a South African–based Israeli. A July 2005 European intelligence report warned that Pakistani efforts to procure for its nuclear program were continuing with the range of materials and components being ordered clearly exceeding the amount required for spare parts or replacements for its own program.[8] The same aluminium tubing that Khan bought for Libya was still being bought even after Khan's activities were revealed. Could someone—or the state itself—still be selling?

Though it may have burned the brightest, Khan's network was only one amidst a wider constellation of proliferators. Khan's great innovation was to offer a full service providing all the required designs and access to the businesses who could supply the parts, allowing a state to shortcut the developmental and purchasing process. Khan was also unique in shifting his work from state control to the private sector. But although Khan's network may have been extinguished, others may now move into its space, trying to grab some of its share in this small but very lucrative market. A European intelligence report listed hundreds of front companies and institutions involved in proliferation, including more than two hundred from Iran. Intelligence agencies continue to see indications of people in the marketplace looking for equipment and, given the huge riches on offer, where there is demand, the chances are that people will try and meet it.

Some sellers are amateurs trying to make a quick buck; others are far more dangerous. A major fear is that organized crime recognizes the profits and could move in to fill the vacuum. As international organized crime networks increasingly overlap and even merge with terrorist networks, this could be a route for terrorists getting hold of technology or nuclear material. There's little doubt of Al Qaeda's desire for nuclear weapons and the more states there are with the bomb and the more technology and material there is on the market place, the more likely it is that Al Qaeda will succeed in its ambition.

The non-proliferation system that was constructed in the mid 1970s in response to India's nuclear test was designed to prevent the spread of technology from Western states with high-tech, dual-use capacity to developing world countries.[9] But since a broader array of countries have themselves developed nuclear technology, it has become much harder to stop them from exporting their know-how to others, as Khan did. Countries can simply buy, share, and sell technology amongst themselves rather than needing to start programs from scratch or import material or steal plans from the West as Khan and Pakistan were forced to do. Even the exposure of the Khan network is unlikely to put a stop to the growth of these activities, for which remedies are hard to find. This so-called "secondary proliferation" has happened for a long time with missile technology but its emergence in the nuclear field under Khan is a major worry, particularly when states like North Korea are involved. It threatens to completely shatter the existing non-proliferation system. It is unclear whether the wreckage will produce a new workable system or a world of many more nuclear states.

Khan's ambiguous relationship with Pakistan illustrates how those engaged in proliferation can now be either individuals or organizations that have either no relationship or a murky, complex one with their state. That remains the case with China where key individuals cooperated with Pakistan and North Korea and continue to operate, although it is unclear whether they operate with the full knowledge of the Chinese state or just some parts of it, like the army or intelligence services. Sometimes, as happened with Khan, individuals strike up relationships that persist beyond the knowledge of their governments or with the clandestine sponsorship of only one part of the government. This all creates the fear that new networks may emerge or grow, perhaps drawing on some the information or technology that Khan has put into the marketplace or some of the individuals linked to Khan who have escaped detection or prosecution.

Khan was clearly a unique figure in many ways. He had the power and political patronage of a state behind him when he started his work, which gave him huge purchasing power and global reach with his network. This allowed him to obtain the technology and, once he had it, exploit his own links and contacts. He was able to turn himself into a global broker, bringing together an array of services, under the protection of his status as a national hero. But that does not mean that similar conditions might not allow another figure to emerge with some of the same capabilities, someone who might once again bring together the supply chain of nuclear procurement in such a forceful way. The very nature of a state-led clandestine nuclear program provides the kind of autonomy, procurement infrastructure, secrecy, domestic and international contacts, and prestige on which Khan thrived and that he used to build his own network. There's no reason why in Iran or North Korea an unknown figure is not already on the path to becoming the next international salesman of nuclear technology. There's also no reason why a similar figure could not emerge from a covert biological weapons program with equally frightening consequences.

Would any new network be detected and dealt with faster? That is partly a question of improving intelligence capabilities but also of diplomacy, ensuring there is a greater global consensus to prevent any recurrence. The question marks regarding intelligence on Iraq may well have made it harder to act against other, more real threats. A 2005 U.S. commission raised serious questions about the state of U.S. knowledge. "Across the board, the Intelligence Community knows disturbingly little about the nuclear programs of many of the world's most dangerous actors. In some cases, it knows less now than it did five or ten years ago," it reported. It called for "broad and deep" change in a U.S. intelligence community that has been slow to adapt and bring in new human and technical capabilities.[10] Khan's activities have piled pressure on an already shaky non-proliferation architecture. Its shakiness derives not just from the growing availability of nuclear know-how and equipment but also a growing demand amongst key states for nuclear technology. This is a demand that Khan stimulated and satisfied only in part; it continues to grow as the actions of his customers lead other states to reassess their stance on acquiring nuclear technology. Khan's support of Iran's work, and to a lesser extent North Korea, could well be the trigger for the collapse of the non-proliferation regime. The non-proliferation system was built on the optimistic ideal that by tolerating and even spreading civilian nuclear technology, states could be diverted from pursuing nuclear weapons technology. In return, the existing nuclear weapons states were also expected to negotiate in good faith to disarm themselves. The bargain largely held firm during the Cold War but since then has been increasingly strained. India and Pakistan both tested and remained outside the system, never really suffering much for it; India if anything has gained in status. Israel still remains outside. North Korea has yet to suffer much for its departure from the Non-Proliferation Treaty (NPT), which governs the regime. As a result, the deterrent factor for those considering embarking on their own nuclear quest is low.

The growing chasm in attitudes between the "old" nuclear and the new and aspiring nuclear states, which Khan exemplified and exploited, is an even more fundamental threat. As the values that underpinned the non-proliferation system diverge, the center ground disappears. Non-nuclear states ask how existing nuclear states can tell others not to acquire weapons when they are so unwilling to give them up. The NPT is the cornerstone and centerpiece of international non-proliferation efforts, but it looks increasingly ragged and out of date with growing tensions between the five declared weapons states and the rest, who are angry at the failure to make any moves towards disarmament while trying to limit the availability of peaceful nuclear technology. From the start, the NPT was seen as an instrument of discrimination and control by many developing countries rather than an even-handed bargain and the divide in perceptions has only grown worse. At the 2005 conference to review the treaty, tensions were so bad that attendees couldn't even agree on an agenda let alone any solutions. The United States sees the ability of Iran (and also before it Libya, Iraq, and North Korea) to develop weapons programs while technically under the treaty's provisions as an example of its fundamental inadequacies. Developing countries see the treaty as a bargain that has never been fulfilled. The failure to de-legitimize or devalue nuclear weapons, and the fact that the permanent members of the UN Security Council are the same five official nuclear weapons states under the NPT, merely adds to their mystique and the desire to acquire them. In 1958 British Prime Minister Macmillan said that Britain had nuclear weapons because it "put us where we ought to be, in the position of a great power," a view that is echoed by many other leaders, including those of India now and maybe Iran soon.

U.S. policy has also contributed to the breakdown in the system. This is partly because some in the U.S. administration believe that the NPT is already broken and remaining wedded to it represents a danger. These voices look towards a policy of multilateral pre-emption to replace it, in which the United States brings together allies to prevent states considered dangerous from developing technology, using a range of tools from interdiction at sea to financial sanctions to military force. In order to improve its capabilities, the United States has also looked at developing new nuclear weapons, such as the so called bunker buster, which could penetrate and destroy the kind of underground facilities that Iran and North Korea are believed to have developed. These moves have in turn heightened the sense that the United States and others are failing to devalue nuclear weapons and are instead making their acquisition more attractive to the rest of the world. Washington has also broken down the universality of the non-proliferation regime by telling Iran that it cannot have nuclear power under the NPT because of the fear it is developing weapons, while at the same time rewarding India, which has never even joined the NPT and actually developed a weapon, with a civilian nuclear cooperation deal in 2006. This again reflects the way in which U.S. policy is now based on Washington's perception of a country, its leadership, and wider strategic priorities rather than on support of the old NPT system. The move is a de facto acceptance that a state can go nuclear outside the NPT if it is important enough to U.S. interests.

Having labelled the North Korean regime as part of the "axis of evil" in his landmark January 2002 speech, President Bush found it hard to swallow the idea of dealing with Pyongyang and offering it the security guarantees it desires to ensure the survival of the North Korean regime. A decision for the United States when it comes to Iran and Syria as well as North Korea is: whether regime change is more important than preventing the development of weapons of mass destruction? Deals modelled on the one with Libya may offer the chance to prevent proliferation but may also entitle a degree of acceptance and even help to countries that are willing to disarm and which may also be intensely disliked by many in Washington.

Libya may be a model more for North Korea than Iran. This is because in a strange way it is easier for dictatorships than democracies to give up overt nuclear weapons programs. South Africa did give up its program but it had been a secret until the end of the apartheid regime. For Gadaffi or for Kim Jong-Il in North Korea, disarming merely takes a decision by the supreme leader. But in a less monolithic country like Iran, nuclear weapons can take on the same aura of power and prestige as they did in Pakistan or India. They become part of the political landscape and something that politicians compete over in terms of protecting. For any leader to give them up would be a far riskier option politically. Also, the more isolated a country is—like Libya was or North Korea still is—the more tempting the offer of reengagement might appear.

Proliferation isn't inevitable. Some countries have been persuaded or have decided to give up nuclear weapons programs. But in the current environment, the general sense of insecurity and uncertainty over the future has led a number of states to want to at least keep their options open. If the only way of discouraging countries from going nuclear is to provide security guarantees, then the danger is that a more insecure world encourages more countries to go nuclear. There is also the danger that the collapse of the non-proliferation regime combined with a U.S. policy that emphasises pre-emption and the development and potential use of new nuclear weapons, increases the sense of global insecurity and heightens the perceived utility of nuclear weapons around the world.

Global insecurity and fears over U.S. power can both contribute to nuclear demand. Some countries look at the advanced militaries of the United States and believe their only hope is through asymmetric and nonconventional tools of warfare, including nuclear arsenals and "the poor man's nuclear bomb"—chemical and biological weapons. In many cases, the likely calculation is that the safest option is to develop a latent nuclear weapons capability by developing advanced civilian nuclear power programs that can quickly be switched from civilian use towards developing weapons if desired. With fears over energy security leading to a growing global trend back towards nuclear power, the situation bears more than a passing resemblance to the mid-1970s.

Not many countries are suspected of actively seeking nuclear weapons but those that are suspected of doing so reside in the two most unstable parts of the world, the Middle East and East Asia. The fear is that declared possession of the bomb by either Iran or North Korea could start cascades of proliferation as demand multiplies. A North Korean bomb, confirmed by a test, for instance, would send shock waves across Asia. Japan, South Korea, and Taiwan would be forced to reassess their current position on nuclear weapons, and all have the technical capability to move forward relatively quickly because of existing civilian programs and research (faster than countries in the Middle East). If Iran were to develop the bomb, the fear is that countries like Saudi Arabia, Turkey, and Egypt would also press ahead with nuclear capabilities, further destabilizing the region.

Would the spread of nuclear weapons be such a bad thing? Some have claimed that the more nuclear weapons there are in the world, the less chance there is that one will actually be used because of the theory of mutually assured destruction and the deterrent effect. But this may be a profound and dangerous misunderstanding, based on extrapolating Cold War dynamics onto much more unstable regions like the Middle East where there are many more friction points between states, more instability within states, and where leadership can be weak.[11] While each state may rationally pursue nuclear weapons as a means to enhance its own security, the result may be the start of a tidal wave that makes everyone less safe. Thanks to both Khan's commoditization of nuclear weapons as well as the policies of other states, there is a danger that nuclear weapons have become almost normalized and that the taboo against their use has eroded. It is hard to know whether the world is really facing another turning point in which the nuclear tide threatens to break again. IAEA Director Mohammed El-Baradei has warned that if we do not deal with countries' legitimate security fears and we fail to create a new international system, "we will have 20 new nuclear powers in 20 years . . . Everyone will have to give up something, because we are standing with our backs against a wall."[12] Pessimists feared proliferation would accelerate in the 1970s and they were largely proven wrong, but if they are right this time, A. Q. Khan may be the individual, more than any other, who bears responsibility for the spread of the technology.

In his thirty-year career as a proliferator, how much damage did Khan do? On one level the charge sheet is long—he played a crucial role in Pakistan's development of the bomb, he provided major assistance to the nuclear programs of at least three other countries, and he increased the amount of knowledge and material available on the nuclear black market. However, because his network was stopped, the damage amounted to less than might otherwise have been the case. Libya has been disarmed, the Iranian program is now public knowledge and under intense scrutiny, and Khan and many of his supporters are out of business. But the real answer to the question of how much damage Khan has done is that no one knows for sure. That's partly because, even now, many mysteries remain about his activities. And those mysteries matter deeply since they speak directly to the larger question of whether the nuclear genie has now been let out of the bottle. Will we, as some predict, now have to learn to live with a new world in which many more states, often in unstable parts of the world, have nuclear weapons and in which the chance of those weapons being used is much greater? Khan may be out of business but the world is still sifting through the wreckage left by his work and looking warily over its shoulder to see what may be next.

Notes

Introduction

1. Quoted in Leonard Weiss, "Atoms for Peace," *The Bulletin of Atomic Scientists* (November/December 2003): 31–41.
2. Douglas Jehl, "CIA Says Pakistanis Gave Iran Nuclear Aid," *The New York Times*, November 24, 2004.
3. Mark Landler and David E. Sanger, "Pakistan Chief Says It Appears Scientists Sold Nuclear Data," *The New York Times*, January 24, 2004.

Chapter 1

1. The account of events is drawn from TV archives of 1971, particularly BBC Panorama, December 22, 1971;Hassan Abbas, *Pakistan's Drift into Extremism* (New York: M.E. Sharpe, 2004), 71; and Owen Bennett-Jones, *Pakistan: Eye of the Storm* (London: Yale University Press, 2005). Khan's reaction is recounted by his biographer, Zahid Malik, in *Dr. A. Q. Khan and the Islamic Bomb* (Islamabad: Hurmat,1992), 16.
2. Zeba Kahn, "Abdul Qadeer Khan: The Man Behind the Myth," http://www.yespakistan.com/people/abdul_qadeer.asp.
3. Information from the "Zembla Report—The Netherlands' Atomic Bomb," Nederland 3 TV Network, November 7, 2005. Translated from Dutch by BBC Monitoring.
4. Mark Hibbs, "Khan acquaintance charged in export of bearings to Pakistan in 2002," *Nuclear Fuel*, May 24, 2004.
5. "'I was born to make a nation': Emotions Focus on Bhutto," *The Globe and Mail*, February 12, 1979.

6. Quoted in Steve Weissman and Herbert Krosney, *The Islamic Bomb* (New York: Times Books, 1981), 44–45, and in "Project 706—Panorama," BBC TV program broadcast, June 16, 1980.

7. Shahid-ur-Rehman, *The Long Road to Chagai* (Islamabad: self-published, 1999), 35.

8. Usman Shabbir, "Remembering Unsung Heroes: Munir Ahmad Khan," *Defence Journal*, May 2004, http://www.defencejournal.com/2004-5/index.asp.

9. Quoted in Weissman and Krosney, *The Islamic Bomb*, 54.

10. "Project 706—Panorama," BBC TV.

11. "Pakistan History" Website, see http://pakistanspace.tripod.com/74.htm.

12. "State Department Proposed Cable to Tehran on Pakistani Nuclear Processing," May 12, 1976, declassified and available at http://www.gwu.edu/~nsarchiv/NSAEBB/NSAEBB114/chipak-3.pdf.

13. The final break came when Bhutto was hanged in 1979. Gadaffi was furious and threatened to expel all fifty thousand Pakistanis living in Libya at the time.

14. Shahid Amin, *Pakistan's Foreign Policy* (Delhi: Oxford University Press, 2000), 144.

15. In return for not asking for payment for oil imports, it is suspected in some quarters that Saudi Arabia received an "option" on the Pakistan program and was placed under a Pakistani nuclear "security umbrella," perhaps with guarantees to use weapons on Saudi Arabia's behalf if required or to pass on technology.

16. Amin, *Pakistan's Foreign Policy*, 133–35.

17. John J. Fialka and Marcus W. Brauchli, "Arrest May Link BCCI to Nuclear Program," *Wall Street Journal,* European edition, August 5, 1998, and Jonathan Beaty and S.C. Gwynne, "Scandals: Not Just a Bank," *Time Magazine*, September 2, 1991. After the bank's collapse, a U.S. Senate inquiry said it had suspicions that BCCI was directly financing the Pakistan nuclear program. "BCCI is functioning as the owner's representative for Pakistan's nuclear-bomb project," said one international businessman at the time.

18. Safrdar Mahmood, *Pakistan: Political Roots and Development 1947-1999* (Oxford: Oxford University Press, 2000).

19. George Perkovich, *India's Nuclear Bomb* (Berkeley: University of California Press, 1999), 176.

20. Ibid., 7.

21. Shahid-ur-Rehman, *The Long Road to Chagai*, 47.

22. Ibid., 5

23. Malik, *Dr. A. Q. Khan and the Islamic Bomb*, 60.

24. Joop Boer, Henk Van der Keur, Karel Koster and Frank Slijper, "A. Q. Khan, URENCO, and the Proliferation of Nuclear Weapons Technology," Report for Greenpeace International, May 2004, see http://www.antenna.nl/amokmar/pdf/KhanvoorGreenpeace.pdf.

25. Mark Hibbs, "Using Catch-all Rule, the Hague Blocked 20 Exports Since 1996," *Nuclear Fuel*, March 15, 2004.
26. Shahid-ur-Rehman, *The Long Road to Chagai*, 50.
27. Author telephone interview with Frits Veerman, June 23, 2005.
28. "Zembla Report—The Netherlands' Atomic Bomb," Nederland 3 TV Network.
29. Shyam Bhatia, "Yours Sincerely, Dr. A. Q. Khan," www.rediff.com, February 11, 2004, http://in.rediff.com/news/2004/Feb/11specl.htm
30. Shyam Bhatia, "Ex-colleague spills beans on A. Q. Khan," www.rediff.com, January 29, 2004, http://in.rediff.com/news/2004/jan/29spec.htm; and David Albright and Mark Hibbs, "Pakistan's bomb: Out of the closet," *Bulletin of Atomic Scientists* (July/August 1992): 38–43.
31. An appeals court overturned Khan's conviction because the original summons had not been delivered properly.
32. Author telephone interview with Frits Veerman, June 23, 2005.
33. Shahid-ur-Rehman, *The Long Road to Chagai*, 51.
34. Author interview with senior official associated with Kahuta who requested anonymity, January 2006.
35. Central Intelligence Agency, Directorate of Intelligence, Office of Political Research, Research Study, "Managing Nuclear Proliferation: The Politics of Limited Choice," December 1975, declassified and located at http://www.gwu.edu/~nsarchiv/NSAEBB/NSAEBB155.
36. Author interview with Joe Nye, London, May 23, 2005.
37. Ibid.
38. Malik, *Dr. A. Q. Khan and the Islamic Bomb*, 93–94.
39. "Project 706—Panorama," BBC TV, and Weissman and Krosney, *The Islamic Bomb*, 183.
40. Frederick Lamy, "Export controls violations and illicit trafficking by Swiss companies and individuals in the case of A. Q. Khan network," Paper for Geneva Centre for Security Policy, August 19, 2004.
41. "Project 706—Panorama," BBC TV.
42. "CIA Weekly Surveyor," January 17, 1977, declassified and available at www.cia.gov, and "Commission on the Intelligence Capabilities of the United States," March 31, 2005, http://www.wmd.gov/report/, 253.
43. Boer et al., "A. Q. Khan, URENCO, and the Proliferation of Nuclear Weapons Technology."
44. "Zembla Report—The Netherlands' Atomic Bomb," Nederland 3 TV Network.
45. "Project 706—Panorama," BBC TV, and also Weissman and Krosney, *The Islamic Bomb*, 187.
46. Interview with Peter Griffin, Bordeaux, France, March 22, 2006.
47. Albright and Hibbs, "Pakistan's Bomb: Out of the Closet," 38–43
48. A. Q. Khan talking to Zahid Malik, cited in Bennett-Jones, *Pakistan: Eye of the Storm*, 201.

49. Mark Hibbs, "Dutch Dossiers Show Ministries Dismissed Khan Role in Pakistan," *Nuclear Fuel*, August 1, 2005.
50. "Nuclear Exports to Pakistan," *Der Spiegel*, February 20, 1989.
51. Author telephone interview with Robert Gallucci, September 21, 2005.
52. Simon Henderson, "We Can Do It For Ourselves," *The Bulletin of Atomic Scientists* (September 1993): 27–32.
53. Author telephone interview with Gary Schroen, June 8, 2005.
54. Bennett-Jones, *Pakistan: Eye of the Storm*, 200.
55. Perkovich, *India's Nuclear Bomb*, 223.
56. Husain Haqqani, *Pakistan: Between Mosque and Military* (Washington, D.C.: Carnegie Endowment for International Peace, 2005), 112.
57. Steve Coll, *Ghost Wars* (New York: Penguin Putnam, 2004), 82.
58. Author telephone interview with Robert Gallucci, September 21, 2005.

Chapter 2

1. Author telephone interview with Richard Barlow, September 6, 2005.
2. Mark Hibbs, "U.S. Repeatedly Warned Germany on Nuclear Exports to Pakistan," *Nuclear Fuel*, March 6, 1989, and "Nuclear Exports to Pakistan," *Der Spiegel*, February 20, 1989.
3. Hibbs, "U.S. Repeatedly Warned Germany."
4. Hedrick Smith, "Inside Pakistan's Continuing Quest for Nuclear Weapons," *The San Francisco Chronicle*, September 3, 1988.
5. Walter Stefaniuk, "Nod of the Head Sparked Nuclear Bomb Probe," *The Toronto Star*, August 10, 1987.
6. Author interview with Richard Barlow, September 6, 2005.
7. Leonard S. Spector, *Nuclear Ambitions* (Boulder, Colo.: Westview, 1990), 92–93.
8. Author telephone interview with Stephen Solarz, March 17, 2006.
9. Author telephone interview with Richard Barlow, August 27, 2005.
10. Information on Charlie Wilson's role comes from George Crile, *My Enemy's Enemy* (London: Atlantic Books, 2003), 478.
11. Author telephone interview with Stephen Solarz, March 17, 2006.
12. Richard M. Weintraub, "Zia Says Pakistan Capable of Building a Weapon," *Washington Post*, March 24, 1987.
13. Crile, *My Enemy's Enemy*, 478.
14. Anwar Iqbal, "Pakistan Can Explode H-Bomb: A. Q. Khan," Jang Newspaper Website, May 30, 1998, http://www.jang.com.pk/thenews/spedition/nuclear/may30.htm.
15. Recounted in Shahid-ur-Rehman, *The Long Road to Chagai* (Islamabad: self-published, 1999), 58–59.
16. From an article by Khan, cited in www.ptvworldnews.com.pk/peopledetail10.asp and http://members.tripod.com/~babajack/azadi_site/aqkhan.html.

17. "The Pakistani Nuclear Program,"—Secret Department of State Paper, June 23, 1983, declassified in 1996, and available at http://www.gwu.edu/~nsarchiv/NSAEBB/NSAEBB6/ipn22_1.htm. Also mentioned in David Albright and Mark Hibbs, "Pakistan's Bomb: Out of the Closet," *The Bulletin of Atomic Scientists* (July/August 1992): 38–43.

18. Simon Henderson, "We Can Do It Ourselves," *The Bulletin of Atomic Scientists* (September 1993): 27–32.

19. George Perkovich, *India's Nuclear Bomb* (Berkeley: University of California Press, 1999), 323, and "Pakistan: Defense Industry Struggles for Self-Sufficiency," CIA Directorate of Intelligence Research Paper, October 1989, declassified September 2000, available at http://www.foia.cia.gov/browse_docs.asp?doc_no=0000107402&title=PAKISTAN:DEFENSE+INDUSTRY+STRUGGLES+FOR+SELF-SUFFICIENCY&abstract=&no_pages=0011&pub_date=10/1/1989&release_date=5/22/1997&keywords=PAKISTAN|PAKISTAN+ORDNANCE+FACTORIES|DEFENSE+INDUSTRY&case_no=F-1995-01050&copyright=0&release_dec=RIPPUB&classification=U&showPage=0001.

20. Posted on Pakistan Defence Forum Website at http://www.pakdef.info/forum/showthread.php?p=63553#post63553. The source for this claim and one of the best ways of watching the rivalry is through discussions on web forums, especially http://www.pakdef.info/forum/forumdisplay.php?f=23.

21. Owen Bennett-Jones, *Pakistan: Eye of the Storm* (London: Yale University Press, 2005), 202.

22. Ibid., and Rai Muhammad Saleh, "Where Mountains Move—The Story of Chagai," *The Nation* (Lahore), May 28, 2000.

23. R. Jeffrey Smith, "U.S. Aides See Troubling Trend in China-Pakistan Nuclear Ties," *Washington Post*, April 1, 1996.

24. Author interview with Gary Milhollin, Washington, D.C., December 14, 2005.

25. Author telephone interview with Richard Barlow, September 30, 2005.

26. "Pakistan's Atomic Bomb," *Foreign Report*, January 12, 1989.

27. Richard L. Russell, *Weapons Proliferation in the Greater Middle East* (Oxford: Routledge, 2005), 117, and Albright and Hibbs, "Pakistan's Bomb: Out of the Closet," 38–43.

28. Robert Karniol, "Vital Aid? Pakistan's Dr. A. Q. Khan Responds to Allegations That His Country Had Outside Help in Developing Its Nuclear Weapons," *Jane's Defense Weekly*, November 4, 1998.

29. "The Pakistani Nuclear Program," Secret Department of State Paper, June 23, 1983,

30. Shahid-ur-Rehman, *The Long Road to Chagai,* 86.

31. Hassan Abbas, *Pakistan's Drift into Extremism* (New York: M.E. Sharpe, 2004), 149.

32. Weintraub, "Zia Says Pakistan Capable of Building a Weapon."

33. Interview with Abdul Qadeer Khan, *The News* (Karachi), May 30, 1998. Available at: http://nuclearweaponarchive.org/Pakistan/KhanInterview.html
34. Quoted in Steve Coll, *Ghost Wars* (New York: Penguin Putnam, 2004), 69.
35. John Glenn, "On Proliferation Law, a Disgraceful Failure," *Herald Tribune*, June 26, 1992.
36. Jeffrey T. Richelson, *Spying on the Bomb* (New York: W.W. Norton & Company, 2006), 344.
37. Seymour Hersh, "On the Nuclear Edge," *The New Yorker*, March 29, 1993.
38. See for instance, General Mirza Aslam Beg, "Who Will Press the Button?" *Saudi Gazette*, May 8, 1994.
39. Interview with Abdul Qadeer Khan, *The News*.
40. Abbas, *Pakistan's Drift into Extremism*, 150, and interview with Abdul Qadeer Khan, *The News*.
41. Peter R. Lavoy and Feroz Hassan Khan, "Rogue or Responsible Nuclear Power? Making Sense of Pakistan's Nuclear Practices," *Strategic Insights* Vol. III, Issue 2 (February 2004). http://www.ccc.nps.navy.mil/si/2004/feb/lavoyFeb04.asp.
42. CIA Internal Report, "CIA Near East and South Asia Review: Prime Minister Bhutto and the Pakistani Nuclear Issue," May 5, 1989, declassified September 1, 2000, at www.cia.gov.
43. Shahid-ur-Rehman, *The Long Road to Chagai*, 107–8.
44. Abbas, *Pakistan's Drift into Extremism*, 136.
45. Jeffrey T. Richelson, *Spying on the Bomb*, 345.
46. Seymour Hersh, "On the Nuclear Edge."
47. Albright and Hibbs, "Pakistan's Bomb: Out of the Closet."
48. Ibid.
49. Perkovich, *India's Nuclear Bomb*, 308.
50. Husain Haqqani, *Pakistan: Between Mosque and Military* (Washington, D.C.: Carnegie Endowment for International Peace, 2005), 217, 253.
51. Abbas, *Pakistan's Drift into Extremism*, 142.
52. Ibid.,145.
53. Ibid., 11.
54. Haqqani, *Pakistan: Between Mosque and Military*, 253, 297.

Chapter 3

1. Author interview with Jafar Dhia Jafar, former head of Iraqi Nuclear program, Paris, July 30, 2004.
2. Jack Boureston and Charles D. Ferguson, "Schooling Iran's Atom Squad," *Bulletin of Atomic Scientists* (May/June 2004): 31–35.
3. Description drawn from Jonathan B. Tucker, *War of Nerves* (New York: Pantheon, 2006), 257.
4. Richard L. Russell, "Iraq's Chemical Weapons Legacy," *Middle East Journal*, April 1, 2005.

5. Akbar E. Torbat, "Brain Drain from Iran to the United States," *Middle East Journal*, April 1, 2002.

6. Vladimir A. Orlov and Alexander Vinnikok, "The Great Guessing Game: Russia and the Iranian Nuclear Issue," *The Washington Quarterly* (Spring 2005).

7. Michael Dobbs, "A Story of Iran's Quest for Power; A Scientist Details The Role of Russia," *Washington Post*, January 13, 2002.

8. Orlov and Vinnikok, "The Great Guessing Game."

9. Safdar Mahmood, *Pakistan: Political Roots and Development 1947–1999* (Oxford: Oxford University Press, 2000).

10. Farzad Bazoft, "Iran Signs Secret Atom Deal," *The Observer*, June 12, 1988.

11. Richard L. Russell, *Weapons Proliferation in the Greater Middle East* (Oxford: Routledge, 2005), 28, citing Ahmed Hashim, *The Crisis of the Iranian State,* (London: Oxford University Press 1995), 296, and John Lancaster and Kamran Khan, "Pakistanis say Nuclear Scientists Aided Iran," *Washington Post*, January 24, 2004.

12. Dalip Singh, "Delhi Dossier on Pak Bomb Daddy," *The Telegraph* (Calcutta, India), February 8, 2004.

13. Leonard S. Spector, *Nuclear Ambitions* (Boulder, Colo.: Westview, 1990), 212, and Kenneth Timmerman, *Countdown to Crisis: The Coming Nuclear Showdown with Iran* (New York: Crown Forum, 2005), 38–39.

14. Dafna Linzer, "Iran Was Offered Nuclear Parts; Secret Meeting in 1987 May Have Begun Program," *Washington Post*, February 27, 2005.

15. Press Conference by National Council of Resistance of Iran, Brussels, September 22, 2005.

16. Louis Charbonneau, "Iran Stalls in Probe of Nuke Smuggling-Diplomats," Reuters, April 18, 2005.

17. "Iran's Strategic Weapons Programmes," International Institute for Strategic Studies Dossier (London: Routledge, 2005).

18. Elaine Sciolino and David E. Sanger, "Pressed, Iran Admits It Discussed Acquiring Nuclear Technology," *New York Times*, February 28, 2005.

19. Spector, *Nuclear Ambitions*, 212.

20. David Albright and Corey Hinderstein, "The Centrifuge Connection," *Bulletin of Atomic Scientists* (March/April 2004): 61–66.

21. Herbert Krosney, *Deadly Business* (New York: Four Walls, Eight Windows, 1993), 263, and "Iran's Strategic Weapons Programmes,"International Institute for Strategic Studies Dossier (London: Routledge, 2005), 14.

22. Krosney, *Deadly Business*, 256–58

23. Press release by inspector general of police in relation to investigation on the alleged production of components for Libya's uranium enrichment program, February 20, 2004. Available at http://www.rmp.gov.my/rmp03/040220scomi_eng.htm.

24. Albright and Hinderstein, "The Centrifuge Connection,"61–66.

25. "Iran's Nuclear Program," Broadcast BBC Two, May 3, 2005.

26. "Iran May Have Received Advanced Centrifuges: Diplomats," Agence France Presse, January 20, 2006.

27. IAEA Safeguards Division reports on Iran, available at www.IAEA.org.

28. Interview carried on Iran Channel 2, April 13, 2006. Translated and provided by Middle East Media Research Institute (MEMRI)TV project, available at http://www.memritv.org/search.asp?ACT=S9&P1=1120.

29. Victor Gilinsky, Marvin Miller, and Harmon Hubbard, "A Fresh Examination of the Proliferation Dangers of Light Water Reactors," Paper from Non-Proliferation Policy Education Center, September 27, 2004, available at: http://www.npec-web.org/Reports/Report041022%20LWR.pdf.

30. Mirza Aslam Beg, "Who Will Press the Button?" *The Saudi Gazette*, May 8, 1994.

31. MSNBC Interview with General Mirza Aslam Beg, February 9, 2004, available at http://www.msnbc.msn.com/id/4223687/.

32. General Mirza Aslam Beg, "Pakistan's Nuclear Imperatives," *National Development and Security* (November 1994): http://www.friends.org.pk/Beg/pakistan's%20nuclear%20imperatives.htm.

33. Mahmood, *Pakistan: Political Roots and Development 1947–1999*.

34. Beg, "Pakistan's Nuclear Imperatives."

35. Husain Haqqani, *Pakistan: Between Mosque and Military* (Washington, D.C.: Carnegie Endowment for International Peace, 2005), 280.

36. Author telephone interview with Robert Oakley, June 30, 2005.

37. Singh, "Delhi Dossier on Pak Bomb Daddy," and Zahid Hussain, "There Is a Conspiracy Against Me By the Jewish Lobby—General Aslam Beg," *Newsline*, February 2004, http://www.newsline.com.pk/Newsfeb2004/cover3feb2004.htm.

38. Farhan Bokhari, Victoria Burnett, Stephen Fidler, and Edward Luce, "Pakistan's Rogue Nuclear Scientist," *Financial Times*, April 6, 2004.

39. Douglas Frantz, "Iran Closes in on Ability to Build a Nuclear Bomb," *Los Angeles Times*, August 4, 2003.

40. Author interview with former Pakistani diplomat.

41. Hassan Abbas, *Pakistan's Drift into Extremism* (New York: M.E. Sharpe, 2005), 148.

42. *Dawn Newspaper*, December 20, 1994, cited in Wilson John, "Iran, Pakistan and Nukes," *The Washington Times*, October 4, 2004, available at http://washingtontimes.com/op-ed/20041004-015707-2087r.htm.

43. Gaurav Kampani, "A. Q. Khan's Clandestine Nuclear Market," *Asian Export Control Observer* (April 2004).

44. Zahid Hussain, "There Is a Conspiracy Against Me By the Jewish Lobby—General Aslam Beg," http://www.newsline.com.pk/Newsfeb2004/cover3feb2004.htm.

45. John Lancaster and Kamran Khan, "Pakistanis Say Nuclear Scientists Aided Iran," *Washington Post*, January 24, 2004.

46. Jeffrey T. Richelson, *Spying on the Bomb* (New York: W.W. Norton & Company, 2006), 506.
47. James Risen, *State of War* (London: Free Press, 2006).
48. Author interview with Gary Samore, London, June 28, 2005.

Chagai Hills—May 1998

1. George Perkovich, *India's Nuclear Bomb* (Berkeley: University of California Press, 1999), 417.
2. Ibid., 375
3. Strobe Talbott, *Engaging India*, (New Delhi: Viking, 2004), 50.
4. Tim Weiner, "Pakistan Looks Ready to Test Its Own Bomb," *New York Times*, May 14, 1998.
5. Talbott, *Engaging India*, 65.
6. Farhan Bokhari, Stephen Fidler, and Roula Khalaf, "Saudi Oil Money Joins Forces with Nuclear Pakistan," *Financial Times*, August 5, 2004.
7. Rai Muhammad Saleh, "Where Mountains Move—The Story of Chagai," *The Nation* (Lahore), May 28, 2000.
8. Ibid.
9. Ibid.
10. The best account of the confusion is in Owen Bennett-Jones, *Pakistan: Eye of the Storm* (London: Yale University Press, 2003), 187–89.
11. Quoted in Shah Alam, "Iran-Pakistan Relations," *Strategic Analysis* (October-December 2004).
12. Bennett-Jones, *Pakistan: Eye of the Storm*, 195, and BBC News, June 3–4, 1998.
13. M. A. Chaudri, "Pakistan's Nuclear History," *Defence Journal*, http://www.pakdef.info/forum/showthread.php?p=83606#post83606

Chapter 4

1. "Kim Il-Sung, Benazir Bhutto Deliver Banquet Speeches," BBC Monitoring Service, December 31, 1993, and author conversation with Pakistani who was present.
2. Stephen Fidler, "Bhutto Disputes Musharraf's Nuclear Stance," *Financial Times*, February 23, 2004, and David E. Sanger, "In North Korea and Pakistan, Deep Roots of Nuclear Barter," *New York Times*, November 25, 2002.
3. "CIA Top Secret: Pakistan Strong Motivation to Develop Their Nuclear Capability," April 26, 1978, declassified in 1997. www.cia.gov.
4. Bill Gertz, "CIA Analyst Says U.S. Winked at Cheating," *The Washington Times*, June 12, 1998.
5. Joseph Bermudez, "A Silent Partner," *Jane's Defence Weekly*, May 20, 1998.

6. Shyam Bhatia, "Musharraf Must Explain Why He Visited Libya," www.rediff.com, March 12, 2004, http://www.rediff.com/news/2004/mar/12inter.htm.
7. Peter Roff, "Bhutto Missile Story Raises Hill Hackles," United Press International, March 7, 2005.
8. "A Talk with A. Q. Khan," *Foreign Report*, July 24, 1998.
9. Gaurav Kampani, "Second Tier Proliferation," *The Nonproliferation Review* (Fall/Winter 2002).
10. Interview with Robert Gallucci, PBS Frontline, March 5, 2003, available at www.pbs.org/wgbh/frontline/shows/kim/interviews/gallucci.html.
11. Author telephone interview with Robert Gallucci, September 21, 2005.
12. Jasper Becker, "Building the Bomb," *The Independent* (UK newspaper), February 11, 2004.
13. Daniel A. Pinkston, "When Did WMD Deals Between Pyongyang and Islamabad Begin?" Center for Non-Proliferation Studies. Available at http://cns.miis.edu/pubs/week/021028.htm.
14. Jasper Becker, *Rogue Regime* (New York: Oxford University Press, 2005), 188.
15. Wieland Wagner, Erich Follath, Georg Mascolo, and Gerhard Spoerl, "The Tyrant and the Bomb Part II," *Der Spiegel*, February 14, 2005.
16. Larry A. Nilksch, "North Korea's Nuclear Weapons Program," Congressional Research Service, March 25, 2005. Available at http://fpc.state.gov/documents/organization/46412.pdf.
17. Sharon A. Squassoni, "Weapons of Mass Destruction: Trade Between North Korea and Pakistan," Congressional Research Service, March 11, 2004. Available at http://www.nti.org/e_research/official_docs/other_us/crs03112004_DPRK_Pakistan.pdf, and Pinkston, "When Did WMD Deals Between Pyongyang and Islamabad Begin?"
18. Salman Masood and David Rhode, "Pakistan Now Says Scientist Did Send Koreans Nuclear Gear," *The New York Times*, August 25, 2005, and David E. Sanger, "Pakistan Leader Confirms Nuclear Exports," *The New York Times*, September 13, 2005.
19. David E. Sanger, "In North Korea and Pakistan, Deep Roots of Nuclear Barter," *The New York Times*, November 24, 2002.
20. David E. Sanger and William J. Broad, "Did North Koreans Fuel Pakistan Bomb?" *International Herald Tribune*, February 28, 2004.
21. Dexter Filkins, "N. Korea Aid to Pakistan Raises Nuclear Fears," *Los Angeles Times*, August 23, 1999.
22. "The Nuclear Bazaar," NHK TV (Japan), English version provided on DVD. Broadcast in 2005.
23. Paul Watson and Mubashir Zaidi, "Death of N. Korean Woman Offers Clues to Pakistani Nuclear Deals," *Los Angeles Times*, March 1, 2004.
24. Author telephone interview with Feroz Khan, November 14, 2005.
25. Ibid.

26. Transcript of PBS interview with General Mirza Aslam Beg. http://www.pbs.org/frontlineworld/stories/pakistan/e.html.

27. "Pakistan Offers UAE Nuclear Training But Not Atomic Bomb 'On Platter,'" *Jasarat Newspaper*, May 26, 1999, translated from Urdu by BBC Monitoring.

28. "Saudi defense minister visits Pakistan's nuclear installations": *Khabrain*, Islamabad, May 8, 1999. Translated by BBC Monitoring. "Saudi defense minister denies intention to buy nuclear arms": *Sharq al-Awsat*, August 5, 1999. Translated by BBC Monitoring.

29. Jane Perlez, "Saudi's Visit to Arms Site in Pakistan Worries U.S.," *New York Times*, July 10, 1999.

30. Richard L. Russell, *Weapons Proliferation and War in the Greater Middle East* (Oxford: Routledge, 2005), and Thomas Woodrow, "The Sino-Saudi Connection," China Brief, Jamestown Foundation, October 24, 2002. Available at http://www.jamestown.org/publications_details.php?volume_id=18&issue_id=661&article_id=4680.

31. Russell, *Weapons Proliferation and War in the Greater Middle East*.

32. Steve Coll, *Ghost Wars* (New York: Penguin Putnam, 2004), 315.

33. Author telephone interview with William Milam, June 30, 2005.

34. Bill Gertz, "U.S. Saw Signs of N. Korea's Work to Enrich Fuel for Nukes," *The Washington Times*, October 18, 2002.

35. Jeffrey T. Richelson, *Spying on the Bomb* (New York: W.W. Norton & Company, 2006), 530.

36. Mitchell B. Reiss, Robert Gallucci, et al., "Red Handed," *Foreign Affairs* (March/April 2005).

37. CIA Unclassified Report to Congress on Proliferation, covering July 1–December 31, 2003. Available at http://www.cia.gov/cia/reports/721_reports/july_dec2003.htm.

38. Unclassified report to Congress on the acquisition of technology relating to weapons of mass destruction and advanced conventional munitions, January 1–June 30, 2002. Available at http://www.cia.gov/cia/reports/721_reports/jan_jun2002.html.

39. Reiss, Gallucci, et al., "Red Handed," and Selig S. Harrison, "Did North Korea Cheat?" *Foreign Affairs* (January/February 2005).

40. Richelson, *Spying on the Bomb*, 527.

41. Bill Gertz, *Treachery: How America's Friends and Foes Are Secretly Arming Our Enemies* (New York: Crown Forum, 2005), 78.

Jordan—August 1995

1. David Albright and Corey Hinderstein, "Documents Indicate A. Q. Khan Offered Nuclear Weapon Designs to Iraq in 1990," *Institute for Science and International Security*, February 4, 2004.

2. A translated copy can be found at http://www.isis-online.org/publications/southasia/khan_memo_scan.pdf.

3. Herbert Krosney, *Deadly Business* (New York: Four Walls, Eight Windows, 1993), 207, 210.

4. "Iraq Survey Group Report," September 30, 2004, available at www.cia.gov.

Chapter 5

1. Andrew Koch, "Khanfessions of a Proliferator," *Jane's Defence Weekly*, March 3, 2004.

2. Transcript of PBS interview with General Mirza Aslam Beg. Available at http://www.pbs.org/frontlineworld/stories/pakistan/e.html.

3. A copy of the video was later found in Libya.

4. Malaysian Police Press Release, February 20, 2004.

5. Ibid.

6. Juergen Dahlkamp, Georg Mascolo, and Holger Stark, "Network of Death on Trial," *Der Spiegel*, March 13, 2006.

7. David Albright and Corey Hinderstein, "Libya's Gas Centrifuge Procurement: Much Remains Undiscovered," ISIS paper, April 1, 2004. Available at: http://www.isis-online.org/publications/libya/cent_procure.html.

8. Author interview with Peter Griffin, France, March 22, 2005.

9. Baradan Kuppusamy, "Nuclear Ring's Alleged Middleman Vanishes," *South China Morning Post*, February 25, 2004.

10. Matt Kelley, "Nuclear Suppliers Were Known to U.S.," Associated Press, February 12, 2004.

11. Sue Clough, "Exporter Helped in Nuclear Race," *Daily Telegraph*, October 9, 2001.

12. Sammy Salama and Lydia Hansell, "Companies Reported to Have Sold or Attempted to Sell Libya Gas Centrifuge Components," Center for Nonproliferation Studies, March 2005, http://www.ntinitiative.com/e_research/e3_60a.html.

13. "Paper Trail Shows Malaysia Ties," Associated Press, carried on CNN.com, February 18, 2004

14. Ibid.

15. Raymond Bonner, "Did Tenet Exaggerate Malaysian Plant's Demise?" *The International Herald Tribune*, February 7, 2004.

16. Frederick Lamy, "Export Controls Violations and Illicit Trafficking by Swiss Companies and Individuals in the Case of A. Q. Khan Network," Geneva Centre for Security Policy, August 19, 2004.

17. Raymond Bonner and Craig S. Smith, "Pakistani Said to Have Given Libya Uranium," *New York Times*, February 21, 2004.

18. Stephen Fidler, "Turkish Businessman Denies Nuclear Goods Claim," *Financial Times*, June 11, 2004.

19. Juergen Dahlkamp, Georg Mascolo, and Holger Stark, "The First Accomplices Head to Trial," *Der Spiegel*, March 14, 2005.

20. Mark Hibbs, "European Suspects in KRL Case May Have Previous Involvement," *Nucleonics Week*, February 5, 2004.
21. Stephen Graham, "Trial Opens Against German Charged with Aiding Defunct Libyan Nuclear Arms Plan," Associated Press, March 17, 2003.
22. Douglas Frantz and William C. Rempel, "New Find in a Nuclear Network," *Los Angeles Times*, November 28, 2004.
23. Seema Gahulat, Michael Beck, Scott Jones, and Dan Joyner, "Roadmap to Reform: Creating a Multilateral Export Control Regime," Center for International Trade and Security, University of Georgia, October 2004. Available at http://www.uga.edu/cits/documents/pdf/CITS%20ROADMAP%20Report.pdf.
24. Sharon A. Squassoni and Andrew Feickert, "Disarming Libya," Congressional Research Service, April 22, 2004. Available at http://fpc.state.gov/documents/organization/32007.pdf.
25. Jan McGirk, "The Mysterious World of Pakistan's Dr. Strangelove," *The Independent*, February 7, 2004.
26. Speech by A. Q. Khan in Islamabad in 1995, quoted in *Dr AQ Khan on Science and Education*, Mujahid Kamran, ed, 47 (Lahore: Sang-e-Meel Publications, 1999).
27. David Blair, "Bleak Future for Pakistan's `Bomb Hero,'" *Daily Telegraph*, February 7, 2004.
28. "Zembla Report—The Netherlands' Atomic Bomb," Nederland 3 TV Network, November 7, 2005. Translated from Dutch by BBC Monitoring.
29. Cited in Brian K. Anderson, Major, USAF, "A Profile of WMD Proliferants: Are There Commonalities?" May 1999, located at http://www.fas.org/irp/threat/99-003.pdf.
30. Zeba Khan, Interview, "Abdul Qadeer Khan: The Man Behind the Myth," available at http://www.yespakistan.com/people/abdul_qadeer.asp.
31. Zahid Malik, *Dr. A. Q. Khan and the Islamic Bomb* (Islamabad: Hurmat, 1992), 227.
32. Transcript of BBC interview (not broadcast) with Zahid Malik, February 2005.
33. Khan, "Abdul Qadeer Khan: The Man Behind the Myth."
34. Ibid.
35. Pervez Hoodbhoy, "The Nuclear Noose Around Pakistan's Neck," *Washington Post*, February 1, 2004.
36. Ardeshir Cowasjee, "The Story Is Recounted in The Depths of Degradation," *Dawn Newspaper* (Karachi), December 22, 2002.

Chapter 6

1. Author telephone interview with Richard J. Kerr, October 21, 2005.
2. Mark Gibbs, "KRL Hid Purchase of Sensitive Goods in Orders For 'Junk,' Records Say," *Nuclear Fuel*, November 21, 2005.

3. John McLaughlin, "Intelligence Community: Not Perfect, But Not Bad," *USA Today*, May 15, 2005.

4. William J. Broad and David E. Sanger, "As Nuclear Secrets Emerge, More Are Suspected," *New York Times*, December 26, 2004.

5. Author telephone interview with Gary Schroen, June 8, 2005.

6. Author telephone interview with William Milam, June 30, 2005.

7. An English translation is quoted at length in Mir Jamilur Rehman, "Opening a Pandora's Box," *The News*, February 14, 2004.

8. Greg Bearup, "Dr. Khan's Shady Nuclear Family," *South China Morning Post*, reproduced in April 2004 issue of World Press Review.

9. Commission on the intelligence capabilities of the United States, March 31, 2005. Available at http://www.wmd.gov/report/.

10. Report of the Select Committee on Intelligence on the U.S. Intelligence Community's Prewar Intelligence Assessments on Iraq, July 7, 2004. Available at: http://www.fas.org/irp/congress/2004_rpt/ssci_iraq.pdf.

11. British intelligence has stood by the claim that Iraq attempted to buy uranium from Africa. An investigation said the assertion was "well-founded" as the British government maintains that it has information from several different sources indicating the purpose of the Iraqi visit was to acquire uranium, although not necessarily that an actual purchase took place. Review of Intelligence on Weapons of Mass Destruction, *The Butler Review*, 156.

12. "International Crisis Group—Islamist Terrorism in the Sahel: Fact or Fiction?" *Crisis Group Africa Report* no. 92, March 31, 2005, 17–18.

13. Edward Harris and Ellen Knickmeyer, "Head of Pakistan's Nuclear Ring Made Repeated Visits to Uranium-Rich Africa," Associated Press, April 20, 2004.

14. Interview with senior IAEA official, Vienna, November 2005.

15. Dulue Mbachu, "UN Atomic Agency Chief Visits Nigerian Nuclear Reactor," Associated Press, January 19, 2005.

16. Ian Traynor and Ian Cobain, "Clandestine Nuclear Deals Traced to Sudan," *The Guardian*, January 5, 2005.

17. "Pakistan Nuke Scientist Khan, Colleagues Met Libyans," *Dow Jones International*, March 18, 2005.

18. Kamran Khan, "Business in Timbuktu," *The News* (Karachi), February 1, 2004.

19. Vladimir A. Orlov and Alexander Vinnikok, "The Great Guessing Game: Russia and the Iranian Nuclear Issue," *The Washington Quarterly* (Spring 2005), 49–66.

20. Author interview with Gary Samore, London, June 28, 2005.

21. Conversation reported in Strobe Talbott, *Engaging India* (New Delhi: Viking, 2004), 156.

22. Quoted in Husain Haqqani, *Pakistan: Between Mosque and Military* (Washington, D.C.: Carnegie Endowment for International Peace, 2005), 235.

23. Steve Coll, *Ghost Wars* (New York: Penguin Putnam, 2004), 481.

24. Hassan Abbas, *Pakistan's Drift into Extremism* (New York: M.E. Sharpe, 2004), 190.

25. Amy Waldman and David Rhode, interview with President Pervez Musharraf, *New York Times*, February 15, 2004. Available at http://www.acronym.org.uk/docs/0402/doc23.htm.

26. Author telephone interview with Robert Einhorn, October 14, 2005.

27. Author telephone interview with Feroz Khan, November 23, 2005.

28. Ibid.

29. Farhan Bokhari, Victoria Burnett, Stephen Fidler, and Edward Luce, "Pakistan's Rogue Nuclear Scientist," *Financial Times*, April 6, 2004.

30. Richard P. Cronin, K. Alan Kronstadt, and Sharon Squassoni, "Pakistan's Nuclear Proliferation Activities and the Recommendations of the 9/11 Commission," Congressional Research Service, January 25, 2005. Available at: http://www.fas.org/spp/starwars/crs/RL32745.pdf.

31. Matthew Pennington, "Pakistan Warned on Nuke Scientist in '98," Associated Press, February 10, 2004.

32. Farah Stockman, "Pakistan Had Case Against Scientist," *The Boston Globe*, February 13, 2004.

33. Zahid Hussain, "There Is a Conspiracy Against Me By the Jewish Lobby—General Aslam Beg," *Newsline*, February 2004, http://www.newsline.com.pk/Newsfeb2004/cover3feb2004.htm

34. Amy Waldman and David Rhode, interview with President Pervez Musharraf, *New York Times*, February 15, 2004.

35. Author telephone interview with Feroz Khan, November 23, 2005.

36. Ibid.

37. Douglas Frantz, "Pakistan's Role in Scientist's Nuclear Trafficking Debated," *Los Angeles Times*, May 16, 2005.

38. William J. Broad and David E. Sanger, "New Worry Rises on Iranian Claim of Nuclear Steps," *The New York Times*, April 17, 2006.

39. Amy Waldman and David Rhode, interview with President Pervez Musharraf, *New York Times*, February 15, 2004.

40. Hameedulla Abid, "Government Decides to Bring Kahuta Research Laboratories Under Nascom," *Jasarat Newspaper*, April 3, 2001. Translated from Urdu by BBC Monitoring.

41. Najum Mushtaq, "Pakistan: Khan forced Out," *Bulletin of Atomic Scientists* (July/August 2001) 13-15 and *Friday Times* (Lahore), March 16–22, 2001.

42. Mushtaq, "Khan Forced Out."

43. Chief Executive General Pervez Musharraf's speech at dinner in honour of Dr. Abdul Qadeer Khan and Dr. Ashfaq Khan can be found at http://www.infopak.gov.pk/CE_Addresses/ce_speech_at_dinner_abdul_qadeer.htm.

44. Ibid.

45. Amy Waldman and David Rhode, interview with President Pervez Musharraf, *New York Times*, February 15, 2004.

Washington, D.C.—September 2001

1. Owen Bennett-Jones, *Pakistan: Eye of the Storm* (London: Yale University Press, 2003), 2, and Rory McCarthy, "Pakistan's ISI Playing Dangerous Game," *The Guardian*, May 25, 2002.
2. From President Musharraf's website. http://www.presidentofpakistan. gov.pk/FromThePresidentsDesk.aspx.
3. K. Alan Kronstadt, "Pakistan-US Relations," Congressional Research Service Report, January 29, 2005. Available at www.fpc.state.gov/documents/ organization/42021.pdf.

Chapter 7

1. "Review of Intelligence on Weapons of Mass Destruction," July 14, 2004. Available at http://www.butlerreview.org.uk/report/report.pdf.
2. Yossi Melman, "Spy vs. Spy," *Haaretz*, February 17, 2005.
3. Remarks by CIA Deputy Director for Operations James L. Pavitt at the Foreign Policy Association, Washington, D.C., June 21, 2004.
4. Douglas Jehl, "CIA Says Pakistanis Gave Iran Nuclear Aid," *New York Times*, November 24, 2004.
5. The George Tenet quote comes from "The Commission of the Intelligence Capabilities of the United States Regarding Weapons of Mass Destruction," March 2005, available at www.wmd.gov.
6. Author telephone interview with Robert Einhorn, October 5, 2005.
7. "The Commission of the Intelligence Capabilities of the United States Regarding Weapons of Mass Destruction," March 2005.
8. Quoted in "Nuclear Jihad," a documentary by the *New York Times*. Available on the web at: http://video.on.nytimes.com. Accessed April18, 2006.
9. "The Commission of the Intelligence Capabilities of the United States Regarding Weapons of Mass Destruction," March 2005.
10. White House Fact Sheet issued December 20, 2001, and David Albright and Holly Higgins, "A Bomb for the Ummah," *Bulletin of Atomic Scientists* (March/April 2003): 49–55.
11. Kamran Khan and Molly Moore, "2 Nuclear Experts Briefed bin Laden, Pakistani Say," *Washington Post*, December 12, 2001.
12. "Scientist Says Osama Sought Nuclear Help," *Daily Times* (Pakistan) December 31, 2002.
13. Daniel Pearl and Steve LeVine, "Pakistan Has Ties to Group It Vowed to Curb," *Wall Street Journal*, December 24, 2001.
14. Peter Baker, "Pakistani Scientist Who Met bin Laden Failed Polygraphs, Renewing Suspicions," *Washington Post*, March 3, 2002.
15. Interview with Tony Blair, broadcast on BBC Radio Four's Today Programme, May 5, 2005.
16. "Review of Intelligence on Weapons of Mass Destruction," July 14, 2004. Available at http://www.butlerreview.org.uk/report/report.pdf, paragraph 285.

17. Memo from Matthew Rycroft to David Manning, July 23, 2002. Reproduced in Michael Smith, "Blair Planned Iraq War from Start," *The Sunday Times*, May 1, 2005.

18. "The Commission of the Intelligence Capabilities of the United States Regarding Weapons of Mass Destruction," March 2005.

19. Doug Struck and Glenn Kessler, "Hints on N. Korea Surfaced in 2000," *Washington Post*, October 19, 2002,

20. Donald Gregg and Don Oberdorfer, "A Moment to Seize with North Korea," *Washington Post*, June 22, 2005.

21. Barton Gellman and Dafna Linzer, "Unprecedented Peril Forces Tough Calls," *Washington Post*, October 26, 2004.

22. Cited in Phillipe Sands, *Lawless World* (London: Penguin, 2006), 204.

23. Ewan MacAskill and Ian Traynor, "Saudis Consider Nuclear Bomb," *The Guardian* (Vienna), September 18, 2003.

24. Ze'ev Schiff, "Iran: Pakistan Helping Saudis Develop Nukes," *Haaretz*, December 8, 2004.

25. "Review of Intelligence Regarding Weapons of Mass Destruction," July 14, 2004. Available at http://www.archive2.official-documents.co.uk/document/deps/hc/hc898/898.pdf.

26. Ibid.

27. Quoted in "The Nuclear Bazaar," broadcast on NHK TV (Japan) 2005. English translation provided on DVD.

28. Around 1980–81, they are suspected of having launched a pan-European campaign targeting those who supported the Iraqi nuclear program. Scientists were found dead in hotel rooms, warehouses storing equipment were blown up, and threatening letters were sent to company directors. Similarly in March 1990, Canadian scientist Gerald Bull was shot dead at the door of his flat in Brussels. He'd been involved in developing the so-called "Supergun"— a new delivery system for unconventional weapons in which Iraq was interested and the Israeli spy service Mossad was again suspected of being responsible. For more on the 1960s, see Michael Karpin, *The Bomb in the Basement* (London: Simon and Schuster, 2005), 207.

London—March 2003

1. Details of the meeting come in part from "Libya and the Nuclear Wal-Mart," Broadcast on BBC Radio 4 and BBC World Service, September 2004. Audio of program at http://www.bbc.co.uk/worldservice/specials/124_dirty_wars/page2.shtml.

Chapter 8

1. Gary Hart, "My Secret Talks with Libya, And Why They Went Nowhere," *Washington Post*, January 18, 2000.

2. Martin Indyk, "The Iraq war did not force Gadaffi's hand," *Financial Times*, February 9, 2004.

3. Author interview with Flynt Leverett, London, May 26, 2005.

4. A copy of the cable can be found at http://www.judicialwatch.org/archive/2006/statedocqadhafi.pdf.

5. Nick Pelham, "From Foe to Ally: Libyan Linked to Lockerbie Welcome in UK," *The Observer*, October 7, 2001.

6. Tony Allen-Mills and David Cracknell, "From Tyrant to Statesman," *The Sunday Times*, December 21, 2003.

7. Douglas J. Feith quoted in Bill Gertz, "Libyan Sincerity on Arms in Doubt," *The Washington Times*, September 9, 2004.

8. Vice-President Cheney, remarks in Dayton Ohio, August 12, 2004, http://www.whitehouse.gov/news/releases/2004/08/20040812-3.html.

9. CBS 60 Minutes II, March 10, 2004.

10. "Libyan Leader laments no 'concrete reward for giving up WMD," interview with Gadaffi on Italian RAI TV, translated by BBC Monitoring, December 30, 2004.

11. The role of Stephen Kappes in the Libyan negotiations was reported in the US media when Kappes was being lined up for a job at the CIA. Among the articles was Peter Baker and Charles Babington, "General formally named to lead CIA; Official who quit under Goss would be Hayden's Number 2," *Washington Post*, May 9, 2006.

12. Information released by the British Ministry of Transport, April 7, 2006, http://www.dft.gov.uk/stellent/groups/dft_foi/documents/division homepage/611515.hcsp.

13. Judith Miller, "How Gadaffi Lost His Groove," *The Wall Street Journal*, May 16, 2006.

14. Details of the flight and photographs of the plane on the runway at Malta were collected by European plane spotters who have been keeping tabs on CIA flights in order to track the process of extraordinary rendition and post details on the web. Also, see information released by the British Ministry of Transport, April 7, 2006, http://www.dft.gov.uk/stellent/groups/dft_foi/documents/divisionhomepage/611515.hcsp.

15. Douglas Frantz and Josh Meyer, "The Deal to Disarm Kadafi," *Los Angeles Times*, March 13, 2005.

16. Colin Brown, Julian Coman, and David Wastell, "How the Deal Was Done," *The Sunday Telegraph*, December 21, 2003; Peter Beaumont, Kamal Ahmed, and Martin Bright, "The Deal with Gadaffi," *The Observer*, December 21, 2003.

17. Stephen Fidler, Mark Huband, and Roula Khalaf, "Return to the Fold," *Financial Times*, October 27, 2004.

18. Brown et al., "How the Deal Was Done; Beaumont et al., "Deal with Gadaffi."

19. Marie Colvin and Michael Sheridan, "Gadaffi's Nuclear Deal with Pakistan," *The Sunday Times*, January 4, 2001; Brown et al., "How the Deal Was Done"; and Glenn Frankel, "A Long Slog Led to Libya's Decision," *Washington Post*, December 21, 2003.

20. "The Commission of the Intelligence Capabilities of the United States Regarding Weapons of Mass Destruction," March 2005, available at www.wmd.gov.

Chapter 9

1. CNN interview with Larry King, transcript posted on President Musharraf's website, http://www.presidentofpakistan.gov.pk/ViewsThoughtsDetail.aspx?ViewsThoughtsID=230.
2. David E. Sanger, "U.S. Rebukes Pakistanis for Lab's Aid to Pyongyang," *New York Times*, April 1, 2003.
3. Sanger, "US Rebukes Pakistanis for Lab's Aid to Pyongyang," and David E. Sanger, "In North Korea and Pakistan, Deep Roots of Nuclear Barter," *New York Times*, November 25, 2002.
4. David Rhode and Amy Waldman, "Pakistani Leader Suspected Moves by Atomic Expert," *New York Times*, February 10, 2004.
5. David Albright and Corey Hinderstein, "The Centrifuge Connection," *Bulletin of Atomic Scientists* (March/April 2004).
6. U.S. Official Briefs on Bush's New York meetings, State Department Press Releases, and Documents, September 24, 2003, from BBC Neon Database.
7. Official website of the President of Pakistan, see http://www.presidentof pakistan.gov.pk/FromThePresidentsDesk.aspx and http://www.president ofpakistan.gov.pk/PersonalLife.aspx.
8. Amy Waldman and David Rhode, interview with President Pervez Musharraf, *New York Times*, February 15, 2004.
9. "Islamabad Received CIA Report on Dr. Qadeer in Oct," *News* (Karachi), February 8, 2004.
10. Kamran Khan, "Washington Put Musharraf in a Spot," *The Straits Times*, February 14, 2004.
11. Simon Henderson, "Nuclear Spinning," *National Review Online*, December 11, 2003, http://www.nationalreview.com/comment/henderson 200312110800.asp.
12. Kamran Khan, "Business in Timbuktu," *The News* (Karachi), February 1, 2004.
13. Kamran Khan, "Pakistani Paper Says Nuclear Program Placed Under Strict Army Control," *The News* (Karachi) website, December 24, 2003, BBC Monitoring Database.
14. Paul Watson, "Pakistan Frees 3 Staff Members of Nuclear Lab," *Los Angeles Times*, July 25, 2004; Shakeel Anjun, "Pakistan Daily Reports Scientists, Officials Questioned," *The News* (Karachi) website, January 19, 2004, BBC Monitoring Database.
15. David Rhode and Talat Hussain, "The Slow Undoing of Pakistan's Father of the Bomb," *International Herald Tribune*, February 9, 2004.
16. David Rhode and Talat Hussain, "Delicate Dance for Musharraf in Nuclear Case," *New York Times*, February 8, 2003.

17. Mubashir Zaidi, "Scientist Claimed Nuclear Equipment Was Old, Official Says," *Los Angeles Times*, February 10, 2004.
18. "Sacked A. Q. Khan's Threat to Hit Back May Save Him from Public Trial," *South Asia Tribune*, February 1–7, 2004.
19. Interview with Dina Khan, Newshour, BBC World Service News, December 24, 2003.
20. Massoud Ansari, "Daddy's Girl," *The New Republic*, March 29, 2004.
21. Simon Henderson, "We Can Do It Ourselves," *Bulletin of Atomic Scientists* (September 1993): 27–32.
22. Interview by Zeba Khan, "Abdul Qadeer Khan: The Man Behind the Myth," http://www.yespakistan.com/people/abdul_qadeer.asp
23. Hussain, "The Slow Undoing of Pakistan's Father of the Bomb," *International Herald Tribune*, February 9, 2004.
24. Rafsqat Ali, "Dr. Khan Seeks Pardon," *Dawn* (Karachi), February 4, 2004.
25. *The News*, February 5, 2004, BBC Monitoring Database.
26. Interview with Senator Sami Ul-Haq on PBS Frontline. Available at http://www.pbs.org/frontlineworld/stories/pakistan/g.html.
27. David Rhode and David E. Sanger, "Key Pakistani Is Said to Admit Atom Transfers," *New York Times,* February 2, 2004.
28. "Qadeer Not Granted Blanket Pardon," *The News* (Karachi), February 10, 2004, BBC Monitoring Database.
29. "Pakistan President Holds Televised News Conference," Pakistan Television (PTV), February 5, 2004, BBC Monitoring Database.
30. State Department interview transcript with Deputy Secretary Asahi Shimbum, February 3, 2004.
31. Remarks by Colin Powell, Islamabad, March 18, 2004, http://islamabad.usembassy.gov/pakistan/h04031805.html.

Chapter 10

1. Author interview with Peter Griffin, London, January 16, 2006.
2. Interview with Mohammed El-Baradei, *Der Spiegel*, February 21, 2005.
3. Author interview with David Albright, Washington, D.C., December 15, 2005.
4. William J. Broad and David E. Sanger, "As Nuclear Secrets Emerge, More Are Suspected," *New York Times*, December 26, 2004.
5. Carla Anne Robbins, "Reaching Out," *Wall Street Journal*, February 12, 2004.
6. "Libyan leader laments no 'concrete reward' for giving up WMD," interview with Gadaffi on Italian RAI TV, December 30, 2004, translated by BBC Monitoring.
7. Flynt Leverett, "Why Libya Gave Up the Bomb," *New York Times*, January 23, 2004.
8. Author telephone interview with John Wolf, October 28, 2005.

9. Dafna Linzer, "Strong Leads and Dead Ends in Nuclear Case Against Iran," *Washington Post*, February 8, 2006.

10. Douglas Frantz and William C. Rempel, "New Find in a Nuclear Network," *Los Angeles Times*, November 28, 2004.

11. Juergen Dahlkamp, Georg Mascolo, and Holger Stark, "The First Accomplices Head to Trial," *Der Spiegel*, March 14, 2005.

12. Carsten Hauptmeier, "Trial Opens of German Engineer Accused of Aiding Libya's Nuclear Ambitions," *Agence France Presse*, March 17, 2006.

13. Juergen Dahlkamp, Georg Mascolo, and Holger Stark, "The First Accomplices Head to Trial," *Der Spiegel*, March 14, 2005.

14. Author telephone interview with John Wolf, October 28, 2005.

15. "Iran Demands Pakistan Head Explains Remarks," *Associated Press*, May 29, 2005.

16. "Iran's Nuclear Programme," *BBC TV*, May 3, 2005.

17. Mark Hibbs, "Four IAEA Campaigns at Natanz," *Nuclear Fuel* (August 18, 2003).

18. "Iran's Nuclear Programme," *BBC TV*, May 3, 2005.

19. *Daily Times* (Lahore), March 14, 2005.

20. Dafna Linzer, "No Proof Found of Iran Arms Program," *Washington Post*, August 23, 2005, and author interview with senior IAEA official, Vienna, November 23, 2005.

21. Christopher Dickey, "Iran: Countdown to Showdown Part 1," available at http://christopherdickey.blogspot.com/2006/01/iran-countdown-to-showdown-part-i.html.

22. Anton La Guardia, "Tailor's Bag That Put the West on the Trail of Iran's Nuclear Secrets," *Daily Telegraph*, March 22, 2006.

23. Dafna Linzer, "Strong Leads and Dead Ends in Nuclear Case Against Iran," *Washington Post*, February 8, 2006.

24. IISS, "Iran's Strategic Weapons Program," September 5, 2005; Dafna Linzer, "Strong Leads and Dead Ends; and Carla Anne Robbins, "U.S. Gives Briefing on Iranian Missile to Nuclear Agency," *Wall Street Journal*, July 27, 2005.

25. IAEA Board Report, November 15, 2004.

26. "John Bolton Talking to Reporters," Associated Press, May 28, 2004.

27. William J. Broad and David E. Sanger, "As Nuclear Secrets Emerge, More Are Suspected," *New York Times*, December 26, 2004.

28. "A Blind Eye to the Islamic Bomb," SBS Television (Australia), Current Affairs Transcript, June 23, 2004, BBC Monitoring Database.

29. Steve Coll and John Mintz, "Saudi Aid to Iraqi A-bomb Effort Alleged," *Washington Post*, July 25, 1994.

30. Contact Pakistan website, September 23, 2000. Available at http://www.contactpakistan.com/news/news107.htm.

31. Douglas Frantz, "A High Risk Nuclear Stakeout," *Los Angeles Times*, February 28, 2005; Douglas Davis, "A Syrian Bomb," *The Jerusalem Post*, September 10, 2004; and Kamran Khan, "Washington Put Musharraf in a Spot," *The Straits Times*, February 14, 2004.

32. Douglas Jehl, "Ex-Officials Say Bolton Inflated Syrian Danger," *New York Times*, April 26, 2005.
33. Wieland Wagner, Erich Follath, Georg Mascolo, and Gerhard Spoerl, "The Tyrant and the Bomb Part II," *Der Spiegel*, February 14, 2005.
34. David Albright and Corey Hinderstein, "Unravelling the A. Q. Khan and Future Proliferation Networks," *The Washington Quarterly* (Spring 2005).
35. Richard L. Russell, *Weapons Proliferation in the Greater Middle East* (Oxford: Routledge, 2005), 111.
36. Author interview with British government official, London, September 23, 2005.
37. Testimony of Porter Goss, Current and Projected National Security Threats to the United States before the Senate Select Committee on Intelligence, February 16, 2005, available at http://www.cia.gov/cia/public_affairs/speeches/2004/Goss_testimony_02162005.html.
38. David E. Sanger, "Pakistan Leader Confirms Nuclear Exports," *New York Times*, September 13, 2005.
39. "Musharraf Defends Decision to Refuse Foreign Access to Nuke Scientist," *Agence France Presse*, November 13, 2005.
40. Author telephone interview with John Wolf, October 28, 2005.
41. Interview with President Musharraf, CNN, March 5, 2006.
42. "New Book by Dr. Khan's Biographer Explains Proliferation," *Pakistan Observer*, October 28, 2004, BBC Monitoring Database.

Epilogue

1. IAEA Safeguards report on Libya, May, 2004.
2. "Iran's Nuclear Programme," *BBC TV*, May 3, 2005.
3. Ian Traynor and Ian Cobain, "Intelligence Report Claims Nuclear Market Thriving," *The Guardian*, January 4, 2006.
4. "Review of Intelligence on Weapons of Mass Destruction," July 14, 2004, available at http://www.butlerreview.org.uk/report/.
5. Louis Charbonneau, "N. Korea Provides Nuclear Aid to Iran—Intel Reports," Reuters, July 6, 2005.
6. "Iran Encourages North Korean Nuclear Work with Free Oil and Gas Offer," *Agence France Presse*, November 26, 2005.
7. Nazila Fathi, "Senior Cleric Tells Sudan that Nuclear Aid is Available," *New York Times*, April 26, 2006.
8. Traynor and Cobain, "Intelligence Report Claims Nuclear Market Thriving."
9. Chaim Braun and Christopher F. Chyba, "Proliferation Rings," *International Security* (Fall 2004).
10. Richard L. Russell, "A Weak Pillar for American National Security: The CIA's Dismal Performance Against WMD Threats," *Intelligence and National Security* (September 2005).
11. Richard L. Russell, *Weapons Proliferation and War in the Greater Middle East* (Oxford: Routledge, 2005)
12. Interview with Mohammed El-Baradei, *Der Spiegel*, February 21, 2005.

Acknowledgments

This book would not have been possible if so many people had not been generous with their time and thoughts. Many of these individuals would prefer not to be identified for a variety of reasons, but they have my thanks. Amongst those I can thank are my publishers Michael Dwyer and Dedi Felman for their help with a first book and to Michael for suggesting taking on the project in the first place. I also extend my thanks to David Albright, Richard Barlow, Owen Bennett-Jones, Robert Einhorn, Mark Fitzpatrick, Robert Gallucci, Siegfried Hecker, Simon Henderson, Feroz Khan, Richard Russell, Joseph Nye, Robert Oakley, Peter Reid, Peter Rickwood, Gary Samore, Gary Schroen, Simon Shercliff, Frits Veerman, Philip Wearne, and John Wolf. Thanks above all to my wife, Jane, for her patience.

Index